Britain's Man on the Spot in Iraq and Afghanistan

Henry Dobbs in his early forties. Courtesy of Henry Wilks.

Britain's Man on the Spot in Iraq and Afghanistan

Government and Diplomacy by Sir Henry Dobbs at the Apex of Empire

Ann Wilks

I.B. TAURIS

LONDON • NEW YORK • OXFORD • NEW DELHI • SYDNEY

I.B. TAURIS
Bloomsbury Publishing Plc
50 Bedford Square, London, WC1B 3DP, UK
1385 Broadway, New York, NY 10018, USA
29 Earlsfort Terrace, Dublin 2, Ireland

BLOOMSBURY, I.B. TAURIS and the I.B. Tauris logo are trademarks of
Bloomsbury Publishing Plc

First published in Great Britain 2024

For legal purposes the Acknowledgements on p. xiv constitute an extension of this
copyright page.

Series design by Adriana Brioso
Cover images: [left] Henry Dobbs, courtesy of Henry Wilks; [middle]
King Faisal I of Iraq © Sueddeutsche Zeitung Photo/Mary Evans;
[right] Amir Amanullah of Afghanistan, courtesy of Henry Wilks.

Bloomsbury Publishing Plc does not have any control over, or responsibility for, any
third-party websites referred to or in this book. All internet addresses given in this
book were correct at the time of going to press. The author and publisher regret any
inconvenience caused if addresses have changed or sites have ceased to exist, but can
accept no responsibility for any such changes.

A catalogue record for this book is available from the British Library.

Library of Congress Cataloging-in-publication Data:
Names: Wilks, Ann (Writer on history), author.
Title: Britain's man on the spot in Iraq and Afghanistan : government and diplomacy
by Sir Henry Dobbs at the apex of empire / Ann Wilks.
Description: London ; New York, NY : I.B. Tauris, 2023. |
Includes bibliographical references and index.
Identifiers: LCCN 2023012720 (print) | LCCN 2023012721 (ebook) |
ISBN 9780755651320 (hardback) | ISBN 9780755651283 (paperback) |
ISBN 9780755651313 (pdf) | ISBN 9780755651306 (epub) | ISBN 9780755651290
Subjects: LCSH: Dobbs, Henry Robert Conway, Sir, 1871–1934. |
Diplomats–Great Britain–Biography. | Great Britain–Foreign relations–20th century. |
Iraq–Foreign relations–20th century. | Great Britain–Foreign relations–Iraq. |
Iraq–Foreign relations–Great Britain. |
Afghanistan–Foreign relations–20th century. | Great Britain–Foreign relations–Afghanistan. |
Afghanistan–Foreign relations–Great Britain.
Classification: LCC DA566.9.D52 W55 2023 (print) | LCC DA566.9.D52
(ebook) | DDC 327.41092 [B]–dc23/eng/20230403
LC record available at https://lccn.loc.gov/2023012720
LC ebook record available at https://lccn.loc.gov/2023012721

ISBN: HB: 978-0-7556-5132-0
ePDF: 978-0-7556-5131-3
eBook: 978-0-7556-5130-6

Typeset by Newgen KnowledgeWorks Pvt. Ltd., Chennai, India

To find out more about our authors and books visit www.bloomsbury.com
and sign up for our newsletters.

To the memory of Sir Henry Robert Conway Dobbs GBE KCSI KCMG KCIE,
who for too long has lingered in the shadows.

Contents

Figures

Maps

Foreword

Ann Wilks's fascinating study of the eventful life of Sir Henry Dobbs is a boon to those interested in the waning years of the British Empire in general and the Raj, Afghanistan and Iraq in particular. As London's 'man on the spot' for a series of crucial episodes that helped to define British rule in South Asia and the Middle East, Dobbs embodied the continuities and changes in late British imperialism. Deftly drawing on the remarkable trove of letters that Dobbs wrote to his family, Wilks gives us a vivid portrayal of the daily workings of a well-placed Indian Civil Servant whose nearly forty-year career covered postings in inter alia India, Balochistan, Afghanistan and Mesopotamia (Iraq). It was in the latter territory during the Mandate era that Dobbs had his longest and most influential posting. He retired in 1929 as the longest serving high commissioner in Baghdad. His tenure in Iraq began with securing the border with Turkey (Mosul question) and securing the Anglo-Iraqi Treaty of 1922, a down-to-the-wire affair, the telling of which is not without back-channel manoeuvres and suspense.

Students of Middle Eastern history will be interested in this recounting of Dobbs's life for many reasons. Unsurprisingly, given his postings and the company he kept, reading Dobbs's biography means meeting a string of important individuals through Dobbs's eyes. In these pages we encounter Henry McMahon, who would go on to fame, or perhaps infamy, as the British half of the Hussein–McMahon correspondence that formed such an important part in contradictory British wartime promises and the problems they led to after the peace. Likewise, there are appearances for Mark Sykes, Gertrude Bell, with whom Dobbs lunched almost daily when high commissioner in Iraq, Percy Cox, Amir (later King) Amanullah of Afghanistan, Mustafa Kemal, the future Atatürk, King Faisal of Iraq, and such important Iraqi figures as Yasin al-Hashimi, Nuri al-Said and Jafar al-Askari. Dobbs's days were rarely dull.

Like the broader empire, Dobbs's career reflects the massive gravitational pull of the Raj. When he began his professional life in 1892, the British Empire was the dominant international power, ruling over a quarter of the land and a fifth of the people on earth, and India was at the centre of that imperial dynamic. Wilks quotes the British Viceroy of India Lord Curzon as saying a few years later, 'As long as we rule in India, we are the greatest power in the world. If we lose it we shall drop straight away to a third-rate power.' That human symbol of the British Empire was undoubtedly more prophetic than he must have realized at the time. As Dobbs's life story demonstrates, within a few decades, Britain's global position had become 'uncertain', to say the least, even though India only reached independence a few decades later still.

Dobbs's Anglo-Irish family had a long-standing connection with British India (two of his mother's cousins had served as lieutenant governors), so it was perhaps not surprising that even as a student at Winchester, young Henry was headed for the Indian Civil Service. After various postings in India, Dobbs was sent to the northern frontier provinces where he was engaged with tribal matters and, increasingly, Afghanistan. A brief stint in Mesopotamia during the Great War left a memorable impression, such that when the opportunity to return arose after serving in Balochistan and Afghanistan, Dobbs was keen to take it. Wherever his career took him, Dobbs was a prolific and shrewd observer and letter writer. The correspondence that forms the backbone of this study was subsequently discovered in seven trunks of papers that had rested undisturbed for over eighty years in Dobbs's family house in Ireland. Wilks has masterfully reassembled Dobbs's career from these letters, supplementing them with papers from the official record and the relevant secondary scholarship. The result is a tautly written study that ably situates its protagonist and his career in the context of this period of remarkable change. Wilks draws freely on Dobbs's letters, which offer remarkable insights into both Dobbs the man and the administrator. A keen eyewitness of all around him, Dobbs the correspondent was at times acid in his criticism of everything from British policy to human foibles, giving the reader an insider's view to the pomp and the travails of an imperial servant at empire's end.

The poignancy of the details in Dobbs's letters are not only fascinating in themselves but also highlight the larger forces at work in shaping what Elizabeth Monroe referred to as 'Britain's moment' in the Middle East. Earlier in his career, when Britain was the foremost imperial power, Dobbs found himself tasked with helping to organize the 'constant pomp' of the Raj – lavish demonstrations of the viceroy's rule, complete with elaborate trains, enormous tents, pianos and even spring beds, all meant to demonstrate British sovereignty and civilizational power. In 1911, while serving in Balochistan, Dobbs had to secure the correct clothing to wear for the Delhi Durbar, a full dress riding costume 'and white silk stockings with ditto lilac underneath to give the proper shade'.

During his final years in Iraq, Dobbs frequently travelled not on horseback or train but by airplane, that symbol of British aspirations to rule on the cheap – and for many Iraqis the delivery vehicle for bombing campaigns that naturally did little to endear them to British rule. On more than one occasion, the plane in which Dobbs was travelling crashed or broke apart around him and he was lucky to emerge unscathed. It is hard not to read these incidents as anything other than metaphors for imperial dilapidation.

Throughout his career, Dobbs was apt to make use of the time and distance separating him from London, and the resulting lag in communications with his superiors, to take his own decisions. This 'independent approach', taken 'sometimes in the face of strong opposition from those in authority', ensured that Dobbs was frequently embroiled in struggles over policy. An ongoing source of friction was the 'Indianization policy' that manifested itself repeatedly in British rule in the Middle East, particularly in terms of administrative and judicial affairs, reflecting the prominence of ex-Indian Civil Service officials in the ranks of British administrators. A significant number of officials involved in formulating British policy on Iraq were committed to deploying ex-Indian officials and to adopting the policies developed there as opposed to maintaining some elements of the systems developed in Iraq during the centuries of Ottoman rule. Foremost among the Indianization policy protagonists were Percy Cox and Arnold Wilson who both resisted the idea of Iraqi independence. Despite or indeed perhaps because of his experience as an Indian Civil Servant, Dobbs stood firmly against the Indianizing influence in Iraq, regarding it as inappropriate for the local conditions of an Arab country like Iraq and doubtless channelling his own iconoclastic spirit. As Wilks writes, 'His career provides an interesting and important counterpoint to the conventional colonial stereotypes.'

The internal jostling over imperial policy was sharpened by the political and fiscal shocks to the British Empire caused by the Great War. Depleted financially and increasingly reluctant to make or extend existing overseas commitments and shaken by the independence movement in Ireland, Britain sought to pare back. Such mental and material retreat left its imperial agents in increasingly unfamiliar territory, and not all adapted to the new dispensation equally well. One of the principal aims of Dobbs's tenure as high commissioner in Iraq, for example, was the difficult balancing act of preparing the country for eventual independence while serving as the League of Nations-appointed mandatory power and attempting to extract favourable terms between the future independent country and Britain. It is against this backdrop that the last two chapters of Wilks's study ought to be read. They reflect the difficult terrain of the post-war situation when a modified form of empire still existed, but the pressure for self-determination was the writing on the wall for imperial rule. In this changed context, Dobbs emerges in greater credit than many British officials. Always keen to learn as much as possible about the local situation, Dobbs could see that 'successes' would henceforth be relative. Securing the controversial Anglo-Iraqi Treaty of 1922 and the Mosul region for Iraq against Turkish claims, both high-wire acts of considerable complexity, were to be the major achievements of his period of rule. They both must be seen as qualified successes when viewed against imperial ambitions of the era in which he had started his career yet far more impressive in the context of the radically changed post-war era.

Dobbs's letters were not without reflective self-criticism, both of his own actions and those of the British Empire more broadly. On one of his first assignments in India, as Wilks narrates, 'His attitude led him to question whether British rule had made the people any better or happier.' These thoughts were also prompted by his romantic notions of an era dominated by 'the elephant-borne rajahs and sultans, the fretted mosques, the quaint stores of Arabic learning, etc.' while 'the English destroyed most things and spread a sanitary peace'. Dobbs's letters naturally contain his own self-appraisal, but it seems clear that over the course of his career, he was on balance only rarely responsible for destruction and could take considerable credit for spreading peace, no mean feat given the frequently difficult circumstances of his postings. But more than merely charting the travails of one individual, Wilks's biography of Dobbs fathoms the larger forces at play during this crucial, tumultuous period, a considerable achievement.

Benjamin C. Fortna
University of Arizona
(Formerly Professor of the History of the
Modern Middle East, SOAS, University of London)

Acknowledgements

This book was prompted by the recent discovery of Sir Henry Dobbs's private papers, many of considerable historical interest. Their owner, Henry Wilks, generously allowed me the free use of them and of related photographs. This new source adds to our understanding of significant events in the changed world that followed the First World War and of Sir Henry's role in them. I cannot thank Henry Wilks enough for giving me this opportunity.

I have greatly appreciated the encouragement Professor Francis Robinson and Professor Benjamin Fortna, who has kindly written the foreword, have both given me to start writing and to persist to publication. My thanks to the reviewer whose very helpful comments and suggestions have strengthened the book, to helpful staff at the British Library, India Office Records, to the Winchester College archivist and to Thomas Marlow for his technology expertise. I owe much too to my editor at Bloomsbury who has nursed my book through to publication.

My thanks are due to many for their steadfast support. Liz Sich has been a constant source of wise advice on the world of publishing hitherto unknown to me. Friends have kindly offered useful comments on my efforts: among them Kate Auspitz, Josh Davis and Franki Ord. My particular thanks to Derek Davis for his firm belief in the importance of the subject, his rigorous scrutiny of my drafts, his welcome suggestions and for his willingness to employ his extensive knowledge to strengthen my text, thus helping me greatly to improve what I wrote.

My biggest debt is to my family. My daughters, Mary and Julia, not only tolerated my preoccupation with the book but also interested themselves in Dobbs and were always ready with much kindly encouragement. Mary made time to give me invaluable help with putting everything together but it is to my husband Victor that I owe the most. His careful analysis of my texts, his eye for detail and his readiness to criticize and challenge spurred me to do better. However, what I most valued was his unshakeable confidence that my efforts would end well, his willingness to discuss any aspects and his thoughtfulness and practical support.

My grateful thanks to all involved.

British India's northwestern frontier and adjacent areas, c.1900

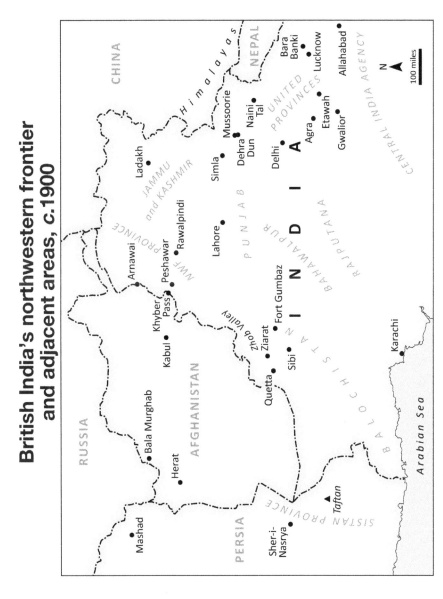

Map 1 British India's northwestern frontier and adjacent areas, c. 1900

Iraq, *c.*1926

TURKEY

RUSSIA

Lake
Van

Birecik

Lake
Urmia

SYRIA

Rawanduz

Mosul   Arbil

Little Zab

Kirkuk

Sulaimaniya

IRAN

Euphrates

I R A Q

Ramadi

Khadimain

Fallujah   Baghdad

Ctesiphon

Karbala

Tigris

Kut

Najaf

Amarah

Qurnah

Nasiryah

*Hammar
Lake*   Basra

SAUDI
ARABIA

Fao

KUWAIT

*Persian
Gulf*

N

100 miles

Map 2 Iraq, *c.* 1926

Introduction

At first glance, Sir Henry Dobbs appears to be just another conventional Indian Civil Servant. However, his atypical outlook, his often innovative approach and sometimes maverick methods led him to put local people and local sensitivities at the heart of what he did, skilfully manoeuvring so that he could also satisfy those in charge in Whitehall and Delhi. His approach enabled him to work constructively with the different communities and leading local figures in some of the world's still most volatile regions – in tribal areas on British India's north-western frontier, in Afghanistan, in Iran and in Iraq. In Iraq, he was greatly helped by his ability to spot trends early and his realization that pressure for self-determination would become irresistible well before it won London's support. As Britain's longest-serving high commissioner (1922 to 1929), his part in the creation of an independent Iraq was the culminating achievement in his career spanning almost forty years. The secretary of state to whom Dobbs mostly reported on Iraq, Leo Amery,[1] commented in 1937:

> I am glad there is a visible memorial[2] but Sir Henry's real memorial is in the actual contribution he made to the shaping of the history of Iraq and of our relation to it, the full importance of which will I hope be increasingly realised as current events crystallise into history.[3]

Dobbs played a leading part in ensuring the survival of Iraq with boundaries as recognized today. Newly arrived, he instructed military forces to take back from Turkish irregulars territory they had seized in Mosul province and in adjacent areas. Subsequently, he exerted unremitting pressure during the international negotiations with Turkey which eventually led to that country formally ceding to Iraq the disputed territory to the north of Baghdad. During his first year as high commissioner, Dobbs, in the teeth of nationalist opposition, had secured Iraq's endorsement of the treaty with Britain. This was critical to continuing the British support which was needed at that point for the survival of the embryonic

Iraq. The guidance Dobbs subsequently gave to the governments in Iraq and Britain was instrumental in enabling the new Arab state to move to early independence – the only country in the Middle East to do so before the Second World War.

Dobbs arrived in Iraq with a strong record of delivering results in troublesome areas. As foreign secretary to the Government of India, he had concluded in 1921 a treaty with India's difficult neighbour Afghanistan – a result widely despaired of following the Third Afghan War. He negotiated the final terms in Persian one-to-one with the amir. This treaty, like the relationships he established with local leaders when in charge of Balochistan, set a pattern which endured until the 1970s.

However, apart from occasional references in the literature on the period, Dobbs has remained relatively unknown. Until now, there has been no significant source to supplement official papers and shed light on his contribution. The current owner of Dobbs's family house in Ireland, his great grandson and my husband's nephew, unlocked a small room opening off the back stairs to find seven sizeable trunks filled with piles of family papers and photographs, undisturbed for over eighty years. Among these were Dobbs's personal papers including some 300 letters to his mother and 450 to his wife. These last had been sorted by date into bundles, lovingly tied together with ribbon or tape. The new owner asked me to review the papers and the intention is to make them publicly available.

For the first time, this new source brings Dobbs out of the shadows. The papers reveal how a distinctive outlook drove his achievements. He was fascinated by other civilizations, tolerant and open to different cultures. Not content with exploring British India, he mounted his own expedition through Syria, Mesopotamia and Persia and later travelled through much of Afghanistan. He had a natural affinity and ease of manner with those he met, whether Persian political activists in opium dens, frontier tribesmen, rural sheikhs or local officials. Always interested to hear what they had to say, he conversed with all of them in their own languages. He was genuinely sympathetic to the aspirations of local communities and willing to support change. He would get to know key local figures and was a shrewd judge of their character, standing and influence.

Dobbs's empathy and understanding combined with an imaginative approach and readiness to act decisively on his own initiative, made him highly effective from early in his career. Aware of how thinly stretched British resources were, his often colourful solutions would reflect the need to minimize effort and the use of force: in 1901, 1,000 Indian Civil Servants and some 66,000 British soldiers and officers administered the Indian subcontinent with a population of 300 million.[4] Thus when Dobbs wanted to protect the inhabitants of his frontier district from marauding Afghan tribesmen, he got the governor of Kandahar (whom he had met previously in Afghanistan) to stop Afghan border raids by threatening to cut off the wool and fruit trade knowing that the governor made 'immense sums' by taxing it.[5] An innovator – he had been criticized at school for being too ready to dismiss 'the old ways'[6] – he tried out various ideas for improving prosperity in his districts – for example getting new crops introduced (he was a keen naturalist) while on revenue matters he devised ingenious schemes for agreeing assessments. Dobbs energetically implemented his initiatives, often with minimal reference to higher authority, and fully exploited the scope that distance and difficult communications gave him to do as he thought best.

Unlike many British contemporaries, Dobbs's understanding of the local environment and his focus on workable solutions made him reluctant to introduce alien British colonial systems with their rigid rules and bureaucratic procedures. His instinct was always to build on what he found in place. In this he was much helped by his eclectic outlook, his respect for local conventions and his sense of what it was fair to expect. This stance was exemplified in 1915 by his bitter quarrel with Sir Percy Cox. The Government of India had sent Cox to head the civil administration in Mesopotamia which was being set up behind the advancing British Army. Dobbs, who reported to Cox, was put under intense pressure to apply Indian regulations and take on staff from India. However he continued to rely on local laws and insisted on employing local people. He stood his ground until he left Mesopotamia in August 1916 to go on long overdue leave in Ireland. In taking his stand, he was warmly supported by Gertrude Bell,[7] who later worked for Dobbs when he was high commissioner and rated him highly.

Dobbs's approach had the further advantages of recognizing the developing uncertainties about the future shape of British rule overseas and of being compatible with the increasing momentum behind the movement for self-government. Ever pragmatic, he believed that pressure to introduce this in former Ottoman territories like Mesopotamia would become irresistible well before the Allies including Britain embraced the policy.[8] As Dobbs realized, an independent government well disposed to Britain would offer the best prospect of maintaining her influence at a time when traditional imperial methods of control were being increasingly challenged and Britain was becoming ever more financially stretched. Unsympathetic to national aspirations, Cox's temporary replacement and former right-hand man, Sir Arnold Wilson, pressed ahead with the Indian colonial model. However, after the serious unrest in Iraq that broke out in 1920, the British government sent Cox back to Iraq and required him to set the country on the road to self-government. Dobbs, who followed Cox to become Iraq's longest serving high commissioner, was instrumental in steering Iraq towards the early independence it achieved in 1932. As the British Empire crumbled, the introduction of self-government into former imperial territories was a trend that would characterize much of political development in the post-imperial world.

Dobbs's career as revealed by these new sources increases our understanding of key events in both Iraq and Afghanistan. At the same time, it shows the scope for an individual to pursue his own approach and to find solutions which advance both the local community's aspirations and the demands of his British masters. Key elements in Dobbs's success were his empathy with local people, organizations and cultures, his focus on the practical, his ability to spot trends, his skill in navigating the system and his determination to follow what he judged would yield the best result, sometimes in the face of strong opposition from those in authority. His career provides an interesting and important counterpoint to conventional colonial stereotypes.

1

Henry Dobbs in the run of his times: The changing international scene and British policies; the context for Henry Dobbs's achievements

Henry Dobbs's career spanned a period that began when Great Britain was the dominant world power and the international order seemed relatively settled. It ended at a time of great uncertainty that followed the tragic upheaval of the First World War when new forces were reshaping the relationships of empires with each other and with those they governed. Dobbs was to make his mark working for the British government in India, Afghanistan and Mesopotamia (later Iraq). His successes were greatly helped by his ability to understand these new realities and use them to deliver results.

At the start of Dobbs's career in 1892, Britain's empire together with its industrial, commercial and financial pre-eminence had, since France's defeat in 1815, established it as the leading European state. Throughout most of the century, Europe had been relatively peaceful, notwithstanding periodic challenges to its stability. These derived primarily from Russia's insatiable appetite for more territory and from the Ottoman Sultanate's weakening grip on its many provinces. Dubbed 'the sick man of Europe', it offered a constant temptation to Russia and opportunistic European governments to encroach on its empire.

However, this international pattern was less settled than appeared. Towards the end of the century, a united and invigorated Germany was competing aggressively in every sphere and seeking to create its own empire. At the same time, within European states and their overseas empires, internal pressures were increasing as those ruled sought greater control over their own affairs. In Britain, the government felt these forces from Ireland to India but was slow to appreciate their implications. The cataclysm of the First World War, with its huge costs in men and resources, quickened the pace of change and forced the government to rethink how best to maintain influence as expenditure constraints tightened. Dobbs's characteristic approach played well in this changing scene. An increasing emphasis on local allies closely matched his own instinctive preferences for engaging with local communities and their leaders. This would become the pattern of relationships in the emerging post-imperial world.

When Dobbs set out to take up his first post in India, Great Britain was still seen as the leading world power. The empire it presided over covered a quarter of the globe's land mass and included a fifth of the world's population.[1] Among all Britain's overseas interests, India was judged pivotal to retaining this global supremacy. 'As long as we rule in India, we are the greatest power in the world. If we lose it we shall drop straight away to a third-rate power'[2] declared Britain's viceroy, Lord Curzon, in 1901. India's importance rested on its natural dominance of the Indian Ocean, its longstanding land and sea connections with the Mediterranean and points further east, its value as a trading hub and its sizeable army of Indian and British troops.

These forces, commanded by British officers, had been initially created by the East India Company (EIC). A trading company set up by royal charter, its trading revenues had funded an army that had enabled it to protect itself from French rivals and hostile Indian rulers, and to extend its control over most of India. In 1857, the EIC nearly lost its grip in a major uprising ('Indian Mutiny') by company soldiers, disaffected princes and landowners. In the aftermath, an army of 120,000 Indian and 60,000 British troops was reconstructed to provide security.[3] The cost amounted to half India's annual budget and was financed by local revenues. In the absence of a large standing army in Britain itself, this force also provided an imperial army which could be deployed where needed. Indeed, in the course of the First World War no fewer than 1.5 million troops from India fought abroad for Britain.

In 1858, the British Government abolished the EIC in the Government of India Act and transferred all authority to the Crown. In Britain, the enormous personal fortunes amassed by early company officials and the self-interested nature of EIC rule had long attracted criticism. The late eighteenth-century trial of Warren Hastings, the EIC's governor-general, for abusing his position had reinforced this impression. The company's governor-general was replaced by a viceroy representing the British monarch and a secretary of state in London who had a council to advise him, which included some members with direct experience of India. These arrangements replaced the president of the board of control who had supervised the EIC.[4] The act set the framework for British

India round which Dobbs later adeptly navigated in negotiating the 1921 Anglo-Afghan Treaty.

In British India, comprising present-day India, Pakistan, Bangladesh and Myanmar (formerly Burma), the viceroy was at the apex of British officialdom. Two-thirds of British India were ruled directly by the viceroy in council, and under him the governors in Madras (now Chennai) and Bombay (now Mumbai) as well as lieutenant-governors and chief commissioners elsewhere. The remaining third comprised 'princely states' whose rulers answered to the British Crown for internal governance under agreements originally reached with the EIC. They were advised by British residents, who reported to the foreign secretary to the Government of India.

Queen Victoria proclaimed in 1858 that this new Government of India would be for 'the benefit of all our subjects'. The Raj did not change its autocratic character but justified it by claiming it would establish 'peace, order and the supremacy of law'. The focus was on good government. For example, George Curzon, viceroy (1899–1905), introduced a number of reforms designed both to enhance efficiency and to make improvements in twelve areas from education to infrastructure.[5] But the paternalistic British rule remained in the hands of an exclusive British cadre. By the late nineteenth century, it faced growing pressure from Indians to have a greater say in the affairs of their country, influenced not least by moves towards more democratic government in Britain itself with its extensions of the franchise. Curzon's partition of Bengal, part of his 'rationalisation' of internal boundaries, ignited a storm of protest from Hindu Kolkata (Calcutta), increasing the momentum behind the Home Rule (*swaraj*) movement. More liberal viceroys attempted to extend the role of Indians in government, and two secretaries of state for India – John Morley in 1909 and Edwin Montagu in 1917 – advanced reforms in this direction.[6]

A key focus for the Government of India was security. India's north-west and western frontiers had always been vulnerable to attack and the government particularly feared invasion by Russia through these gateways. Russian advances into Central Asia from the 1860s onwards had taken them to the frontiers of Afghanistan and Persia. Both bordered India, both were weak and unstable and offered no effective barrier to an invader. Unruly tribesmen on these borders, who looked for plunder where they could get it, added to the difficulties of defending the frontier. Tribal leaders or the amir of Afghanistan could always raise the cry of jihad to unite followings against the infidel British. Russia and Britain competed for influence in Persia, but Afghanistan was a greater concern. Here, the Government of India's approach vacillated between a 'forward policy' and 'masterly inactivity'. Applying the first, it invaded and attempted to install a pliant amir. After the massacre of its troops in the First Afghan War (1838–42) and the murder of Britain's representative in the Second Afghan War (1878–80), the Raj fell back on 'masterly inactivity', and looked to protect its interests through indirect means. In 1880, the Government of India installed Russia's candidate, Abdur Rahman, as amir. He proved an independent and highly effective ruler, undertaking to have external relations only with the British in return for protection from Russia and a subsidy. Russia responded by seizing a slice of Afghan territory. It took seven years and a Joint Afghan Boundary Commission staffed by representatives from the three countries to agree on Afghanistan's northern frontier. The border between Afghanistan and British India was separately agreed in 1893 (the Durand Line).[7]

Another Government of India security concern was the Persian Gulf. The main coastal shipping route to India since ancient times, the area was brought within its sphere of influence by the government through agreements with the rulers along its littoral, thus promoting freer commerce and bolstering Britain's overseas trade. Winston Churchill's 1912 decision that royal navy ships should be powered by oil to be provided by the Anglo-Persian refinery at Abadan[8] enhanced the Gulf's strategic significance. Earlier, in 1869 with French completion of the Suez Canal, Egypt had come into focus as a new 'strategic hinge of Anglo-Indian defence'.[9] The canal enabled shipping dramatically to cut journey times, including importantly to India. In 1875, the British Government bought a 44 per cent share in the canal (the French held the majority). When serious unrest erupted in 1882, the British occupied Egypt and took control in order to protect the shipping route and their investment. They provided British advisers to the Khedive (its ruler) and displaced the previously dominant French. Britain had effectively turned Egypt into a protectorate, a status formalized in 1914 after the Ottoman Empire, of which Egypt was nominally part, joined the Central Powers in the First World War.

India's frontiers, the states bordering them and their borders with Russia remained constant Government of India concerns. But by the end of the century, the British government in London had other preoccupations. A burgeoning German economy and growing industrial competition in Europe were already challenging Britain's dominance. After the Prussian defeat of France in 1871, German influence was increasing both within and beyond Europe and by 1897 Britain had lost its absolute naval supremacy.[10] The creation of a powerful German fleet prompted the British government to embark on costly Dreadnought battleship construction. Higher government spending for defence or overseas purposes was always unpopular in Britain itself and the increased expenditure was only agreed with the greatest reluctance by the Cabinet and Parliament. The government in London accordingly looked to strengthen its international position through foreign alliances.

In 1904, the government arrived at an entente with France which incidentally left Egypt to the British. Three years later, in another entente, the British and Russian governments agreed their spheres of influence on India's frontiers: southern Persia and Afghanistan would fall within Britain's and northern Persia within Russia's.[11] Britain, France and Russia formed the 'Triple Entente' to counterbalance Germany's ambitions and its Austro-Hungarian alliance (the Central Powers). The British government was unmoved by strong protestations about appeasing Russia from India's former viceroy Lord Curzon, a fervent Russophobe. In the event, the Bolshevik government, which came to power after the Russian revolution of 1917, abrogated this and all other agreements made with its Tsarist predecessor.

The British government continued its energetic diplomatic efforts until the eve of the First World War. By then, the stable international system that had underpinned Britain's pre-eminent nineteenth-century position no longer existed. Despite the strenuous efforts of the British Foreign Office and the Foreign Secretary, Sir Edward Grey, diplomacy ultimately failed to prevent the outbreak of hostilities after the assassination of the Archduke Ferdinand.[12] On 4 August 1914, Britain declared war on Germany in support of its allies France and Russia, following the German violation of Belgium's neutrality.

By October 1914, troops from India were on their way from Bombay to theatres of war in Europe. However, when the Ottomans decided to join the Central Powers on 5 November 1914, these troops were diverted to protect British interests at the head of the Persian Gulf and to invade the Mesopotamian provinces of the Ottoman Empire, which was now enemy territory. On 6 November, troops landed in the most southerly of the Ottoman provinces making up Mesopotamia (later Iraq), Basra.

In Cairo, the military intelligence section at the British High Commission became the centre for advising London on the Middle East, displacing the Government of India from this role. In 1916, with the agreement of the section's head, Gilbert Clayton, it was reconstituted as the Arab Bureau at the instigation of MP Sir Mark Sykes, who was advising the government on the area.[13] The unit included Arab experts and enthusiasts, notably T. E. Lawrence and later Gertrude Bell. Another member, Ronald Storrs, put forward the idea of weakening the Ottomans by encouraging an Arab uprising led by Sharif Hussein of Mecca.[14]

This became a particularly appealing prospect, given defeats in the Dardanelles, the disastrous failure in Mesopotamia to relieve British forces besieged at Kut and the stalled campaign there, as well as the Allies' continuing high casualties and lack of success on the western front.

In the summer of 1915, Britain's high commissioner in Egypt, Sir Henry McMahon, contacted the sharif. The sharif asked for British support for his claims to all the Arab lands in return for raising an Arab revolt. Such support conflicted with the French claim to Syria which Britain had already implicitly accepted. The British foreign secretary, Sir Edward Grey, very anxious at this point not to upset the French, told McMahon to make no commitments to the Arabs but to avoid antagonizing them. McMahon's carefully worded correspondence with the sharif raised Arab hopes.[15] Later the prioritization of French claims to Syria would leave a legacy of mistrust and misunderstanding among the Arabs and the correspondence became notorious.

Despite the faltering British military campaigns, the government in London remained confident that the Ottoman Empire would be defeated. France and Britain were planning to divide the Arab lands between them, and Russia raised no objections in return for the promise of territory in eastern Anatolia.[16] The prime minister, Herbert Asquith, was keen to reach agreement with France about the partition. Advised by the MP and self-styled expert Sir Mark Sykes,[17] who had travelled extensively in the Middle East, Asquith and the Cabinet readily accepted his proposed division together with the delineation of respective spheres of influence. Sir Mark rapidly reached agreement with the French diplomat, Georges-Picot, on this basis. The boundaries were later modified, first to take account of the Balfour Declaration which promised a Jewish homeland in Palestine, and then also to reflect Lloyd George's agreement with Clemenceau, reached in December 1918, that the proposed British-controlled areas should include Mosul.[18] Indeed, when the Armistice of Mudros had supposedly ended hostilities between the Ottomans and the Allies on 31 October 1918, the British had nonetheless gone on to seize Mosul province from the Ottomans.[19]

Keen to retain influence over Middle Eastern issues, the Government of India had resisted the role of the Arab Bureau. It argued that encouraging Arabs against the Ottoman Sultan, who was also the Caliph or religious leader, risked provoking jihad against infidel British. This was lent credence by the *Khalifate* (Caliphate) movement led from Lucknow and extending to Afghanistan which lasted from 1919 until Mustafa Kemal (later known as Atatürk) abolished the Caliphate in 1924. But backing from the viceroy, and many of his officials in Mesopotamia, for administration on Indian lines encouraged revolt there in

1920 and was completely at odds with the growing sympathy for Arab aspirations which had the support of the Arab Bureau. When British forces took Baghdad in March 1917, General Maude had read out a proclamation drafted by Sykes, agreed in Cabinet and endorsed in Parliament, inviting the Arabs to manage their own affairs in collaboration with the British.[20] Then in October 1918, British troops under General Allenby and Arab forces under the sharif's son Faisal rode into Damascus, and Faisal proclaimed an Arab government. This was followed by the Anglo-French Declaration, again drafted by Sykes, which announced the commitment of the British and French governments to self-determination in both Syria and Mesopotamia.[21]

Self-determination was gaining increasing support as the most practical and acceptable means of retaining influence and a degree of control over the Middle East. Curzon commented, 'We ought to play self-determination for all it is worth knowing in the bottom of our hearts we are more likely to benefit from it than anybody else.'[22] Lloyd George shared this view and thought it might have the added bonus of helping the British expand their territorial claims at the expense of the French. Ministers assumed that the Arabs would have a continuing need for British support, which would give Britain an enduring influence. Lloyd George had no difficulty with indirect control, provided Arab leaders were guided, like Indian princes, by the British.

The British government had another reason for supporting self-determination. It would make it much easier to present their claims in the international discussions among the Allies that were being arranged following the defeat of the Central Powers. The Allies were due to open peace talks in January 1919. A key player would be President Woodrow Wilson. The United States had entered the war on the side of the Allies in April 1917, and the president had presented the war very much in moral terms as an opportunity to advance American ideals of freedom, democracy and independence. The war was to make the world safe for democracy and to be a war to end all wars.[23] In his Fourteen Points speech given in January 1918, Wilson had made a commitment to autonomous development or self-determination for communities in defeated empires.

At the peace talks, Wilson proposed to the Supreme Council, made up of the Allies' leading peacemakers (from March 1919 comprising the prime ministers of Great Britain, France and Italy and the president of the United States), that former Ottoman and German colonies should be administered by the League of Nations, the body Wilson envisaged would bring about a new world order. Previously, defeated powers' territories would have been divided up between the victors and then annexed, a practice which Wilson considered completely unacceptable. His scheme provided for League of Nations 'mandates' under which territories would be administered in the interests of their inhabitants. Only Lloyd George supported Wilson's proposals. He managed to secure approval for them by introducing three levels of mandate related to the territories' readiness to conduct their own government. In addition, the wishes of the community were to be taken into account in selecting the mandatory. The Supreme Council agreed to these arrangements on 30 January 1919, and they became Article 22 of the League Covenant.[24]

The aspirations of minorities, such as the Armenians and the Kurds, often persecuted within the Ottoman Empire, were more difficult for the Allies to accommodate within the League structure. They had been ready to take at face value vague American hints that they might take on mandates, for example for Armenia and Anatolia, home to many of these minorities. However, once a sick President Wilson had returned to America in September 1919, it became clear that the United States would not do so. Russian Armenia soon became a Soviet Republic and the other Allies proposed dividing much of Anatolia between mandates for Italy and France. They also envisaged creating a neutral zone around Constantinople (Istanbul) and allocating Smyrna (Izmir) to Greece. These plans were reflected in the Treaty of Sèvres (1920), which was signed by a representative of the Ottoman Empire.[25] This agreement would have effectively dismembered Turkey. However, Turkey's most successful general, Mustafa Kemal (later known as Atatürk), had reorganized their army. He drove the Greeks out of western Anatolia and thwarted the proposed Italian and French mandates. Thus freed of foreign control, Turkey's boundaries, with the exception of Mosul, were agreed in the Treaty of Lausanne (1923).[26] Atatürk swept away the remnants of Ottoman rule and turned the country into a modern secular European-style nation state. Whatever the constitutional forms, he effectively ruled the Turkish Republic until his death in 1938.

Progress in agreeing the detail and setting up the new League of Nations as a functioning organization was very slow. The British and French governments argued endlessly over their respective territorial claims, eventually settling on the modified Sykes–Picot agreement carried forward into mandate boundaries. The Supreme Council allocated mandates for Syria and Lebanon to France and for Palestine and Mesopotamia (including Mosul), later known as Iraq, to Britain. All were Class A mandates. The agreement was formalized at San Remo in March 1920.[27]

In his last and most testing post as high commissioner in Iraq, Sir Henry Dobbs was expected to satisfy the conditions of the League of Nations mandate and to deliver the continuing influence which the British government still hoped to exercise. Class A mandates were for the 'most ready' communities 'whose independence could be provisionally recognised subject to the supply of advice and assistance by the mandatory power until the community could stand alone'.[28] However there was no practical guidance on how the proposed mandates should be set up or put into effect and none on how soon full independence might be granted. In practice, the mandatory power held the reins. The London government saw control of Iraq as important to communications with India and later to oil interests. Overseas expenditure was however capped and Atatürk was contesting control of Mosul province (Iraq's northern third), now infiltrated by Turkish irregulars. Displaced from Syria by the French, Faisal was chosen as king of Iraq. He and Iraqi leaders soon became restless under British supervision. They chafed against League requirements, which had to be satisfied for Iraq's independence to be recognized. Dobbs navigated through all these conflicting pressures making it possible for Iraq, Mosul included, to become accepted intact as an independent nation in 1932. It had been created by the British only thirteen years previously and was the first mandate to achieve independent status. Its progress heralded a future international order in which ex-imperial powers would attempt to influence once subordinate territories by building close relationships and exploiting residual 'soft' power. As Dobbs's career shows, he recognized this trend early and was active in promoting the transition.

2

Home and away 1871 to 1900: Family connections; education; early experiences in British India

On 12 November 1892, Henry Dobbs set sail from Trieste to join the Indian Civil Service (ICS). His background and education were typical of those who, like him, were appointed through open competition. Many came from the professional classes, and disproportionately many from Ireland. Dobbs's Irish father Robert Dobbs was a lawyer and member of Lincoln's Inn, whose family had left England in the sixteenth century to settle in Ireland. Dobbs's British mother was descended from the Broadwoods of piano fame – they had after all made Beethoven's favourite piano – although the firm by then was struggling to adapt to new technologies and markets.[1] More pertinent to Dobbs's prospects, his mother's first cousins, Sir Alfred and Sir James Lyall, had a long family connection with India through the East India Company (EIC) and had themselves enjoyed successful careers in the ICS. Both had become lieutenant-governors, the former also serving as foreign secretary to the Government of India and after retirement as a member of the British Government's Council of India in London. While Sir Alfred told Dobbs's mother he had done nothing to assist Dobbs's career except influencing his first posting to a sought-after province (North-Western Provinces and Oudh),[2] family connections were very common among those joining the ICS and made it an obvious career to be considered especially by a young man who, as Dobbs did, would need to earn his living.

Born in London on 26 August 1871, Henry Dobbs grew up in southern England. He went to Ireland from time to time to stay in his grandparents' house, Ashurst, near Dublin and after 1890, when his own family moved to Ireland, either there or on Kenmare Bay where they took a house first at Derryquin and then at Kenmare. Henry was the second of three brothers; he also had three younger sisters. He and his brothers went away to school first in Devon, then for a year near Guildford. He won a scholarship to Winchester and arrived at the school in September 1885. Even as a schoolboy, he showed his readiness to set his own course, which became very evident during his career. He thus preferred more solitary pursuits, including writing verses, to team activities.[3] In his work too, he would take an independent line as Dobbs's headmaster, Dr Fearon, soon recognized. He noted that Dobbs showed 'a remarkable amount of freshness, originality and force in all he does … spirit and ability' while his work was 'bright and vigorous'. However, Fearon also commented that 'his fault is that he enjoys saying things that are paradoxical and occasionally goes beyond the bounds of good taste'. Fearon then warned that 'his danger is that he may be inclined to think old fashioned ways and beliefs not worth consideration simply because they are old'.[4]

One of the notes from Dobbs's headmaster, written after less than two years at Winchester, implies a clear expectation he would sit for the ICS. There is no evidence to suggest that Henry himself had positively chosen this career. He did not appear to have any sense of 'imperial mission' nor at that stage any romantic spirit of adventure which India might appeal to. Indeed, after a year or two in the ICS, he wrote that he wished he had devoted his life to 'composing' verses even if it had meant living on a crust in a garret.[5] Given his family connections, the improbability of his receiving any significant inheritance and Winchester's role as a prolific provider of ICS recruits, it is perhaps no surprise that Henry Dobbs found himself impelled towards the ICS. Later in his career, Dobbs was to show 'Winchester bred mentalities', namely reserve, commitment to work and a life devoted to the public service.[6] However, Dr Fearon, his headmaster, warned him that as a prospective ICS applicant, if he was to succeed in the competition for the ICS, he would need to improve his 'scholarship'. Dobbs then worked 'magnificently'[7] and in the summer of 1890, he was placed twenty-first in the ICS exam and also won an open scholarship to Brasenose College Oxford.[8]

Open competition for appointments to the ICS had been introduced by the government in 1853, a model followed eventually throughout the British civil service. In an effort to improve the quality of ICS recruits, Lord Salisbury had in 1879 redesigned the selection process that Henry Dobbs was to go through. Candidates sat a competitive examination on leaving school for a place in the ICS. The successful candidates then had to spend two 'probationary years' at a university (in Dobbs's case Oxford) studying the languages of their chosen province in India as well as other prescribed subjects.[9] Henry arrived in the autumn of 1890 and left in the summer of 1892. He had to make frequent trips to

London in order to meet the conditions of his ICS appointment. These included language exams, a medical examination and attending court sessions to observe how cases were conducted. While at Oxford, Dobbs found time to row in the Brasenose College boat, and to participate in the college essay and play reading societies.

En route to India, Port Said gave Henry Dobbs his first taste of the East. When his ship docked, he saw 'veiled women with only their eyes peeping out … their dresses picturesque as well as filthy'.[10] He watched Arabs loading coals onto the big steamers in the same way as he would study the Indians and later the Arabs around him and the methods they employed:

> Big barges full of coal are brought up alongside and two planks leant up from the edge of the barge to the ship. Then a large boatful of chattering natives with little baskets is brought over and soon the end of the ship where the coal is presents the appearance of an ants' nest – two continuous lines of black creatures one going up and the other coming down making the while a horrid crazy droning noise.[11]

At Suez, 'crowds of Arab dhows with rakish sail – I believe that is the proper adventure-book term – came fluttering round us. The whole place looked just like the pictures you see of Eastern places.'[12] He described Aden as

> choked with trains of camels, mere bags of skin and bone evidently full of malice and all uncharitableness laden with stacks of dry wineskins or brush wood. The hot sandy road was full of dark-skinned people of every sort, many of them wonderfully handsome though others were distorted by strange dyes incongruous nose-rings stuck into one nostril and heads shaved absolutely bald.[13]

He was also, and remained throughout his life, a keen observer of the natural world, now describing for his family flying fish, pink flamingos, blue beetles and other exotica.

Henry Dobbs arrived in Bombay at the beginning of December 1892. He then travelled by train some 800 miles northwards via Allahabad to Etawah, the civil station and district headquarters in the North-Western Provinces and Oudh (NWP and Oudh),[14] to which he had been allocated. There, he had to report to the district officer or collector, Mr Alexander. This initial assignment, like his other early assignments, followed a standard pattern for all young men who had successfully competed to join the ICS. During his first three years in India, Dobbs worked in many different areas within his allocated province (NWP and Oudh), responding to the collector in charge. Collectors had a vast range of responsibilities, and they set Dobbs to work on a very broad and varied range of tasks. He spent the next three years in the secretariat of the province, most of the time as private secretary to the lieutenant-governor, Sir Antony MacDonnell. Secretariat work, as Dobbs realized, increased the chances of being appointed to some of the more prestigious and interesting posts. Much as he disliked self-promotion, he also appreciated the need to make himself better known in order to secure such opportunities. After another year of district work in the province, Henry Dobbs was appointed to the Political Department, this time at Ootacamund[15] and Coorg[16] in the southern province of Madras (now Chennai). Eight months later, in January 1901, he got the frontier appointment, which he had long wanted. He was to go as a political agent to the Zhob Valley: 'all sorts of interesting things are always happening on the frontier' which can offer 'splendid opportunities'[17] he wrote.

In preparation for their ICS appointments, Henry Dobbs and his fellow recruits had to acquire some knowledge of the relevant local languages and the law. However, there were no formal arrangements to equip them with any of the practical knowledge and skills they might need when they first started work.[18] It was assumed that such elite generalists supported by Indian subordinates would be equal to tackling whatever they faced. Nor was there any systematic effort to give them in advance some understanding of the country to which they were going – its diverse peoples and their different religions and customs, how the new arrivals would be expected to behave, or to tell them about the sort of conditions in which they could be working. How much they knew about what might confront them when they reached India would have largely depended on their own personal contacts.

When he reached Etawah, Dobbs's instructions were to recruit three servants – a bearer, a table servant and a sweeper or general servant – before joining the collector in camp. Dobbs, who had probably never recruited even one servant before, was helped by an official in the station who unfortunately recruited a cook whom Dobbs did not need and failed to provide a sweeper. Relying on his hitherto little used native languages, Dobbs sent back the cook and procured a sweeper 'of which feat I am very proud'.[19]

The next morning, Dobbs rode out to find the collector. As the man on the spot, the collector or district officer was the 'symbol and executive agent of Britain's imperial administration', and not just in India but in other parts of the British Empire. In addition to their responsibilities for revenue collection, collectors oversaw the arrangements for real estate, settling disputes and managing indebted estates. They also supervised the general administration of the district including famine relief and were responsible for law and order. As district magistrates, they oversaw the courts and directed police work.[20] Many collectors spent half the year or more in camp as they toured their district. It was seen as an essential part of running a large district to the extent that provincial governments specified how much time had to be spent on tour.[21] Moving around allowed officials to understand their district and its people better, to settle local disputes and to see things for themselves. It was also an important part of demonstrating the authority of the Raj. Apart from a few days around Christmas, Dobbs was in camp for the next three months. Indeed, for many periods of his life much of his time was spent on the move. On this first tour, the tents were 'about 18 ft every way inside and a sort of tent veranda runs all round them. It is rather queer having no doors but reed curtains and when I was in bed a horrid pariah dog entered the tent … The jackals make a fearful howling.'[22]

Dobbs and the collector never stayed more than two days in each place and generally had to ride about 10 miles to their next stop. There were fourteen 'huge camels' to carry the camp's baggage. Half the tents and luggage were sent on in advance during the night. 'It is rather a desultory life continually packing up and having half your own things sent on in advance.'[23] Henry was at first impressed by the 'palatial tents and appurtenances' and the innumerable servants. However, a few weeks later when he was in camp on his own, he commented, 'I shall feel very small as I have only three tents and 3 bullock carts while the Lieutenant-Governor has 50 tents 300 camels and 100 carts.'[24]

Dobbs was to have direct experience later of organizing these large-scale and elaborate camps, but his current preoccupations were with district work. Each day, he rode out with the collector while they inspected 'fields, villages and all sorts of things', heard complaints and settled disputes. At the same time, he was expected to be improving his language skills and adding to his knowledge. He would have to sit further exams covering criminal law, revenue administration, Hindustani and two scripts – Persian and Nagri.[25] After Christmas, when he would have been in the country for barely a month, he was told to go out into camp on his own. He complained of a 'continual scurry' in his arrangements. Hardly had he reached his destination, inspected papers and registers and questioned the local merchants about anything he wanted to know than he had to move on. As he travelled around, he wrote as an interested observer about subjects ranging from the land and its crops, the bird life with examples such as demoiselle cranes and adjutant birds – ('enormous creatures over 6 ft high with black feathers tremendous bills and heads and necks quite bare from the shoulders who will eat anything from a cow to a snake 5 ft long'[26]) – to local customs or the commercial acumen of the Indian dealer and money lender. Detailed observations and reflections on his surroundings were to characterize both his official writing and his private correspondence throughout his career.

A few weeks later, and back at Etawah, he had his first experience of responding to a natural disaster – a terrible hail storm: 'The hail was a terrific sight. Every stone was about double the size of a large marble and all our windows against which the wind was blowing were smashed ... universal desolation spread around'.[27] The storm had destroyed a third of the spring crops.

> It meant an enormous amount of extra work for everyone as the Government demand will have to be remitted on most of the villages ... I had an awful time inspecting the damage ... wearily wandering on horseback through countless villages taking reports of smashed up crops in a note-book amidst howling villagers ... Every drop of moisture oozed out of me ... At some of the villages they brought me out water to drink in magnificent brazen vessels but I did not drink partly because I should probably have got cholera or something and chiefly because the unfortunate people would have had to destroy their vessels after my drinking from them which would have been rather hard luck considering their present calamities ... The space outside the block of court buildings has been a howling mass of about 10,000 people for the last three days who assert that they and their children are all dead and demand all sorts of things. We are looking forward to the great increase of crime during the rest of the year in consequence of the dearth produced by the hail.[28]

At the same time as Dobbs and the collector were riding around amassing information from their inspections – an essential prerequisite for setting government revenue demands – they were also stopping to hear complaints and settle disputes. These were innumerable since as Dobbs immediately observed, everyone was 'occupied in quarrelling with everyone else; if not the Hindus with the Mohammedans, then one Hindu caste with another'.[29] Indeed, he complained that 'if I go out by myself people start up howling from every bush, put their hands together in front of them, and begin with "hail, nourisher of the poor" and then proceed with some complaint against some enemy or other, but I always tell them imperiously to go away'.[30] He also commented that 'their only weapon seems to be false accusation'. He had an early demonstration of this. A man accused another of attacking him but when the collector made him wash his wound, it disappeared. In this atmosphere, as Dobbs observed, 'It is very trying not to be able to believe anyone in the least. You simply have to decide a case by probabilities which makes it very worrying'.[31] The only exception was if the authorities happened to come across a crime that had just been committed and statements could be taken at once so that the victim had no opportunity to cook up evidence against their private enemies.

Throughout these early years, Dobbs spent a considerable amount of his time dispensing justice and keeping order. He dealt with cases which ranged from petty crime to public order and corruption. A few years after his arrival, he was particularly proud of his handling of a 'tremendous' outbreak of burglaries which occurred during his time in Bara Banki (about 20 miles east of Lucknow) in August 1898.

> I had all the reputed bad characters secured in one night, got the most wealthy and influential citizens to give evidence as to their bad reputations and, after sitting in court recording evidence from 9.00am to 7.00pm, trying them in gangs, I sent 20 of the worst specimens to jail for a year. There has not been a case of burglary since, so I feel I was justified in my coup.[32]

He subsequently held other judicial appointments and drew on his experience to suggest changes to Indian civil and criminal procedures. He soon came to the conclusion that order could be better maintained by allowing some offences to be dealt with by tribal rather than 'stupid English law'. This conviction was reflected later in his approach in the North-West Frontier Province and later still in Mesopotamia.

Dobbs's early responsibilities included not only applying the law but also maintaining the administration needed to underpin it. Thus, he was responsible for overseeing the keeping of proper records and reports and, after his first year, was commended for his 'thorough and efficient' supervision of the office.[33] However, this approach forced him to take very unpleasant actions to deal with embezzlement and corruption. In June 1898, less than a month after his arrival at Bara Banki, he suspended three of his clerks for embezzlement of public moneys.

> I suffer from a constitutional disability to sign my name to a register or bill without looking through it; so that criminals who have been jogging along comfortably for years under other people and have thus become careless get tripped up and found out. And then it seems rather horrid in the end when you have broken a man for life to hear that he has a large family dependent on him … It always seems to be my fate to discover and punish these things wherever I go.[34]

A more serious case involving the police was to arise four months later. A well-known figure in the district bribed the whole of the local police force and many of the clerks in the office before murdering an enemy. Dobbs became suspicious and so put together a pretext to arrest him. He was found to have with him papers which detailed his false alibi, named those who had been persuaded to give false evidence and those of Dobbs's staff who had been involved. Dobbs then discovered duplicate false papers in his office and had everyone connected with the conspiracy arrested and tried. The perpetrator, who was defended by European barristers, was committed to the Sessions where he might be hung. 'I will be glad to leave after all this work and worry, having brought so many officials to grief. I think they must think me a fiend thirsting for blood and slaughter.'[35] From the moment he arrived, Henry Dobbs took swift and immediate action against dishonesty and incompetence wherever he found it as he was to do throughout his career.

As well as dealing with burglaries, robberies, assaults and murders, the judicial system had its part to play in preserving public order, peace and security – constant preoccupations of India's British rulers. Thus, Dobbs found himself handling an enormous riot case. In July 1895 at Dehra Dun, he wrote, 'I have had a tremendous riot case with 20 prisoners, 30 witnesses for the prosecution and 60 witnesses for the defence dragging along in my court for the last three weeks.'[36] But outside the court room, officials could often play an important part in calming tensions. At the same time, they had to be careful that their actions did not inadvertently inflame them. At Etawah, the collector intervened when a new Hindu temple was built touching the mosque – riots ensued, and people were killed. He then required the temple to be taken down and peace was restored.[37] Dobbs wrote about the efforts of the lieutenant-governor to improve relations between Muslims and Hindus[38] and the anxieties of the authorities when large religious festivals took place because offence could so easily be given by one community to another, sparking riots. Dobbs describes how Muslims while celebrating their Muharram rituals were inclined to take their Taziya shrine too close to the peepul tree sacred to the Hindus and how fights ensued.[39] Indeed during Henry Dobbs's first summer in India, the serious unrest in many areas made him very conscious of how religious differences could threaten law and order. Whatever the circumstances, Dobbs did not hesitate to take risks in order to enforce the law. Thus a few months after his arrival, he threatened grain sellers – who persistently disregarded a prohibition on spreading their grain over the public highway – that he would spoil the grain with oil if they continued. They did. Dobbs poured paraffin on the grain and a riot almost ensued. He was reprimanded for this, although it effectively stopped the practice.[40] Some years later, Dobbs, then in Mysore, rode into Bangalore[41] to find thousands of street sweepers holding a mass meeting to declare a strike in circumstances that would have increased the risk of plague spreading. Accompanied by only six soldiers, a few policemen and the local magistrate, he set up a court then and there (one of the posts he held was Sessions Judge of the Bangalore Ceded Tract) and got the magistrate still on horseback to try and to sentence the ringleaders.

After sentencing, they were at once marched away to prison before the mass of sweepers could realize how few keepers of the peace were actually there, and the sweepers immediately returned to work. The resident however, while relieved, thought his assistant, Dobbs, had exceeded his authority.[42] This was not the first time he had been ready to constitute a court in unusual circumstances in order to resolve pressing matters. A year earlier he had got witnesses to take their oath on the sacred emblem in a Hindu temple because the two parties to an important case had agreed to be bound by it. Dobbs was then amused by the witnesses' efforts to dodge the drops that fell on them from the constant dripping of water arranged in the hot weather to keep the sacred emblem cool.[43]

Dobbs had not expected to find the constant demonstrations of the dignity of office that were part of the system to maintain and uphold the authority of the Raj, nor had he anticipated the responses these prompted. Soon after his arrival at Etawah, he writes, 'I could scarcely keep from laughing out loud when I passed a crowd of village policemen whom their superintendent hustled into line and caused to salute magnificently. However, I tried to look as if I was accustomed to it.'[44] Two weeks later at Christmas, he had to 'sit in state to go through a tremendous course of interviews with native magnates and landlords … At the end, you have to say with a wave of your hand "now you have permission to depart".'[45] This was just a foretaste of the pomp and ceremony that Her Majesty's representatives in India were expected to maintain and which Dobbs would see a great deal of in his later private secretary role.

Henry Dobbs always enjoyed the variety of work as a district officer. Furthermore, the widely held view among the governing classes that intelligent generalists from the public school system could turn their hands to anything – a view that persisted in the British Civil Service until the follow-up to the Fulton report of 1965 – meant that Dobbs was often asked to work in rather specialized areas of which he had no previous knowledge. Six weeks after his arrival in India he had to act as returning officer for the local elections. The liberal Viceroy Lord Ripon had wanted to see elected self-governing local authorities and by 1892 the Indian Councils Act had established municipal corporations and district boards for local administration with elected Indian members. Dobbs commented, 'Election fever is so keen among the natives in India that they have to be driven to vote in municipal elections by force otherwise no vote would be recorded and the whole thing would be a farce, at least that is the case in the northwest … I shall have to gather people together and compel them to vote.'[46] Much later, as high commissioner in Iraq, Dobbs had to work with a recently enfranchised electorate in a new self-governing state.

Other requests on sometimes abstruse topics followed. One required him to deal with Etawah's 'dreadful stenches' and devise a means for cleaning out the city latrines. He was also sent to write reports on specialized subjects – the first on brasswork, the second on transport and the third on the glass and pottery of Oudh. Although he grumbled about this work in addition to his 'day job' in the district, he was told that being asked to do it marked him out as a coming man. His approach to the brasswork report was typical of his dogged persistence. When he tried to make a start, long-serving local officials told him no brasswork industry existed for him to write about. Undeterred, he 'poked about' in the houses of the caste traditionally involved in brassmaking to discover a 'hidden industry' – so little was known about it. He writes that 'I then [undertook] a two day expedition into a remote village, which I could reach on an elephant only, the road being about 5 ft. deep in water. I lived and slept in the village schoolhouse, and all the population gathered to see me pay my tribute to nature.'[47]

Hardly had he finished his brassware fact finding than he was asked to spend three months investigating the effect of the proposed Lucknow to Benares railway on traffic and trade in various districts. This involved moving every two days and travelling over 800 miles on horseback.[48] The resulting report was very well received. Dobbs noted that subsequent decisions on new railway routes were in line with his recommendations and later commented on how very satisfying he found it to see such a tangible result.[49] Shortly after writing this report, he was invited to join the secretariat for his province (North-Western Provinces and Oudh) although he did not in fact do so for another two years. His move was held up after an incident in court when Dobbs had just returned to work after a bout of influenza. He had lost his temper, thrown an ink pot at one of the clerks which hit him and covered him with ink. The details were widely reported in the Indian papers and followed episodes involving other officials striking Indian clerks. These had prompted criticism in the British Parliament where liberal opinion was becoming much more sensitive about the treatment of Indians. It was therefore feared that to advance Dobbs shortly after the ink pot incident might prompt criticism in London. His move was consequently delayed.[50]

A few months after this incident in May 1894 and after less than eighteen months working in the districts, Dobbs asked his cousin Sir Alfred Lyall if he could open the way for him to join the Foreign and Political Department. The Political Service offered the biggest spread of postings – in the princely states, in countries beyond the boundaries of India such as the Persian Gulf or Persia itself and on the northwest frontier area, and these Dobbs thought would offer more excitement. Dobbs was free to apply once he had passed all his exams, but the support of a relative from the department would increase his chances of selection[51] and Sir Alfred had been foreign secretary. However, he advised Dobbs to remain in his current province for a year or two because the experience and training there would be invaluable.[52] Dobbs took this advice and in due course got an appointment in the Political Service.

Dobbs had also appreciated that he needed to 'network' to improve his chances of being considered for promotion when he was working not from camp but from administrative centres or 'stations' and so living among colleagues. At first, he took an energetic part in the social life and was very proud of organizing a complicated moonlight picnic, 'a great spread' with aspic, jellies and blancmange at which the entire police band played and there were dances, games and musical entertainments.[53] However, he soon came to dislike the endless round of social calls, and the society of the many young ladies who 'seem to make it their open aim to hunt for a husband' so that 'there is a sort of permanent and blatant expectation of marriage in the air'. He reflected that this may be why they had little success and commented that 'I am afraid they think me rather brusque and rude because I do not eagerly seek their company and pretend to enjoy their stupid ways and silly cackle.'[54]

Rather than socializing, Dobbs preferred to explore his surroundings. He wrote enthusiastically for example about his Christmas expedition to the Shivalik Hills where he spent his holiday in 'the midst of the impenetrable jungles among wild elephants, tigers, leopards, deer of all sorts, pheasants, jungle fowl, partridges etc.: it was like the adventure book descriptions'.[55] He was interested in plants and, later in India, put this to good use in his efforts to introduce more productive crops. He was very fond of gardens and loved to plant them out wherever he went. He enjoyed riding, polo, pig sticking and all kinds of hunting. This last activity in many different forms provided him with much amusement sometimes in splendid circumstances with local dignitaries. Six months after his arrival, he writes enthusiastically to his friend Wainewright about how efforts to deal with criminals turned into an exciting hunt with encouragement from the local rajah:

I had very good fun last week. There have been some rather bad dacoits [gangs of armed robbers; fugitives from rural landowners] on the border of the district, several villagers being shot, so the Collector, the Superintendent of police and I sallied forth to see the scene of operations, and try to catch the dacoits. The latter task we found hopeless, as they had taken refuge in the immense ravines stretching for miles and miles on each side of the Jumna, overgrown with

Figure 2.1 Henry Dobbs with his dog during his early years in India. He preferred his own company to the constant social round. Courtesy of Henry Wilks.

acacias, wild dates, & citrons. But we used our arms – revolvers and carbines – against the more harmless black buck. We had a splendid ride of about 3 miles after a herd, and finally cornered them so that they had either to fall down a cliff or run past us. They chose the latter, and singularly enough all got off unscathed. Next day a rajah the other side of the Jumna came to pay a visit, and afterwards sent us three elephants whereon we mounted to make a return call ... Finally we returned as we had come, taking back with us two hunting leopards or cheetahs, which the old man lent us to hunt black buck with. That same night another local magnate sent us many bottles of the best champagne with quantities of ice, peaches, figs etc., being determined not to be outdone by the rajah, so we had a very fine time of it.[56]

However, perhaps in part as the novelty of these exotic activities wore off, Dobbs wrote that 'I am fonder of my own society than ever and am never so pleased as when I can get away for a walk quite by myself with my dogs.'[57]

Nonetheless, he did recognize that some social activities could be very helpful to him in advancing his career. One of these was acting. Indeed, he became so much in demand for his acting skills that he was asked to go to the hill station

Naini Tal (the summer administrative centre for the lieutenant-governor of his province (North-Western Provinces and Oudh)) to take part in the theatrical productions.[58] Not only was this more pleasant than remaining down in the heat, it also provided an opportunity to meet more senior officials whose patronage was an important element in securing more desirable and interesting appointments.

In February 1896, Dobbs started work in the secretariat for his province. He believed this was an opportunity that might lead to 'all sorts of good things'. Indeed, after three months he writes, 'to my own great surprise and that of everyone else I have suddenly blossomed into Private Secretary to Sir Antony MacDonnell [another Irishman], the Lieut. Governor of these Provinces'.[59]

Dobbs accepted the post although he was somewhat apprehensive about his suitability for it. It was normally filled by a military man. In addition, it would mean a 'complete loss of independence'[60] because he would have to be entirely at Sir Antony's beck and call. Furthermore, Sir Antony was perceived as being notoriously difficult to work for. The post did however give Dobbs the opportunity to observe first-hand how a job at lieutenant-governor level was done and to meet the many senior figures who either worked with the lieutenant-governor or who sought his support. The post also required very effective organizational skills not least because the lieutenant-governor was constantly on the move either in camp or between various administrative centres – most often Lucknow, Allahabad and Naini Tal – or travelling around his province which extended over some 110,000 square miles.

Dobbs had preferred being in camp to being in civil stations or district headquarters where he could be pressed into activities that were intended to strengthen the 'esprit de corps'[61] but were not to his taste such as the empty social round, cricket or going out with the Agra Volunteer Corps. However, in camp touring with the lieutenant-governor was rather a different matter. Dobbs commented: 'I shall be very glad when this tour is over as the burden of all the arrangements falls upon me – special trains, interviews with Rajas, conferences, and deputations all have to be planned out and assigned their proper times, all officials concerned informed, carriages and escorts to be in waiting and a number of other details gone into.'[62]

Another reason Dobbs did not enjoy camp with the lieutenant-governor was because

> one feels like an army of locusts moving over the face of the earth and one knows
> that the horrible red-coated native servants are looting the whole countryside

wherever they go taking everything they can get for nothing because they are in the train of the 'Lord Sahib'. I try my best to stop this wholesale spoliation but it is a hopeless matter.[63]

Dobbs also complained:

I am never off duty. It gets upon my nerves a little at times. I have a lot of extra work too writing out résumés of the extemporary speeches Sir Antony is fond of making and minutes of the proceedings when he receives any deputation to go to the papers. The big natives who have been granted an interview have to be talked to and entertained in my room until he can see them and countless fussy and aggrieved Europeans are always coming to see me to try to get interviews so that altogether a tour is not a period of unmixed bliss.[64]

Dobbs's day-to-day work was largely determined by the way in which the lieutenant-governor chose to meet his responsibilities. Touring in camp enabled the lieutenant-governor to see large areas of his province, to meet local figures and understand local problems at first hand. It was also an opportunity to demonstrate the power and dignity of the government. Any attempt to move away from constant pomp was not well received. Dobbs explains that the then viceroy, Lord Elgin, annoyed 'the good people of Simla by walking out with a cap and stick instead of using the carriage and four in which he is supposed to go forth'.[65] Elgin then failed to get his council to agree

to do away with the special trains by which the Viceroy and Lieutenant-Governors are accustomed to travel. He apparently wishes to fight his way through a crowd of natives on the platform and take a seat if he can find one in an ordinary carriage. As all the pettiest rajahs habitually charter special trains it is felt that this would hardly suit the dignity of the Queen's representative.[66]

Dobbs later observed that the viceroy's train was 'considerably more splendid than anything I am in the habit of providing for Sir Antony'.

The need to impress added to the already enormous and complex logistical task of organizing the camps. At the extreme was Sir Antony's Christmas camp – especially elaborate because Lady MacDonnell and several other ladies accompanied their husbands:

We met an enormous special train with about 100 servants, pianos, spring beds and I know not what else and trundled during the whole night up to a small station in the middle of the jungles called Palia. The camp was six miles from there over a bad road and Sir Antony had insisted on bringing carriages and horses by rail when everyone knew the road was too bad to be used. Fortunately

Figure 2.2 One of the lieutenant-governor's camps which Dobbs, as his private secretary (1896 to 1898), had to organize. Courtesy of Henry Wilks.

there were eighty elephants waiting at the station and about 100 bullocks and the whole fearful paraphernalia had to be ponderously moved off to the camp. The camp consisted of at least 30 enormous tents containing drawing rooms dining rooms boudoirs and everything possible with furniture to match ... All this had to be done at a week's notice and every little detail arranged by me down to the number of cows to be taken by train ... I had to arrange for six other camps to which we are now scurrying like gigantic mushrooms all over the Provinces so you may imagine that I felt like going off my head.[67]

This complicated context created a great deal of work for Dobbs especially as he had sacked his head clerk for 'gross misdemeanours' and Sir Antony was constantly changing his plans so that everything had to be reorganized at short notice. At the same time, the regular administrative work had to continue.

Shortly after Christmas, famine in the province came to dominate the agenda. At its height, there were famine conferences every other day. Dobbs commended MacDonnell's detailed grasp of the system of famine relief which he had largely developed and the way in which MacDonnell interviewed, consulted and listened to the 'big natives' and landholders of every district. He also admired his energy: over two months they had visited twenty-six districts, each about the size of Yorkshire. Dobbs was convinced MacDonnell's handling of the famine had greatly improved relations with those 'in whose breasts memories of the mutiny continuously rankle'.[68] When the famine was over, the leading landholders in Oudh and Lucknow fêted Sir Antony. Regarded by Lord Curzon as one of his most able senior officials, Sir Antony's methods greatly influenced Dobbs, both early on when he himself was a famine commissioner and more generally. Like Sir Antony, Dobbs also saw it as essential to go out and about and see for himself, to have the support of the local community, to establish who the key players were and to win them over. He adopted many elements of this approach in his subsequent posts.

Dobbs was rather less impressed, however, by 'Sir Antony's yearning to keep himself before the public by constantly making speeches though in a country like India where there is no necessity to solicit the suffrages of the people and men hold permanent appointments, I have never been able to understand why it is necessary to shout about things at all. They can be done quite quietly'.[69] Scornful as he was of self-promotion, Dobbs did acknowledge that 'nowadays everyone has an eye to home opinion and to the chance of being reported in *The Times*'.[70] Later on, Dobbs himself used the press with great effect to influence local opinion in Iraq in 1924 when it helped to win a vote crucial to the country's political future.

Dobbs found various aspects of his private secretary role trying. He commented that it was worse than being at school and described how much he disliked having to be a courtier and work among those in camp whom he saw as 'so self-seeking and always trying to administer the grossest flattery to Sir Antony'.[71] At headquarters, he deplored the companies of officials who 'in their quest for place must sacrifice their independence and to some extent lose sight of the good of the country' but was honest enough to admit that he too was driven by ambition, not wanting to be outdone by others, and that he 'played for [his] own hand like the rest'.[72]

Dobbs's position as private secretary provided a vantage point for observing how government at more senior levels might be carried on. Earlier when he first joined the secretariat he reflected on its role:

> Apparently what is expected of me is to continually carp at generally and expose commissioners and collectors old enough to be my grandfather. I call it a silly method of government that local officers of high position and great judgement should not be trusted to do a large number of things without the sanction of a lot of secretaries probably far more ignorant of the matters in question.[73]

He later made a more direct criticism saying that he had spent much time revising draft municipal byelaws and similar regulations which he thought the local officials should have been compelled to draw up properly themselves. This led him to comment more generally on the role of government which he thought tried to do too much, 'It has made itself an immense caretaker and consequently instead of having to deal chiefly with broad big questions, it is over head and ears in petty details which the officers on the spot whose real business it should be trust the Government to put it straight.'[74]

While private secretary, Dobbs met the viceroys in post – Lord Elgin then Lord Curzon – and was prompted to reflect on their approach and that of the lieutenant-governors. While he dismissed Elgin as a 'disappointing apparition', he took the view that

> the constant attempt of Viceroys and Lieutenant-Governors to leave their mark on the administration by doing something striking and startling in their five years' term of office distracts and worries India ... Nowadays the people never get time to understand our methods for they are ever changing and new and I really believe that some of them look upon us as annoying and irresponsible lunatics who may do anything the next moment ... I believe the best thing for India would be to have a lot of dummies as Governors and Lieutenant-Governors for the next ten years who would mainly look wise and do nothing.[75]

Dobbs then met the new viceroy, Lord Curzon, who was clearly determined to leave his mark. He thought Curzon 'posed' a great deal and was not the kind of man in whom he would have confidence. 'I am sure all he thinks of is his own brilliancy and reputation – not like the great solid noblemen with few personal ambitions whom one is accustomed to look for in a Viceroy.'[76] Curzon had many schemes and plans for changes in India but one idea he advanced soon after his arrival in 1899 was to change practice in India to resemble more closely that in the British Foreign Office and thus reduce the amount of paper coming before him. Dobbs commented that the Foreign Office in London didn't look at the relevant correspondence properly; 'which perhaps accounts for [their] many blunders'.[77] Dobbs did though find Curzon kind in his manner and he was later to be instrumental in Dobbs's appointment first as consul in Sistan[78] and next in 1903 to the Indo-Afghan Boundary Commission. Thus was to begin a significant element in Dobbs's career – his sometimes important work on British India's relations with Afghanistan.

Sir Antony,[79] worn out by his efforts on the famine, departed for leave in England. Dobbs, who had decided after a relatively short time in the secretariat that he much preferred district work, was delighted when he persuaded Sir Antony's successor to release him for such work in the province. However, his time as private secretary had given him a perspective on instructions from the centre that was to remain with him throughout his career. He now appreciated that when a request or instruction came from the centre, this was usually a note 'only written by some clerk and a chaser authorised by an official' whereas he thought that those without this experience often believe 'the Lieutenant-Governor is palpitating with rage and waiting for an answer and so they live under a constant sense of shock and despair. These things now pass by me unheeded.'[80] At many points in his future career he was to apply instructions from the centre selectively – depending on how well they fitted with what he considered would work best.

Initially Dobbs went to a district in the province, Bara Banki, where he found the work 'more interesting and responsible ... and one is much more one's own master'. He preferred dealing with

> facts and men instead of merely writing about them ... I suppose partly it is a feeling that it is better to reign in hell than serve in heaven. It is somehow rather pleasant to feel that one is at the head of a large tract of country and that one can regulate everything without question as one thinks best. There are of course great responsibilities for if anything goes wrong in the district one is held to blame.[81]

He found the work heavy but better than writing 'continual précis'.

Dobbs always had an instinctive empathy with the local communities he worked in and a wish to accommodate the cultures he encountered. He contrasted the unique and beautiful ancient Indian buildings with the depressing utilitarian English schools, hospitals, courts and police stations. His attitude led him to question whether British rule had made the people any better or happier. These thoughts were also prompted by his romantic notions of an era dominated by 'the elephant-borne rajahs and sultans, the fretted mosques, the quaint stores of Arabic learning' and so on while 'the English destroyed most things and spread a sanitary peace'.[82] He suggested that the English approach was not suitable for the people's temperament. He also reflected on the unpopularity of British efforts to prevent the spread of life-threatening diseases. Shortly after his arrival, there was an outbreak of smallpox and he saw how hostile the natives were to the vaccination programme when he had to go to an area in the district where there was a particularly virulent outbreak and be vaccinated as an example. This did not persuade the villagers.[83] Later, while private secretary, when it came to a number of outbreaks of plague and associated riots against measures designed to stop it spreading, he began to think that these were so strongly opposed that they ran the risk of making 'the whole people of India loathe us', which would be a most dangerous situation.[84] As his career advanced, he became increasingly reluctant to impose alien or new systems on local communities. Whether in Balochistan, Mesopotamia or Iraq, he always looked for ways of using the systems he found in place in preference to making changes, whether he was relying on local laws and customs or on local leaders and their influence.

Since his arrival in India some eight years before, Dobbs had spent roughly two-thirds of the time in posts at district level and the remainder in the secretariat – mostly as private secretary to Sir Antony MacDonnell. During those eight years, Dobbs had worked in an enormous variety of situations and on a broad range of issues. At district level, the main elements in his work were administering the law and inspecting the country generally for revenue assessment purposes. There were constant unexpected situations to deal with such as strikes, unrest and natural disasters while the special reports he was commissioned to write added to the many subjects he had to familiarize himself with and the areas he had to visit. His period in the secretariat particularly as private secretary offered frequent close-ups of the ceremony and pomp that was one characteristic of the British Raj. It also enabled Dobbs to observe a severe and extensive famine being effectively handled. His work would have put him in touch with many senior figures – valuable in a world where personal connections greatly mattered. Dobbs also got his first insights into the workings of government at more senior levels. He was to develop this understanding and become very skilled at managing the ways of government to get what he considered the best results – as he was to do many years later in the Anglo-Afghan Treaty of 1921. From early on, his secretariat experience had encouraged him to give little weight to instructions from the centre. This increased his readiness to ignore them and exploit the freedom that distance offered to do things his own way. He was at the same time in no doubt about the considerable risks he could be taking.

Although Dobbs had usually met his varied and demanding responsibilities very successfully, he apparently thought that he had achieved little that was worthwhile. On the eve of his twenty-eighth birthday in August 1899, he reflected on his years in India. He dismissed his work as a district officer on the grounds that he felt he had never done much, or been of any particular use except in the same way as 'thousands of others' might have done. He regarded his time in the secretariat as absolutely wasted except that 'it taught me something of the workings of government' and thought that his writing a great deal had possibly influenced the odd policy decision. What he longed for was 'some tangible result to one's labours' such as exploring a new country or building a railway; so he claimed to have derived most satisfaction from contributing through his report to railway construction in Oudh.[85] Dobbs did however think work in a frontier area would be fascinating, 'All sorts of interesting things are always happening on the frontier.'[86] He was therefore delighted when, in January 1901, he was offered the frontier appointment he so much wanted. He was to be assistant political agent in the Zhob Valley. The move marked the start of a new phase for Dobbs: involvement with tribes, frontiers and international questions – elements that were to dominate the rest of his career.

3

Neighbours, frontiers and tribes 1901 to 1914: Exploring Arabia and Persia; the Russian threat and Afghanistan; working with tribal leaders in British India's northwest frontier provinces

Henry Dobbs had now been in India for just over eight years, five of them working at district level and over two as private secretary to the lieutenant-governor of the North-Western Provinces and Oudh. He was about to expand his already extensive experience in government to include British India's frontier areas and relations with the neighbouring states. From now until he left for Mesopotamia at the start of 1915, much of his time was spent working with their volatile and often wily rulers and with tribal leaders.

In March 1901, Dobbs arrived in the Zhob Valley – part of Balochistan south of the Indo-Afghan border – as assistant political agent. He was delighted he would be 'dealing once more with men instead of with papers' (Dobbs's underlining).[1] The frontier context was new to him and his appointment was unusual because posts like his were more often filled by military men working in the Political Department. Most arrived able to speak Pashto, the local language, while Dobbs, who had learnt Persian, which was generally spoken by Afghan officials, had to undertake to study Pashto for an exam six months later. He was also unused to working in a sensitive international political context. The area was part of the battleground in central and southern Asia where rivalry between Britain and Russia continued to play out. This rivalry – later described as 'the Great Game'[2] – was fuelled by Russian expansionist ambitions and by the consequent increase in British focus on the security of the northwest and western approaches to India. Restless frontier tribes took little notice of the Indo-Afghan border or of whatever agreement British India had reached with the amir of Afghanistan to constrain cross-border raiding. Raids into British

India were common. These were often ignored and sometimes encouraged by the neighbouring Afghan rulers. To the north, Russia had extended its empire to the Afghan frontier and was always on the lookout to increase its influence over this buffer state by intriguing with its rulers. The situation meant that clashes in these frontier areas could have far-reaching international consequences.

Henry Dobbs was however undaunted by such complications. He soon showed his readiness to act boldly in order to safeguard what he saw as the interests of those for whom he was responsible. It was a characteristic he demonstrated elsewhere, sometimes incurring the disapproval of his superiors. He commented to his mother:

> I nearly caused war with Afghanistan by seizing the person of the commander of the Amir's frontier posts and holding him as hostage until 400 camels belonging to British subjects which his subordinates had carried off from our territory with their attendants had been returned safe and sound. The levies in the Amir's posts nearly attacked us to attempt a rescue. But by displaying my most menacing aspect to my prisoner and pointing out to him that the Amir would be sure to cut off his hands and feet for having allowed himself to be made a prisoner I forced him into arranging for the return of the property carried off. I see no reason why we should meekly submit to the depredations of the Amir's subjects as we have done in the past and I now imprison every single person who comes over from Afghanistan unless he can get someone in our territory to stand heavy security for him. Thus I hope to prevent the visits of these cut throats who come in to prospect the country and after having reconnoitred make a sudden raid and carry off our people's cattle.[3]

By his own account, Dobbs spent little time in the civil stations and most of his time out and about in his district riding 20 miles a day and 'constantly wandering'. However, this came to an abrupt end in October 1901 when he became so ill, possibly with typhoid (he thought he might not recover), that he was sent back to England to take long leave.

Dobbs had for some time had ambitions to expand his horizons and ideally travel to places new to him. Whilst recovering at home, he decided he would return to India via Arabia and Persia to reach Balochistan, where he expected to resume his previous appointment. He had got a taste for exploring both from some of his travels in India and from books written by authors such as Percy Sykes and Francis Younghusband, both of whom he subsequently met. He thought the Government of India would be 'not unwilling' to let him undertake such an expedition, particularly if he paid his own expenses, and that it would be 'immensely interesting' and perhaps useful.[4]

British India had been drawn into the 'Arabian frontier of the Raj' and also into Persia by vying with Russia to gain influence. Dobbs's intended route would take him to places in these two areas which he had read about and were entirely new to him. Some of the time he would be travelling through country that was still relatively unknown and where occasionally he had to find his way with rudimentary sketches that passed for maps. He decided he would like to go down the Euphrates by boat, a 'rich and rare untravelled route'.[5] This had last been taken nearly seventy years before by the Irish explorer, Colonel Chesney, who had written extensively about his journey, and reported to the British government.[6]

After a year's convalescence, Henry Dobbs set out in December 1902. He called first at Constantinople (Istanbul) where the British ambassador to the Ottoman Empire, Sir Nicholas O'Connor, another Irishman, facilitated Dobbs's journey with introductions.[7] Military intelligence had suggested a number of matters Dobbs might investigate, something for which he was well suited. He was always extremely observant, interested in and curious about what he saw whether it was the terrain, commerce, local industry, native customs, local personalities or the workings of the local Ottoman bureaucracy.

Sailing from Constantinople, Dobbs arrived at Alexandretta (Iskenderun), the starting point for his journey, on 6 January 1903. He set off for Aleppo where he spent three days and explored the city, 'the streets are delightfully quaint, far more oriental than anything in India or Egypt and like one's dreams of the Arabian nights'.[8] Dobbs dismissed his guide or dragoman, 'whose ideas were too magnificent for my style of travelling'. He then hired two horses, two mules, a cook and a muleteer and set out across country to reach the start of his projected journey down the Euphrates. Beyond Aleppo, there was no road, merely some tracks, and Dobbs had to find his way with a map given him by the military to which he added details and made many corrections. Three days later, he started down the Euphrates from Biredjek (now Birecik). He travelled often in 'icy misery'[9] in a specially made boat. When he got to Fallujah, he left the river and rode across the desert at night to Baghdad where he spent a week writing up his report on the navigability of the Euphrates. From there, Dobbs travelled southwest following the Persian pilgrims' route via 'the sacred place of Kerbala (Karbala)', a Shia pilgrimage centre, to the border with Persia. On his way, he talked to chiefs, slept in 'the houses of Kurds' and hunted with a powerful Kurdish tribe.[10]

Persia he wrote 'is in the most interesting state in which it has ever been, a prey to the contending influence of Russia and England, full of intrigue and yet full also of its old customs'.[11] Just into Persia, his route took him near the oil exploration activities which were part of the extensive D'Arcy oil concession. The concession was won by the British in the teeth of Russian opposition. (This was the start of the Anglo-Persian Oil Company and in due course BP.) Dobbs spent several days visiting the operations and sent in a report on the situation to the governments in both London and Calcutta.

Beyond Isfahan, as Henry Dobbs made his way east through Persia towards the frontier with India, the stages of his journey became increasingly tough and demanding.

> I had a violent ride from Isfahan to Shiraz at the rate of 70 miles a day on post horses of the worst description. At one place, they refused to supply me with horses and I had to stand in front of the post-house with a whip in my hand and declare that no-one should either eat or sleep until I got them (it was 8.00pm). Finally they produced splendid horses and I rode rejoicing through the night.[12]

In Shiraz, Dobbs who by then was 'bearded and suntanned', had some respite as the guest of a Nawab and had

> rooms in a delicious courtyard with large square tanks full of goldfish, an orange tree still covered with fruit shading a bed of jonquils in full bloom and a bathroom lined with exquisite pale blue tiles ... A high-stepping horse is at my disposal and four attendants with floating scarves and high astrakhan caps ride behind and in procession through the arcades of the bazaars clearing my way. I have to be helped to mount by three; as it would be a terrible scandal if one mounted one's horse without being assisted into the saddle. If I go out at night attendants with sort of Chinese lanterns not far from 5 ft long go with me as rank is indicated by the size of one's lantern.[13]

Dobbs left for Kerman 'by untravelled ways'.

> I have had the greatest difficulty getting muleteers as they declare that no one knows the way and that we shall die in the wilderness; so I have had to pay treble prices; but it is much more amusing than going by a beaten track. I have got two mounted soldiers as escort as we shall travel the territory of some notorious robbers ... We had no trouble with robbers; but at a fortified village on the edge of a great strip of salt desert we were taken for robbers by the headman who was keeping guard on his watch tower and he discharged his rifle at us without doing any harm. When he was satisfied of our peaceful intentions he divested himself of all his powder horns and cartridge belts and was most hospitable.[14]

When Dobbs arrived at Kerman some two weeks later, he was met by Major Sykes, the author of one of the books on Persia he had read (another was Lord

Curzon's volumes[15]). While in Kerman, Dobbs heard from the Indian Foreign Department that he had been appointed consul in Sistan and must go there at once. He then prepared for the most 'trying' part of his journey 'through desert [the Lut desert] with salt water and considerable heat'. He had to take supplies for five days to cross it 'as there is nothing for man or beast to eat or drink'.[16] However, it took Dobbs over a week to procure the minimum seven 'fast' camels he needed because 'the Governor of Kerman has established a reign of terror and all the camel men have fled'. The consul there however was able to provide him 'with tents etc. sufficient to enable me to enter Sistan with suitable magnificence'.[17] Dobbs was 'rather pleased' with the appointment since

> Sistan is at present the great battle-ground between Russia and England in Persia as it is a great oasis capable of feeding a large army on the flank of Afghanistan in a desert commanding all the principal routes across Afghanistan; and the Russians are straining every nerve to acquire influence there. My principal employment will be watching the intrigues of the Russian Consul and cultivating friendly relations with Baluchis and Persians.[18]

Dobbs reached Sistan at the end of May, and just over a month later, he described a Russian attempt to force the British out of the capital city, Sher-i-Nasrya (now Nosratabad) and how he countered it:

> The Russians got up a big anti-British agitation and a mob marched into the city yelling insults and threatened some of our subjects. I rode off to the Amir's house, found the mob yelling there and demanded that the ringleaders should be instantly bastinadoed[19] in my presence. The governor refused and the next five days were spent in a long series of bluffing manoeuvres on my part and threats to the foremen while on the side of the agitators ... But I triumphed in the end and compelled [one of] the foremen to do what I wished though he wriggled and wiggled and wiggled. So on 2nd July I rode with my whole escort in triumph through the town and solemnly witnessed the bastinadoing on the feet of the ringleaders while the Russian consul hid in deep humiliation in his house unable to save his protégés from punishment.[20]

Dobbs followed up by going

> with only 3 horsemen into camp at the town where the agitation had had its rise and where the gathering of the tribes had taken place. They sent me repeated messages that they could attack my camp. But as I took no notice and sat calmly on, they all came round and I had a lot of straight talks with them ... Finally I bought carpets from some of the people whom I had caused to be bastinadoed

and today am returning to the city after giving a great display of tent-pegging and wrestling and other amusements.[21]

As to the Russian presence, Henry Dobbs hoped that he had been instrumental in 'securing British paramountcy in Sistan' at any rate for the present. The Russian consul left in disgrace, while the Government of India congratulated Dobbs on his handling of the situation.[22] However, he confessed that he had found the strain considerable and was glad that a British military escort was in the vicinity accompanying the British-led Perso-Afghan Arbitration Commission, which was determining the boundary.

While on his travels, Dobbs frequently sent back reports to India and sometimes to London on what he had observed. These would include opportunities for British and Indian business and comments on the varying effectiveness of the British consuls in cities he visited. He was keen to see the promotion of British and Indian commercial interests and appreciated how helpful an active presence in local business and trade could be in extending and consolidating British influence. In Aleppo, for example, he spent much time drinking cup after cup of sweet Turkish coffee with the 'principal men of business' enquiring about the indigo trade with India and the possibility of combating the advance of the synthetic indigo produced by the Germans, about which he then reported back to the Indian government. He commented on the absence of English commercial travellers due to 'sheer laziness and want of interest'.[23] It was in fact one of these reports – his report about 'the oil and people on the Turko-Persian frontier' in the area being prospected under the British D'Arcy oil concession that favourably impressed the viceroy, Lord Curzon, and led to his having Dobbs appointed first as consul in Sistan and subsequently as British commissioner on the Russo-Afghan boundary. Curzon, who earlier had travelled extensively in Persia and Afghanistan, took a particular interest in both areas on account of his belief in the gravity of the Russian threat and his fear that these areas could provide a springboard for a Russian attack on India.

After only three months, Curzon ordered Dobbs to leave Sistan and go at once to Herat in Afghanistan and to continue further north from there to the Russo-Afghan frontier on what Dobbs described as a 'mystic mission'.

Dobbs soon discovered that he was being sent to repair the pillars marking the boundary between Russia and Afghanistan, which had been erected jointly by the Russians and the British between 1884 and 1886. The Afghans had asked the British to repair them. The British had then asked the Russians to join them. Instead, the Russians invited the governor of Herat to send Afghans to

Figure 3.1 Dobbs in turban and Major Wanless, who accompanied him, at Bala Murghab near the Russo-Afghan border. November 1903. Courtesy of Henry Wilks.

join just the Russian representatives at the frontier and refused to collaborate with the British. This contravened what at the time was regarded as the 'cardinal principle' of British India's Afghan policy, as Dobbs commented.[24] This was that the Government of India controlled all Afghan external relations. The principle had been accepted by the then current Amir Habibullah and by his predecessor Amir Abdur Rahman, in return for British protection and a subsidy. The British prohibition on Afghan direct dealings with foreign powers had also been accepted twenty years previously by the Russians. Now however, the latter, who had extended their empire to the borders of Afghanistan, would only deal directly with the Afghans.[25]

The initial British instructions to Dobbs were to allow the governor of Herat to reply to the Russians and for him to go up to the border merely in the capacity of adviser to the Afghans. Indeed Curzon repeatedly sent warnings to Dobbs to be circumspect and conciliatory towards the Russians. Instead, Dobbs told the governor not to answer the Russians, wrote to them himself and later got Government of India approval to repair all the border pillars unilaterally in company with the Afghans. However, the Russians, who had ignored him, had repaired some pillars on their own and left. Earlier, while he was in Herat, Dobbs had observed,

The Governor [of Herat] was very cordial; but after taking leave of him, as I was passing out of the door, I turned round and intercepted a most vindictive glance directed at my back … Beneath it all, the Governor was furious because he has been carrying on intrigues with the Russians and he wishes to promote the policy of direct communication with the Afghans. So he placed every obstacle that he could in our way.[26]

Dobbs had decided to disobey his initial instructions because of his concerns that the local Afghans would conclude the British had now given away their control over relations with Russia and only reported his actions afterwards. He was well aware of the risks to his career that he was taking and wrote, 'I am momentarily expecting to be dismissed from the service for contumacy and disobedience to orders'.[27] Dobbs's decision was typical of the independent approach he was ready to take throughout his career. Whilst it was daring, the risks to his career were well judged. Curzon's views on Russia and the need to take a tough line against the Russians were well known as was the government in London's more conciliatory position.

An escort of 300 Afghan troops, led by the old Afghan general Ghausuddin, had been ordered by Amir Habibullah to accompany Dobbs from Herat to the frontier. However, on instructions from the governor of Herat, the general would not allow Dobbs to take any unilateral action unless he had express instructions from the amir to go ahead without the Russians. These instructions the amir refused to give, despite repeated requests from the viceroy, who pointed out that many pillars needed repair.[28] The amir had a difficult relationship with the governor of Herat and furthermore had possibly been alarmed by his exaggerated reports of Russian troop movements. Seven months of stalemate ensued while Dobbs's party lived in tents during a bitterly cold winter coping with 'trying snowstorms' and snowbound for twenty-eight days. Dobbs summarizes some of the problems:

I am much disenchanted with the Afghans. Although we are here to help them, they are so dreadfully suspicious of us, and so fanatical. Their whole object is to prevent us obtaining information about their country, and they lie to us on every opportunity. One has to work very cautiously, with the Governor of Herat intriguing with the Russians against us, the non-Afghan Tribesmen ready to rise against the Afghans, and go over to the Russians at any moment and the ordinary Afghan tribesmen planted in large colonies to guard the marches, secretly set against us by the Governor. And here we are at their mercy for supplies and everything. Every word we say is reported to the Russians across the frontier immediately by their spies in our camp … We feel rather unhappy because the

Afghans are growing more and more suspicious of us and are only too evidently playing purposely up to the Russians. These webs of intrigue are very wearing to the temper and make one jumpy and irritable. One has to appear unconcerned and serene when one is quite the reverse.[29]

Eventually, the Government of India told Dobbs to accede to the amir's request to leave the frontier, report to the amir in Kabul and take messages from the amir to the viceroy.

Somehow throughout their seven months together Dobbs and the Afghan delegates had remained on very good terms, although the Afghans had repeatedly tried to keep Dobbs away from the frontier on one pretext after another which Dobbs had not hesitated to expose as patently false. On 20 June 1904 when the party arrived at the border between the Herat and Kabul districts, where they had to part, the general and Dobbs took a tearful farewell of each other.[30] Accompanied by another military escort, Dobbs then travelled to Kabul by 'wild unexplored and unsurveyed country'. The terrain was terribly bleak, the 'inhabited places' were at or above 10,000 feet but the amir sent Dobbs 'mule loads of champagne and cakes and soda water over these terrible passes to meet me on the way! The champagne has rather lost its fizz.'[31]

After his 470-mile journey from Herat, Dobbs had seven meetings with the amir during July, one lasting more than two hours. Dobbs described him as: 'Round-faced, red-cheeked and with a scrubby beard, an exceedingly pleasant, smooth faced, handsome young man with a most winning manner, and altogether very French in appearance. In repose his face has a heavy and almost sullen expression; when he is talking it lights up and becomes extremely vivacious. He stammers a good deal and gesticulates continually.'[32]

Dobbs soon 'conceived a very great liking for him and I do think his sole thought is the good of his people – though his methods of securing that good may not always commend themselves to us or fit in with our views'.[33]

The amir readily gave Dobbs his views but at the same time was keen to draw Dobbs into a debate on British government policy. Following instructions, Dobbs successfully sidestepped these attempts while still maintaining cordial and friendly relations. Indeed, the Government of India commended him for his patience, tact and discretion generally and for his 'well-judged' report to the amir, on Herat and on the Russo-Afghan frontier which had highlighted Russian activity and influence in the region.

Although Dobbs had failed to achieve the objective for which he had been sent, namely to repair frontier pillars on the Russo-Afghan border, the Government of

India wrote that Dobbs deserved great credit for 'the way in which he comported himself often in very trying circumstances.' They recognized that many difficult situations had been created not only by the Afghans but also by the physical conditions.[34]

Over the next two years, the Government of India exploited fully Dobbs's experience of working with Afghan officials and the good relationship he had established with Amir Habibullah. Apart from a period of home leave and six months in Rajputana where he worked for several weeks as famine commissioner, Dobbs was employed almost exclusively on Afghan affairs. He returned to Afghanistan in November 1904, two months after completing his boundary commission assignment, as secretary to the British mission to Kabul, whose purpose was to agree that country's future relationship with British India. The foreign secretary to the Government of India, Louis Dane, headed the mission, and the amir told him that Dobbs, whom he knew extremely well, 'will be a most efficient aid to you.'[35]

The amir, who feared that British India wished to impose tighter controls on Afghanistan, had only reluctantly accepted the mission. The talks took three months to arrive at an agreement, which essentiality reinstated the arrangements the Government of India had made with Habibullah's father. This result met the wishes of the amir and of the British government in London. The latter did not want to risk a breakdown in relations that might follow if the Government of India insisted on their requirements and were nervous that failure to conclude discussions between the British and the Afghans could provide an opening for Russia. For their part however, the Government of India had wanted to respond to continuing Russian pressure with changes in the agreement with Afghanistan, which would allow for a British military presence there.[36] The agreement the mission eventually managed to reach with difficulty simply confirmed the status quo, and Dobbs then wrote from Kabul, 'There is now great enthusiasm on both sides.'[37] This was not shared by Curzon who had supported a tough line. He regarded Dane as a duffer and had doubts about how effectively he had negotiated with the amir.[38] When Dane and Dobbs got to Simla, 'we found the Viceroy furious because we had carried out the orders of His Majesty's Government' and there was a 'disgraceful atmosphere of squabbling between Curzon and the Secretary of State for India over the Kabul Mission'. Dobbs claimed that 'no such rude and violent telegrams have ever passed between two highly placed officials before.'[39] Dobbs later put to good use this experience to play on differences between London and Simla when he came to negotiate the 1921 Anglo-Afghan Treaty.

In 1904 the Kabul mission had undoubtedly come very close to breaking off negotiations at several points. However, in Dobbs's view, 'at any rate we had done a great deal better than we had at one time expected and we had left the Afghans in a very friendly frame of mind'.[40] He was 'rather pleased because there has been a marked increase in the friendliness of his [the amir's] attitude since my visit to Kabul'. Dobbs had also struggled to avoid unnecessary irritations by getting the members of the Dane mission to 'observe the most elementary rules of oriental etiquette'.[41]

Less than a year later, the amir was ready to consider visiting India for 'friendly interviews, sightseeing and tiger shooting' and arrived in January 1907. Sir Henry McMahon[42] was put in charge of the tour with Dobbs as his assistant. Dobbs started work on the visit in September 1906 and, according to McMahon's report on it, the lion's share of the work fell to him.[43] The tour took the amir and the 1,100 accompanying him to – among other places – Agra, Delhi, Calcutta, Bombay, Lahore, Amritsar and Peshawar and was a considerable feat of

Figure 3.2 Amir Habibullah on tour in India (January to March 1907). The amir is seated with Dobbs on his right and Sir Henry McMahon immediately behind him. Courtesy of Henry Wilks.

organization. Dobbs's responsibilities included accommodation – designing and constructing large camps including the vast 'base camp' at Agra – arranging the financing, the detailed programme, railway and other transport and overseeing local hosts from maharajahs to lieutenant-governors.

McMahon commented that the at times unreasonable Afghan ideas of duties of hosts and rights of guests as well as the sudden and frequent changes in the programme they requested – sometimes with only three or four hours' notice – made the work still more 'strenuous and trying'. McMahon reported that 'the smooth running and absence of any hitch in the carrying out of the tour was a result on which its success so largely depended and the visit therefore from the Amir's point of view was a complete success and in this result the object of our endeavours was accomplished.'[44] He credited this largely to Dobbs's great ability and energy. The British were later rewarded for the goodwill generated in that, despite a determined German effort, Habibullah kept Afghanistan neutral during the Great War.

For Dobbs, the tour must have turned into something of a nightmare. First, he had to handle all the difficulties created by the vagaries of the amir and his enormous party. He wrote, 'The Amir has been very happy but also very trying. He refuses to be bound by his programme; and has stayed on and on in Calcutta shopping and enjoying himself generally and has refused to go to the shooting camp in the Central Provinces which [was] prepared with such care and at such expense.'[45]

A further worry for Dobbs was that the amir's repeated deferrals of his departure from India meant that instead of leaving a week before Dobbs was due to get married he was still there:

> the Amir had put off his going day after day, and had finally insisted on staying at Lahore for the wedding, instead of having been across the frontier on the 1st March as he should have been ... I had to do work on the Amir's business up to the evening before the wedding [and] had been so worried by attempting to combine the work on the Amir's tour with preparations for the wedding and afterwards, that I was really quite worn out and apathetic the day before, and felt that I did not much care what might happen.[46]

Dobbs got married as planned on 4 March in Lahore Cathedral and all went well.

> Kifayat and Yousuf, my two faithful servants were allowed in the back of the Cathedral to their great excitement. The Amir, much to his annoyance, was not allowed in, or at least I induced him not to go, as the Bishop had apparently objections to his presence. He came to the reception however: and slipped a beautiful pair of gold bracelets on to Esmé's arms.[47]

Dobbs's new wife, formerly Esmé Rivaz, had impeccable credentials for marriage to a rising Indian Civil Servant. Dobbs's second cousin, she was the daughter of an Indian Civil Servant, George Rivaz;[48] she had herself grown up in India and was extremely well connected. One of her mother's brothers was Sir Alfred Lyall, a distinguished Indian Civil Servant; another brother, Sir James Lyall, had been lieutenant-governor of the Punjab while her father's brother, Sir Charles Rivaz, held that position when she got married. He gave her away and the reception was held in Government House, Lahore. Afterwards, the couple had a delightful honeymoon in Dehra Dun. As Dobbs told his mother, they had seen very little of each other and he 'was a little nervous about how we should get on, being almost strangers'.[49] Luckily, Dobbs found his wife 'very very charming'. It is clear from their voluminous correspondence that they became extremely fond of each other. Before long, she was in addition a friend and a confidante, as can be seen from Dobbs's many interesting and colourful letters to her.

In April 1907, Henry and Esmé arrived in Simla, where Dobbs started work as one of the deputy secretaries in the Government of India's Foreign Department. Nine months later in January 1908, he resigned from the department on a point of principle, protesting that the viceroy, Lord Minto, had ignored an undertaking which his predecessor, Lord Curzon, had given.[50] Curzon, in response to acute and widespread discontent, had assured the department that top posts, which its members might reasonably expect to fill, would not be offered to outsiders with no relevant experience. Dobbs learnt in November 1907 that Lord Minto had nominated Harcourt Butler to succeed Sir Louis Dane as head of the Foreign Department. Dobbs pointed out that Butler lacked any experience of foreign department business and had not shown any interest in Indian foreign policy questions. He believed that Minto had chosen Butler for two reasons: because he had written a long series of anonymous articles in the Indian newspaper *The Pioneer* attacking Lord Curzon who 'was anathema to Minto'[51] and because Butler's brother had married Minto's private secretary's sister. Dobbs complained to Dane about the implied slur on the competence of those in the Foreign Department and the widespread discontent the appointment would cause. He said he would resign if the appointment went ahead, and that he felt he could not loyally serve under Butler. Dobbs at the same time wrote to all the 'principal members' of the Political Department about the proposed appointment, thus setting off a stream of protests to the viceroy. Lord Minto went ahead with Butler's appointment and was 'furious' with Dobbs. As Dobbs wrote to his mother, 'my present prospects are bad but Lord Minto cannot last forever and I have the sympathy of the whole Political Department which is one comfort'.[52]

After resigning in January 1908, Dobbs took leave while he waited to be offered an appointment he considered suitable. He then decided to go with Esmé to Tehran, 'where all sorts of exciting events are occurring'.[53] This trip also indulged his fondness for travel and for exploring areas new to him. (While on his travels in 1903, he had written 'I am only afraid that the routine of official life in India will seem absolutely unbearable after my delightful wanderings.'[54]) It took them a month to reach Tehran, where Dobbs went to the Majles (Persian Parliament) and was presented to the shah. He enjoyed himself with Persian companions – one day smoking opium for five hours and on another evening drinking and singing with them.[55] After a month in Tehran, he had met his objective, which was to understand the present 'queer situation' in Persia by talking to different parties and factions himself so that he did not have to rely on the view of the 'somewhat blinkered' British legation.[56] The 'queer situation' was the opposition of the current shah to the constitution which had been established by the Persian constitutionalists and accepted by his predecessor. Indeed, on 23 June 1908, about a month after Henry and Esmé had left Tehran, at the request of the shah, the Majles was bombarded by the Russian army and leaders of the constitutional movement executed.[57] Dobbs was later to be very critical of British policy towards Persia and in particular the decision not to support the constitutionalists.

After eight months on leave in the British Isles, Dobbs and his wife returned to India at the end of January 1909. He had accepted an appointment in Balochistan where Sir Henry McMahon was agent to the governor-general (AGG) and chief commissioner and whom Dobbs knew from their work on the amir's tour of India. Dobbs described the Balochistan post as an appointment he had 'long coveted', and so concluded that his resignation from the Foreign Department had not done him much harm.[58] Reflecting on its implications some years later he thought he would have tired of 'dealing with all those petty everlasting Native States', was glad to have avoided 'falling into secretariat grooves' and 'kept my independence'.[59]

The coveted appointment was the first of a number of posts in Balochistan which Dobbs held between 1909 and 1914. Whatever his job title, his responsibilities were very similar to those he had held earlier when working at district level: revenue collection, the local economy, dealing with natural disasters such as earthquakes and famine, the administration of justice and the maintenance of law and order. He worked from Sibi, Ziarat and Quetta. He describes a typical working day at the hill station at Ziarat:

Behind the house is a large juniper arbour with windows and doors among the tree-trunks in which I sit most of the day and do my work and interview hill notabilities. I have a nice young assistant, a civilian, Mr Cater ... I start out for a ride with my two poodles about 7 leaving Esmé asleep. We breakfast at 9.30, I work till lunch at 2, and then again till 5.30. Then we have tea and I either play tennis or walk out in front of a tiny little strong hill-pony on which Esmé perches herself, and which never goes out of a walk. About 8 we get back, I work for ¾ of an hour and we dine about 9. My work is fairly heavy – a steady grind of about 8 hours a day.[60]

He was also frequently based in camp. At the end of 1910 after a three-month tour, he writes to his father:

I have been busy camping through the vast tracts of my district ... There are such an immense number of tribes and sub tribes – Pathans and Baluchis – all speaking slightly different dialects that it takes a very long time to grow familiar with the conditions of the district. One portion of my district has mountains over 11,000 ft high and another part is the flat plain only 300 ft above the sea. And of course the habits of the people, the agriculture and everything differs totally in these two parts.[61]

Although the range of Dobbs's responsibilities was similar to those he had held at district level, his greater seniority gave him more scope to focus on what he saw as local priorities. He was determined to reduce bureaucracy and use the resulting savings to improve the local economy. After a few months in Sibi (Balochistan), he writes:

I have been engaged lately to the great annoyance of the old long-planted European officers in Baluchistan in carrying on a campaign against the multiplication of codes, regulations and clerks in this wild and unprogressive country with its immense arid stretches of mountains and only 400,000 inhabitants. They rage when I tell them that they are foolishly aping the Punjab and Bengal with their immense populations; that their clerks and officers exist only to discuss one another and write about regulations which this unprogressive country does not want; and that instead of spending all their money on unproductive bureaux they should drive roads through the tribal areas and teach the people how to improve their apricots, peaches, and grapes for which there is unlimited demand in the plains of India. I have had a great fight and have overwhelmed them with statistics as to the extraordinary growth in the numbers of clerks and returns and the actual deterioration of the roads; and I have at last won much unpopularity <u>and</u> my way. (Dobbs's underlining)[62]

The Government of India agreed to an increased spend on roads in Balochistan and that there should be an enquiry into reducing the number of clerks.

Dobbs then put a lot of effort into developing fruit production. He won approval from the secretary of state for India to have a special fruit expert for Balochistan, a fruit growers' association, special railway rates and fruit vans in order to supply the plains of India with fruit during the rainy season when none was available there. By May 1911, a large model fruit farm was set up in the hope that 'Balochistan will soon supply the whole of India with peaches, nectarines, grapes and tomatoes.'[63]

Establishing fruit production was only one of several agricultural 'experiments' which Dobbs tried, often at his own expense. He imported merino sheep from Australia to improve the quality of the wool from the sheep kept by the Marri tribe, maize seed from America to increase the yield from the plants in the upper valleys and Egyptian clover into the plains around Sibi. He had 200 olive trees imported from France, obtained a tract of land where wild olives already grew and after three years was ready to have hundreds of European olives grafted on to the wild trees. He hoped that if his scheme was successful the local production of olive oil would bring great prosperity to the area because there was the necessary water power to extract the oil and the price of olive oil was continually rising.[64] He introduced bees from Kashmir to an area near Quetta and later near Ziarat. However, initially he had to summon a private serving in the Essex regiment who understood bees to ride out and deal with their swarming every other day.[65] Dobbs persisted, and today Ziarat honey is a tourist attraction and can be bought online.

Dobbs also took a close interest in irrigation arrangements which could be essential to local agricultural success. Irrigation was often provided by Karezes – a system of underground tunnels taking water from mountain springs to the plains. Typically, the landowner had to borrow from the government to finance them. Dobbs tried to assure himself that there was worthwhile land to water, that there was some prospect of the advance being repaid and that the landowner would not be unduly burdened with debt. Sometimes he found himself in the middle of heated disputes over the sharing out of what had previously been tribal land held in common but which irrigation was now making valuable – on one occasion the quarrel had been going on for over eighty years. He also sought to ensure that Balochistan was not disadvantaged by irrigation schemes beyond its borders.[66]

Dobbs's schemes were not confined to agriculture. He also encouraged oil exploration in a promising area by granting leases. His most exotic project was the creation of a spa near a 'splendid radio-active hot sulphur spring which has got the Quetta doctors to boom for the sake of the many persons suffering from gout, sciatica and rheumatism in Quetta'.[67]

At the same time as pressing ahead with his various schemes, Dobbs also had to keep the peace and oversee the administrative and judicial system. He reorganized the clerks, reducing their numbers, and reformed the revenue assessment system. On one of his tours, he found the assessment had been set so high that no one cultivated their land, so he publicly castigated the serving official. He explained that when on tour, 'I would sit down before the house of the headman of every village through which I pass and the inhabitants sit in a vast circle in front of me and pronounce their grievances and requests.'[68]

Dobbs's more senior role also meant that he was now involved in grander ceremonial events: maintaining the dignity of the Raj was regarded as an important part of emphasizing the British right to rule. However, he saw these events as unwelcome and expensive distractions but found he often had a part to play in such occasions. In May 1910 he had to assemble the tribesmen in an enormous hall at Sibi, built as a Victoria Memorial Durbar Hall for the whole of Balochistan.

I have pranced thither twice in full dress uniform with the thermometer at 110F in the shade first to announce King Edward's death and to make official appropriate observations and then to proclaim the accession … I am afraid the King is a very distant personage indeed to these tribes … However, they all profess to lament the King's death greatly. Of course they attribute it all to the Comet.[69]

Eighteen months later in December 1911, Dobbs and his wife went to the most magnificent ceremonial occasion organized during the British Raj, the Delhi Durbar. This was the only time a reigning sovereign, King George V, ever visited India. Its official purpose was to crown the king and queen as emperor and empress of India and demonstrate Indian loyalty to the Crown. Dobbs and his tribesmen had a small part in the ceremonies. Dobbs wrote amusingly about the event with his sharp eye for detail:

Esmé has all sorts of new dresses for the Durbar … and I have had to undergo a good deal of expense because I have to ride in the King's procession at Delhi; and so have had to get a full dress riding costume which I hadn't got before – not to mention white kerseymere court breeches for Investitures and things; and white silk stockings with ditto lilac underneath to give the proper shade. It would have been a relief to everyone if the complications at home[70] had prevented the King coming out. But as he is coming we must go through with it smiling.

We arrived a fortnight before the Durbar ... The plain behind the ridge on which all the happenings were concentrated was one sea of immense white tents amid lawns and gardens laid out for the occasion intersected with well-oiled roads crammed with gay traffic. There were over 3,000 motor cars but no dust and this I think was really the chief triumph of the occasion.

From where I saw it the actual arrival was quite impressive. I stood in charge of a line of 6 Baluchistan chiefs about 10 feet from the two thrones ... With fanfares of silver trumpets, heralds, two noble persons walking backwards with white rods, the King and Queen came through the arch and into the tent and stood by the thrones. Afterwards, the King got onto a black horse looking rather ordinary; and the Queen, looking magnificent, got into a carriage with umbrellas and ceremonial fly-flappers and the like. The king was quite indistinguishable among the other mounted officers including the Viceroy; and it seemed rather poor to see him waiting about on horseback like an outsider while the Queen slowly got into her carriage. Off they started; and it appears that throughout the procession the millions of native spectators and even most of the Europeans were unable to discern which was the King; and after it was over, the people said that the Queen only had come out to India.

When our proper place came, I started off at the head of my Baluchi chiefs on horseback. It was interesting riding slowly between the crowds for about 3 miles; and they mostly clapped our Baluchis loudly because, I suppose with their wild flowing locks, loose white clothes, shields and matchlocks, they formed an agreeable contrast to the fat pampered chiefs in carriages who had preceded them. [When the processions had dispersed] ... we rode off onto the principal road, and swept along it dashing the frightened native policemen who were trying to supervise the traffic aside.

The Durbar itself was a truly splendid sight ... especially the procession of the King and Queen along the causeway between the thrones when they received the homage.

The most impressive ceremony was the Garden party when the King and Queen showed themselves from a balcony in the Fort to millions and millions of natives passing below and shouting, the King and Queen wearing their hot and uncomfortable crowns and ermine robes.

The investiture in the evening was alarming owing to the fire in a tent nearby. We had been saying for weeks that if a big tent caught fire, we should all be burnt with the King and Queen like rats in a trap; and here suddenly were fire whistles blowing outside and the flames of the burning tent reflected in the Investiture tent with 3000 persons packed together on chairs. A number of people stood up; and the King from his throne shouted 'sit down' and went on with the Investiture.

I think that after all the big tents which had been burnt it was monstrous that the King and all of us should have been exposed to such risk.[71]

There was however one element in Dobbs's Balochistan responsibilities of which he had almost no previous experience. Apart from a very brief period in the Zhob Valley, he had not worked in tribal and frontier areas where border raids had to be dealt with. To try to reduce raids across the Afghan frontier into Balochistan, he threatened the Governor of Kandahar (whom he had met in Afghanistan) with stopping the wool and fruit trade unless the governor handed over a criminal 'of the deepest dye. This brought him to his knees as he makes immense sums by taxing the trade.'[72] Dobbs also took firm action against one of the tribes which operated on both sides of the Indo-Afghan border. His predecessor had always let them off when they produced the Koran and promised to stop but the raids had greatly increased. 'I have had to refuse to yield even to the sacred name of the Koran and of course they think me a beast. But raids have diminished and life and property are more secure during the past few months.'[73]

More generally, working in the frontier and tribal areas of both Balochistan and the North-West Frontier Province led Dobbs to take a different approach especially to security and the administration of justice. Dobbs now based his approach to governing on the 'Sandeman system', the principles adopted by Sir Robert Sandeman in establishing British influence in Balochistan.[74] Its key characteristics were to work through tribal leaders who had the support of their people creating a community of interest through the power of patronage. There was an emphasis on the jirga (council) and on fairness, although Dobbs argued that these principles needed to be underpinned by overwhelming force. Thus when Dobbs found that for the past two years a subset of the Marri tribe were refusing to accept the authority of the local chief and did not come to the jirga to settle their disputes he set off with the members of the Marri tribe and established a small fort to collect tax and revenue from the insubordinate tribe by way of punishment 'as we can't let the whole country fall into disorder.'[75]

Dobbs enjoyed working with the hill tribes, 'most of the Pathans and Baluchis speak out their minds and have no hesitation in telling one of one's mistakes; and I have a great deal of affection for them.'[76]

He also seems to have been well regarded by them. When they heard he was leaving Balochistan,

all the tribesmen from far and near rushed at me with petitions asking me to settle all their disputes before I went. Water disputes, boundary disputes, cases about wives and marriages water rights and land. I toured distractedly about

Figure 3.3 Henry Dobbs in Balochistan with a group of the chiefs, probably in 1913. Courtesy of Henry Wilks.

>	trying to settle as many as I could writing advice and decisions far into the night, surrounded by crowds of people; then in the early dawn a march of twenty or thirty miles and other crowds and other disputes.[77]

When he was on the point of departure, 'The chiefs of the great semi-independent Marri and Baluchi tribes, rode in with all their headmen more than 300 miles to say goodbye; and others assembled from distant corners. They blocked the approaches to the station and the platform so that all railway business had to be suspended.'[78]

After four years in Balochistan, Henry Dobbs left for the North-West Frontier Province to be judicial commissioner. There he was based in Peshawar and Nathia Galli until his departure for Mesopotamia in January 1915. Dobbs believed his approach to law and order based on the Sandeman system had proved very effective in keeping the peace in Balochistan. For example, in the six months to June 1910, there had only been seven murders, which compared favourably with the rate in more settled parts of India.[79] It also compared well with the North-West Frontier Province. When he arrived in January 1914, he commented that 'This Province is in a bad way – murders and raids every day – and ladies forbidden to ride out unprotected outside their gardens.'[80] Dobbs ascribed this to 'sheer brutal hanging' and the refusal to allow the tribesmen to settle their feuds according to tribal custom in line with the Sandeman system. Five months later he wrote a highly critical report on criminal administration in the province. He described his point of view to his mother:

> I have dwelt as tenderly as I could on their [British officials] mistakes in dealing with the frontier tribes to which I attribute the extraordinary increase during the last few years in raids, murders and robberies. To my mind they haven't the least idea in this province, of the way in which to treat the tribesmen or to work the tribal system – a lot of earnest industrious young men, pegging solidly away under masses of rules and regulations without looking to the right or the left, without a glimpse of understanding of the happy go lucky feelings of the Pathan – imprisoning, fining, hanging, when they get the chance with the result that all the population is so set against them and their methods that no one will give evidence or help in the detection of crime and that only about 5 persons out of 150 murderers get caught and punished. The more heavily that we punish the very few persons convicted, the more does the average tribesman refuse to help in catching the criminal. Yet all the officials go on uttering the parrot cry that heavy enough punishments are not inflicted on the few persons caught. And the blood feuds go on spreading more and more widely until there is not a village in which there are not three or four factions thirsting for one another's blood. If only they would adopt my principle of compensation to the injured and blood money according to tribal custom … we should soon stop all this crime as I stopped it in a few years among the Marris and the Bugtis in Baluchistan. But these young boys are so wedded to their old rigid legal system that they won't choose to try and work any other.[81]

This approach has been criticized on the grounds that it denied tribesmen who might wish to challenge arbitrary and unfair decisions by the tribal leaders access to the British justice system. However, following traditional and accepted practice was more effective in maintaining general order. It is also argued that locking the inhabitants of the area generally into the tribal system created economic dependence and made it difficult for them to share the greater prosperity enjoyed by the non-tribal people in the plains.[82] Dobbs's approach to this latter issue was to try and introduce changes which would improve the local economy in the tribal areas without challenging the way of life.

Dobbs did not enjoy his work in the North-West Frontier Province where he was mainly hearing appeals. He had to listen to many barristers and pleaders and could not readily apply 'a commonsense view of the law'.[83] He worked hard to deal speedily with cases – he attached much importance to crime being punished promptly – and drafted a special regulation for summary criminal trials which would allow cases to be handled more speedily. It was later accepted in a rather modified form and applied throughout India.[84] He also found the living arrangements less attractive and had enjoyed Nathia Galli less than Ziarat. Although he liked taking his son and daughter out to catch butterflies and identify plants in Nathia Galli, the constant mists made everything melancholy and wet.

Following the outbreak of the First World War and the British invasion of Mesopotamia (later Iraq), Dobbs left Peshawar at the beginning of 1915 to take up the post of revenue commissioner in the civil administration that was being established in Mesopotamia in the wake of the advancing army. Over the previous ten years, Dobbs had worked with Afghans, with different tribes and their leaders and in sensitive frontier areas. He had had to make decisions on a huge variety of diverse issues and was always ready to take an independent-minded approach. This had often included a pragmatic willingness to build on what he found in place when traditional British practices did not seem to be working. He had also found time to introduce and actively promote imaginative schemes to enhance the well-being of the communities he was responsible for. Dobbs would now need to call on his accumulated experience, his combination of resourcefulness, patience, persistence and firmness to meet the demands of working in the entirely new context of a war zone – Mesopotamia.

4

Mesopotamia 1915 to 1916: Administration in a newly occupied territory; Battle of Ctesiphon; working unescorted among the marsh Arabs; opposing the imposition of the Indian model

Henry Dobbs was delighted when the Indian Foreign Department told him in July 1914 that he was to go to Baghdad. He was to be appointed resident in Turkish Arabia for British India and consul general in Baghdad (a province of the Ottoman Empire) for the Foreign Office. Although he recognized that his present post as judicial commissioner in the North-West Frontier Province gave him useful experience, he was pleased that his 'monotonous judicial work' was over and was eager to return to political work.[1]

Dobbs already knew something of the area from his travels in 1903 and from a report he had written at that time on the navigation of the Euphrates. However, following the British declarations of war on Germany and Austro-Hungary in August 1914, Dobbs was asked to remain where he was for almost another six months until it was known whether Britain would be at war with the Ottomans.

On 5 November 1914, Great Britain, like France, declared war on the Ottoman Empire. Both did so in support of their Russian ally after Ottoman attacks on Russian seaports and the consequent Russian declaration of war. The next day, British and Indian troops landed at Fao (Al Faw) on the southern extremity of Mesopotamia, which comprised the Ottoman Empire's provinces of Baghdad, Basra and Mosul. The troops were part of Indian Expeditionary Force D. This had sailed from Bombay a month earlier and was initially expected to go to Egypt or the western front. However, the force was diverted to await developments in the Gulf and then stationed in the 'quasi British protectorate' of Bahrain. The area, 'the Arabian frontier of the Raj', was strategically significant as the main sea route to India and because of British trading and defence interests. Once

Figure 4.1 Henry Dobbs, judicial commissioner, North-West Frontier Province in 1914, shortly before going to Mesopotamia. Courtesy of Henry Wilks.

in Mesopotamia, the troops immediately took the fort at Fao, advanced rapidly inland to occupy Basra and then consolidated their position in the surrounding area by taking Qurnah, 40 miles to the north.[2]

As well as sending troops, the viceroy had also sent Sir Percy Cox to take charge of all non-military matters.[3] Recently appointed foreign secretary to the Government of India, Cox had been for the previous ten years its resident in the Persian Gulf. He secured the viceroy's agreement to establish a civil administration and Henry Dobbs was then ordered to go to Mesopotamia as revenue commissioner. His role was to set up administrative systems and collect revenue in the wake of the army as it advanced through Mesopotamia. He was to report to Sir Percy Cox and also to the military commander, initially Sir Arthur Barrett and later his successor, Sir John Nixon.[4]

Dobbs's new assignment separated him for the first time from his wife and young family for what both expected to be a lengthy period. From now on, it was primarily his wife to whom he wrote. Because he and his wife were so often not together, Dobbs's 450 letters to her cover much of his working life. They were apart for much of the Great War, and after that when he was away on official assignments as well as subsequently for more than half of his six years as high commissioner in Iraq. During those years, she and the family would remain in the British Isles to avoid the searing Baghdad sun in the hot months. Dobbs wrote lively and often amusing accounts of events, decisions and the personalities he encountered. He also frequently confided in his letters what he would have told his wife face to face. She replied giving reassurance about his handling of the often difficult situations that he had to confront. These confidences reveal for the first time many of Dobbs's thoughts, plans and actions and their significance.

Dobbs's letters also show how important his family and his wife were to him. He writes wanting to 'hear anything about the children … Don't let the children forget me … I don't want to be a stranger to them when I see them again.' Three years later looking at the residency garden in Balochistan, he commented sadly, 'it is constantly my fate to gaze on daisies which I have planted for my children and which they do not come to pick'. He took a close interest in all their activities and insisted that he be involved in every important decision about them. He also much missed his wife and writes, 'I think of you constantly … you are the centre of my life.' He particularly dreaded the 'long separations' from her and thought that it was only a 'miserably small proportion of happiness' they had been able to enjoy together. These themes recur throughout the many and usually lengthy letters Dobbs wrote to his wife.[5]

At the end of January 1915, Dobbs reached Basra. He had speculated earlier, 'I shall perhaps end up as governor of Mesopotamia and warden in chief of the Garden of Eden.'[6] This, according to legend, had been at Qurnah where the Tigris and Euphrates meet. After a couple of weeks, Dobbs wrote to his mother about some of his impressions and his hopes:

> It is immensely interesting dealing with a quite new situation and types of men. I don't know much Arabic yet and have to deal with Arabs largely through interpreters. The Arabs are fine independent men with great ideas of hospitality and a kind of chivalry of their own … One hears great tales of Turkish corruptness and incompetence. But I have a sad suspicion that, even so, the Arabs are happier under them than they eventually will be under us – when we have irrigated the Mesopotamian deserts and regularized everything and screwed everyone up to concert pitch and allow no dirt or slackness and rule with the vast and crushing minuteness of our records. So, I look upon it as an act of providence that I have been sent here to help in laying the foundations and to have an opportunity of countering from the very beginning the methods of excessive red tape. If I have my way, everything will be done to revive a true Arab civilisation, and the lines of administration will be so set that an increase in prosperity shall not mean spiritual decay and the dying out of all local custom and native force of character.[7]

Before long, he was extremely busy 'trying to get elements of civil administration into some sort of order' and found it 'slow work' with everything under military rule and constant 'alarms and excursions'.[8] Furthermore, the responsibilities of the embryonic British civil administration expanded rapidly as British forces secured more territory. After the troops had defeated Turkish attempts to retake Basra at the battle of Shaiba in April 1915, they enjoyed a number of relatively cheap early successes which were achieved with few British but considerable Turkish losses. The troops' swift advance brought extensive new areas within British control. In the absence of agreement as to its objectives, the army had advanced both west and also north towards Baghdad under its thrusting new commander, Sir John Nixon. The troops first secured the whole of the Basra vilayet. By 24 July, they had gained control of Nasiryah on the Euphrates to the west. Going north, they captured Amarah on the Tigris in June, and took Kut-al-Amarah in September.[9]

When Dobbs arrived in January 1915, he had begun by collecting information about existing arrangements. He had also started to put in place systems for raising revenue and a general administrative framework. In her report on the civil administration of Mesopotamia during the British occupation, Gertrude

Bell outlined some of the difficulties. Apart from registered title deeds which were relatively well ordered, such Turkish records as remained were scattered over the floors with the rubbish, and the administration had to try and make a strange and complicated system work without either up-to-date records or the help of experienced officials.[10] Dobbs was always ready to take an imaginative approach to the problems he faced. At Qurnah he was told that the Turks had removed all the revenue records. He was pleased with how he resolved the problem as he explained to his wife:

> I sent for some of the principal sheikhs and said I was so very sorry that all the records had disappeared as I should now be obliged at great inconvenience to myself and them to take the Govt share of dates instead of the light cash assessment. This meant an enormous increase in their taxation, as the cash revenue represents nothing like the Govt Share of dates. They immediately said they had all the records hidden away and produced them. So now we have all that we want.[11]

Dobbs also had considerable difficulties with the officials. He regarded working with the existing Ottoman system and such officials as were in place, mainly Turkish-trained Arab clerks, as the most practical option. However, he noted that the officials were 'not much pleased with us'. He employed a total of about 200 and decided to continue with them but they were

> continually running away to the Turks in spite of our giving them ever so much better pay ... I know for certain that my three most trusted men are in receipt of regular Turkish pay; and I have all the details of who brings the money down and how much each Superintendent receives. I called a number of them together today and told them I knew exactly what was going on; but that I would take no action. I wished them to know, however, that I was aware of everything ... It is a little disappointing.[12]

Dobbs did not replace them because he thought replacements would do exactly the same. The officials were also frequently ill – at one point hardly any of Dobbs's fifty clerks were fit to come to his office. He introduced free coffee hoping it would maintain their strength.

Even when well, Dobbs's officials were unwilling to take any responsibility. They came to him about every detail and he found himself overwhelmed.

> It is no use writing orders, though I write ever so many. They pass by the local officials like the wind. They think an order is an end in itself, a beautiful paper to be looked at and put away. They seem astonished to hear that it is intended

to be <u>acted</u> upon. And they don't think of acting on it unless one asks every day
whether they have done so and raves if they have not. (Dobbs's underlining)[13]

Dobbs had an extremely broad remit – much broader than his position as revenue
commissioner might imply. In addition to revenue collection, his responsibilities
included land records, crown lands, customs, Ottoman public debt, excise, the
tobacco monopoly and its taxation, the oversight of 'pious foundations' (awqaf),
some educational institutions as well as municipal organization and funding. As
Gertrude Bell's report explained, the Ottoman government regarded all lands
in their conquered territories such as Mesopotamia as belonging to them and
revenue officials consequently had a much wider-ranging interest than simply
taxation.[14] Dobbs wrote plaintively to his wife about how overworked he was:

> Those vast domains, Crown Lands and religious endowment lands (about one
> quarter the whole area of the occupied territories I suppose) which I manage
> direct bristle with problems – bad tenants who cut down trees and let their houses
> go to ruin (I am landlord of about 1,000 houses baths, bazaars and tea-shops) …
> I try to get the accounts kept in order and all the dozen Turkish Departments or
> so run properly; sometimes [I am] darting off to the customs house, and finding
> out whether smuggling is being checked, and whether the goods impounded are
> being properly valued for customs (a terrible lot of swindling goes on in this,
> I am afraid). Then a hasty letter about schools and teachers; and a telegram to
> the Consul General at Salonika ordering 1000 tons of a special brand of cigarette
> tobacco (which is a government monopoly).[15]

Dobbs also complained about Army Commander Sir John Nixon's many requests
for statistics. As Dobbs commented, he forgets that 'we have no machinery
to ascertain them as in India and that all the Turkish records are destroyed'.[16]
Dobbs rode out every morning to inspect the lands and properties 'discovering
all sorts of curious abuses', supervised his clerks and gave time to meeting local
dignitaries: 'had up lots of people who were to be punished for not paying their
taxes' and heard petitions.[17]

These responsibilities gave Dobbs a very full day. Initially, he was out riding
soon after 5.30 am and carrying out inspections. He was punted back to his
house for lunch, and returned 'worn out' before the curfew at 6.00 pm. By the
end of May 1915, he was able to tell his wife, 'Everything is going very well here.
I have broken in the Arab clerks and now have far less to do than I did and we
are receiving quantities of money. I feel that if I were to go now, I should have
laid down the lines pretty completely and that people coming after me would
have little difficulty.'[18]

From his first days in the Indian Civil Service, Dobbs had always attached great importance to going out and about in the area for which he was responsible to see things for himself. As in India, this was to make his presence felt and to inspect what he taxed. After two months in Mesopotamia, Dobbs left Basra to go into camp for about ten days. As he told his wife, 'I will be able to see how my various orders and schemes really look when applied over the land and discussed among the Arab villagers.'[19] He was also frequently called on to settle local disputes. He commented on these excursions that 'I always discover unsuspected facts.'[20]

Dobbs made several tours from his base in Basra to see how his initiatives were working out. These were primarily concerned with the management of the Ottoman Crown lands, the collection of revenue from these lands and from other taxation. Dobbs declared, 'I have done all I can for Basra and must get to know all new territories as we conquer them.'[21] The advances to Nasiryah to the west and beyond Amarah to the north greatly increased the number of districts for which Dobbs was responsible. These additions immensely expanded his workload because he found that the Turks had no consistent approach and the system in each area was different. Consequently, he could not simply apply elsewhere the arrangements that he had already worked out for Basra. In Amarah, the records were in such a muddle that no one knew what rights they had and there were therefore endless disputes. The local sheikhs were much more powerful than in the Basra area and Dobbs worried that because 'every man's hand is against everyone else's' his decisions might unwittingly 'light up conflagrations all round'.[22]

The powerful landowning sheikhs whose crops were at that moment on the threshing floor were also pressing Dobbs to know what payments they would be asked for. He described the situation: 'I have had a terrible time attempting to settle disputes between tribes whom we have not yet subdued and know very little about and simultaneously deciding on the revenue. It is the total lack of knowledge that is so wearing and the feeling that any slip may set a whole tribe with its chief careering over to the enemy.'[23]

After a month Dobbs decided he must move on to Nasiryah where he was if anything even busier:

I have been busy from morning till night the last three days; and am now starting off tomorrow at 7 am for a six day trip up and down the river confiscating estates of enemies. There are about 100 estates, all large blocks of land covered with date palms. I shall land at each estate, call up the head tenant and tell him that the estate now belongs to the British Govt and that all the dates are to be paid over to it.[24]

Dobbs was there in August and September, at the time when the dates were harvested:

> It is a full moon; and all the date palms with their bunches of yellow fruit stand out clearly along the river. So many squabbles are taking place all over the country about dates between landlords and tenants and all come up to me for decision. I have invented rather a neat solution. The landlord sends an estimator to estimate the total amount of the date crop and says that it is say 150 maunds[25] of dates. The tenant has a right to a third. The tenant says the crop is only 90 maunds. By the tenant's estimate the landlord should get only 60 maunds. I say to the tenant 'Very well. I accept your estimate of the crop is 90 maunds. According to that your share would be only 30 maunds. Now I turn you temporarily out of the grove until the crop has been picked and you shall get your third viz 30 maunds; and the landlord gets the rest.' So if the crop is really more than 90 maunds the tenant loses by his low estimate and the landlord gains. Thus the tenant is hoist with his own petard. This solution is admired and the tenant cannot possibly raise his voice against it.[26]

Dobbs, who normally never took an armed escort with him, discovered that Nasiryah and its environs were less peaceful than he had hoped. At nearby Suq al Shuyukh, he found:

> One can't go into the streets without a guard … The tribes in the neighbourhood are troublesome and won't pay revenue; and we have at present no force to use against them. So one is utterly powerless.
>
> Most of the Arabs round about are practically independent and laugh at the idea of paying any taxes; and the landholders can't get them to pay any rents either.
>
> None of the people here outside the town will do what I tell them; and they shoot at my messengers and are generally impertinent … I go out myself to settle some matters and they haven't taken any notice of me so far; but they abstain from attending if there is any danger that my decisions will go against them.[27]

Dobbs moved on to Nasiryah itself where he was concerned about increasing unrest among the Arabs who were being encouraged by the Turks to attack both Nasiryah and Suq al Shuyukh. There were attacks on Nasiryah every night and several guards were killed. Dobbs was not aware of any proposals to deal with the attacks. His experience on British India's northwest frontier persuaded him that these would only stop if tough action was taken against the attackers:

I went to the General and told him the Arabs would get worse and worse if no active measures were taken and said that he must blow up some towers and burn a village or two. Well. No one was in favour of this plan. However by dint of much urging I converted the General; and we set forth with 500 men and two guns against a village 6 miles off. We sent a message to the village that we were going to destroy it. They said they would resist; but two shots sent them streaming into the desert. At last the [sappers] came running out towards us and up went the towers like fountains of clay and collapsed into crumbled heaps. Then the houses were set fire to, and there was a splendid blaze. Columns of black smoke above and the flames reddening the smoke below, while desperate hens ran clucking out of the houses and yards. I felt like Nero. At the last moment, [some] said they thought the blowing up of the towers was enough and that the houses of the poor people should be spared. But I made a great fuss; and said that either we should do the thing thoroughly or not at all. We had come to show that we were in earnest; and no one would believe it unless we extirpated the village. Half and half was no good. So I had my way. Then the General announced that every night there was an attack one village of one tribe and one village of [another] would be burnt. Since then (that was a week ago) there has not been a single shot fired at night and distant tribes have been tumbling in to make submission. This I feel as rather a triumph. It is curious that the civilian should be more blood thirsty than the military.[28]

Dobbs spent much of August and September based in Nasiryah where the sporadic attacks had largely restricted him to overseeing the workings of the offices. Returning to Amarah, he went on tour when

[I] was overwhelmed as usual with interviews with Shaikhs, all wanting to have boundary disputes of their estates leased from the government decided or their revenue [assessments] reduced. I spent five days inspecting the estate of several hundreds of square miles and settling boundaries between the sheikh I was with and two truculent neighbours, with crowds of Arabs yelling at the tops of their voices explaining their own points of view.[29]

Dobbs hoped to go further north behind the army knowing that Army Commander Sir John Nixon and Sir Percy Cox were keen to advance further. However, views in both London and Delhi had been divided between those who saw Mesopotamia as a holding operation and the expansionists.[30] In late October, it was at last decided to give Nixon formal approval to go on to Baghdad.[31] Although Dobbs had spent much time relatively close to the army while he established a working administration behind them, he had seen very little of the fighting. He regretted this contrast with his brother, William Dobbs, who had been wounded at Ypres and again on the Somme. He was therefore delighted that in the middle of November he was asked to join Sir Percy Cox and Sir John Nixon's staff as they made their way towards Ctesiphon[32] for the battle which it was hoped would open the way to Baghdad 30 miles to the north. There, the Turks were mainly entrenched and the British and Indian troops would face the numerically superior force of Turks and Arabs.[33]

On 19 November, Dobbs and Sir Percy Cox arrived at the battlefield where Dobbs would be an interested observer. The main attack began at dawn on 22 November and continued until 24 November when, after heavy casualties on both sides, the British and Turkish generals ordered a withdrawal. Dobbs describes his experiences on the two days of fighting (22 and 23 November):

> The body of troops we were with marched slowly forward in scattered blocks over a very wide front towards the arch of Ctesiphon which rose in front of us through the morning mist; and we saw the whole panorama – detached masses of troops moving nearer and nearer to the invisible trenches which we knew were dug all round the arch and away from it. The Turks made no sign; and many thought they had bolted. … When our troops were about ¼ mile from the first trench a tremendous crackling of rifle fire began. After some time a message came that the first line had been carried. We rode forward until we came to the deep narrow trench and passed a number of bodies of our men lying in front of it.
>
> The Army Commander went off and sat behind a low mound to which also I went. Bullets kept coming down among us. The man next to me had one through his helmet and a gunner at my feet was wounded in the arm. Shells still fell everywhere. Then away to our right a great fusillade began and we saw a number of our men running back. They rallied again and went forward; but could not get on. We left the shelter of the mound and moved nearer to the middle of the battlefield; but everywhere shells seemed to be following … The Turks still held the second line of the trenches behind the great arch, cutting us off from the river. The sun set and the almost full moon rose. A large mass of troops came within the first trenches and wire entanglements left by the Turks. Our horses had been without water for 24 hours; and all the transport carts had been sent back to the advanced base. I had 2 tins of mutton in my bag and some biscuits and chocolate and my old knife. Sir Percy and I ate half a tin of mutton and some biscuits and I gave 2 biscuits to my syce.[34] Then there was a call for people to help in taking horses to the water; and I joined … We got through the entanglements and jumped two ditches and so out onto the plain across which we rode towards the arch. Then suddenly the Turks in the second trench stretching towards the river awoke to our presence and began firing and

we all galloped away out of reach or out of sight in the dusty moonlight. Then we crossed a ditch full of corpses of one British regiment and one native. The wounded were sitting up everywhere and calling to us – sitting alone there in the cold. We could do nothing. It was dreadful. There were so many. At last we came to a small trench where there was water. We led our horses down. I loosened my mare's girths and she drank and drank. We made a long detour back to camp having great difficulty in getting the sowars[35] together in the dim light and finding our way. Then we passed a dreadful night. I slept with my head on my saddle, just on the lip of a trench with 4 dead Turks below who smelt horribly. No bedding – shivering through and through until I bethought me of a trenching tool I had picked up and dug me a shallow grave and raked the loose earth over my legs and up to my waist. That kept me beautifully warm. In the centre of the camp were masses of wounded men moaning and over them blew the dust all night. Hardly anyone had water. In the early dawn [23 November] we were all up walking to and fro to get warm. The headquarters Staff gave us some tea. Nothing was decided until the afternoon. Shells burst all day from the same guns across the river. I rode about 11 in the Army Commander's train towards the back. The ground was strewn with dead. Every 20 yards or so there lay a corpse. We dozed in a long line against a hillock – our batteries booming and the Turks' shells falling; and at last it was decided that we must swing back towards the river, rather behind the positions we had gained. So off we went and trains of carts full of wounded and camped below a long southern ridge over which shells fell until after dark, and bullets whizzed all over us. But our transport carts had arrived and we were in comparative comfort; with bedding ... Sir Percy's horse was shot in the night. None of us was touched. At dawn [24 November] we moved off with the wounded and the Army Commander and I are then going back on the launch [to Basra].[36]

For Dobbs, the Battle of Ctesiphon was the closest he came to a major battle. Although he was an onlooker and not directly involved, he wrote to his wife that 'I thought how pleased you would be to hear that I had at last been in the middle of a real hard fight.' He then commented, 'I feel rather worn out; but was surprised to find that I only felt interest, not frightened. However, of course moving under shells and bullets in the background was very different from leading troops against trenches. That must be a great test. Our men have all fought splendidly; but the entrenched positions are too strong' (Dobbs's underlining).[37]

While 'it was not a defeat' the battle failed in its objective, namely to open the way to Baghdad. The British casualties amounted to some 40 per cent of the force. Army Commander Sir John Nixon had left the operational command to General Sir Charles Townshend who, whatever his subsequent errors and misjudgements, had maintained that his forces needed to be strengthened and the logistical support improved before advancing against the Ottomans. Townshend soon concluded that his position at Ctesiphon was untenable, that the troops must retreat and make for Kut until reinforcements arrived. Townshend then despatched his cavalry to Basra, and led the infantry to take refuge in Kut where they arrived on 3 December and were besieged for the next five months.[38]

The failure to break through towards Baghdad after Ctesiphon ended a run of relatively easy British military victories in Mesopotamia and marked the change to a very different military context for Dobbs's work. The earlier successes had encouraged British government hopes of conquests in Mesopotamia to counterbalance the disasters in the Dardanelles. The British increased their forces but the Ottomans did so too and instead of the expected military gains and rapid advances, which had brought new territory under British control in 1915, the army struggled to hold its position. Worse still, British forces were not able to relieve General Townshend and his troops besieged in Kut. Three attempts to relieve the troops were made in January 1916, and three more in March and April. A secret mission led by T. E. Lawrence and Aubrey Herbert to buy out the troops also failed and on 29 April, General Townshend surrendered. For the remainder of Dobbs's time in Mesopotamia, no further offensive action by the army took place and there was no increase in the geographical extent of British control. It was not until Nixon's eventual successor General Maude had put in place what he considered adequate logistical support previously sadly lacking and secured reinforcements that an advance to Baghdad would be attempted. Led by General Maude, the city fell to the British in March 1917. They then went on north to occupy Mosul province.[39]

Back in Basra after the battle of Ctesiphon, Dobbs was in no doubt about what he should do:

> I am going up the river to Amara to the furthest edge of the country which we hold to do revenue and administration. Well; with all these wild rumours among the Arabs about our defeats, I shall insist on showing myself and working as if nothing had happened. It doesn't do, I am sure, for us all to be bunched in Basra.[40]

He saw the situation as providing excellent reasons for concentrating on the part of the job he most enjoyed – going out on tour:

> I am touring about the country doing most of my marches on horseback towing a barge full of my servants and clerks while my launch goes round by river … I carry tents for my clerks to sleep in at night. Thus I can command both the

river and the land and am having a most delightful tour, seeing a great deal of the country and the people … I have been slowly coming up the river making investigations and deciding disputes. I thought it important to do so early, as the tribes are full of rumours after our retreat from Ctesiphon and also full of Turkish emissaries; and it is a calming thing for them to see me going on administering and demanding revenue, as if nothing had happened.[41]

They also voiced their many complaints to Dobbs which were generally property related and extended to runaway slaves.

Dobbs then spent much of his time among the sheikhs who dominated the marsh Arabs. Dobbs always took great care to follow local customs and not give offence. For example, having settled a dispute in Sheikh Majid's favour, the sheikh pressed Dobbs to eat with him. However, Dobbs believed that the Arab food made him ill, so while Majid's dishes were brought through the door of Dobbs's launch with great pomp they were disposed of by the servants and his own dishes were pushed through the window of the launch on the side away from Majid's house.[42] The military stalemate made the situation more difficult. Dobbs took no guard with him 'so as to seem quite confident'[43] but was well aware that apparently friendly sheikhs were often taking money from the Turks and promising to raise their tribes against the British. He did not think they should be blamed for sitting on the fence and 'waiting to see who wins, poor things'.[44]

Dobbs's journeyings into the interior took him into areas where the Turks were sometimes much in evidence. Indeed, his next principal host, Sheikh Shaway he knew to be also working with the Turks, 'playing a double game'.[45] He thought 'the only policy is one of bluff and showing absolute confidence'[46] so had decided to entrust himself to Arab escorts although he did from time to time have concerns about his own safety. As he advanced down the tributaries of the Tigris in his launch he invited the local sheikhs on board to continue their negotiations. However, the launch soon stuck in the mud. They all got off and continued in mashufs – narrow boats of reeds covered in pitch.

Dobbs, who had intermittently been running a high fever, wrote:

I myself sat with Shaway in a mashuf still feeling very feverish. The grey evening came on, heavy clouds sweeping over the shallow lake, a drizzle and high wind. It was wretched. Here I thought am I, stricken with fever, in a boat with a treacherous sheikh in a swamp in the middle of Mesopotamia half way between the British and Turkish spheres, wet through and cold and being hauled to an unknown destination through the night. Sometimes we were paddled,

Arab Village on the Bank of the Tigris

Figure 4.2 Marsh Arab village on the bank of the Tigris (*c.* 1910). Dobbs visited many villages, sometimes travelling in traditional boats (mashufs) and staying in the local chief's reed house (mudhif). Grenville Collins Postcard Collection /Mary Evans.

sometimes poled; sometimes the whole crew sprang out and hauled us forcibly over the mud. It seemed unending. I could make out no land. At last we got to Sheikh Shaway's fort and house of mud on the shores of the great shallow lake up a side channel called the 'Gate of the Winds'.[47]

Dobbs spent five days inspecting Shaway's lands but for some of this time Dobbs had to retire to bed with a temperature of 104°F. Initially Shaway had a spring bedstead put together for him in his fort but later he had to lie down under 'dirty quilts and carpets' at the end of a smoke-filled mudhif[48] where many members of Shaway's tribe were meeting. Although Shaway had strongly denied any links with the Turks, Dobbs's specific purpose in visiting the next sheikh, Sikar, was to persuade him to provide information about any Turkish moves that might cut off British lines of communication. In addition, Dobbs had been expressly asked to look into Turkish efforts to encourage a tribal uprising. Revenue business, as Dobbs commented, enabled him to 'poke about in these back regions without exciting so much opposition or suspicion as someone with no ostensible purpose'.[49] Dobbs had also been asked to find out what possibility there was of the Turks using water routes to mount an attack. The British knew almost nothing about the area and there were no maps. Dobbs was able to make a rough sketch and reassure those concerned that an attack from that direction would be practically impossible. Furthermore, Dobbs collected the information needed to draw up a plan to create extensive flooding and so prevent the Turks getting through should this be necessary.[50]

Dobbs did not enjoy being back in Basra where

> as usual when I got down here, I found such an immense amount of things that had been piling up for me – customs and financial matters, town planning regulations, arrangements for buying up lands for cantonments, dockyards and railways – every kind of horrible and rather uninteresting matter which I had managed temporarily to get rid of while careering about up the Tigris and settling the affairs of the tribes.[51]

Dobbs had at the same time been doing a great deal of work on administrative arrangements for the tribal areas. The Ottomans had largely left the sheikhs to their own devices and had focused on controlling the cities and towns. In an attempt to introduce some degree of order beyond the towns, Dobbs issued the 'Tribal Criminal and Civil Disputes Regulation' in February 1916.[52] 'The working of order out of chaos has been rather a strain,'[53] he told his mother. The regulation reflected the land, revenue and tribal policy under the occupation which Dobbs as revenue commissioner had largely created.[54] Dobbs was very sympathetic to the tribesmen. The Turkish government had made grants of their lands over their heads to townsmen, thus transforming them into mere tenants. Dobbs believed that 'the whole countryside has been in turmoil for the last twenty years in consequence.'[55] He was very much on the side of the tribesmen as opposed to the nominal landlords and anxious to restore the authority of the sheikhs. Essentially the regulation reinforced their traditional authority by recognizing their judicial authority over their tribe. It also enabled them to act as landlords and revenue collectors. It had particular advantages during the period of occupation because it proved effective in controlling crime and was very cheap to administer. It took a broadly similar approach to that Dobbs had followed in Balochistan.[56] However, in the absence of the sort of oversight that existed for similar arrangements in British India, it was more open to abuse in Mesopotamia.[57]

Dobbs had spent much of the first three months of 1916 among the marsh Arabs. He had done his best to ignore his frequent bouts of fever, but after an attack when he spent 'quite a long time' running a temperature of 105°F, the doctor and Sir Percy Cox insisted he take a short trip to India to recuperate. He was sent by sea to Quetta where he found everything quiet on the Indian frontier and commented that the amir of Afghanistan was 'behaving well'. Despite a determined German effort, the amir did not abandon the neutral stance implied by the terms of his agreement with the British. Dobbs was 'rather grieved though to find things going on as if there were no war – Anglo-India hopping and chirping undisturbed. I fear the Indian government has not … made a proper effort … determined to be disturbed from their ruts as little as possible'.[58]

Dobbs returned from India to Mesopotamia at the beginning of May 1916. From the start of that year until the end of July when he left to go home on leave, increasing amounts of Dobbs's time were being taken up by the work he was asked to undertake for the military. More and more often he was expected 'to do all sorts of things that are not my job'.[59] A big project assigned to him in January was to collect and despatch supplies up river. He found this surprising when the military 'had so many special officers and departments for the job'. He was soon arranging for livestock to be driven up river by tribal herdsmen and for boats full of grain to be sent to Amarah where it was ground into flour. He also distributed seed so that the troops could be supplied with fresh vegetables in due course and abolished tax on the growers to encourage them. Some five months later Dobbs, complaining bitterly about 'Transport and Supply's' inability to manage things better, took over negotiations to buy the whole of the barley crop for the use of the troops. The only permitted buyer of the crop was the government. 'Transport and Supply' were paying 'preposterous prices' to a single contractor who could charge the military as high and pay the growers as low a price as he liked. Dobbs arranged for six or seven contractors to compete, saved the government money and got a better price for the growers.[60] Dobbs was always being given miscellaneous tasks and odd jobs, and they always had to be done in a hurry.

While on his tours, the military had often asked him to provide information for them. He was very critical of their general unwillingness to find out for themselves about the terrain in which they were fighting. On his first excursion from Basra into the back lands in January 1916, he saw many detachments of troops stuck all along the river. He believed that this situation arose from the military telegraphing for lorries and ordering camels to move the troops at a time when the water, mud and weak bridges would have made them virtually useless – as Dobbs had previously told them.[61] Some six months later, Dobbs used his local knowledge to quash an unwise scheme for the Tigris and Euphrates river basin. Dobbs, as he told his wife, had been 'coping with' Sir George Buchanan, a civil engineer with expertise in rivers and harbours who had been appointed director-general of port administration and river conservancy to advise on improving shipping channels to Basra. His proposal was to force water into the main river channel by damming the mouths of the principal branches of the Tigris. This would have cut water off from all the crops and 'laid waste the countryside thereby'. Dobbs took him down the principal side branch of the Tigris in his launch 'past stacks of wheat and barley and rice and prosperous settlements for miles and miles; and he ended by saying that he had no idea that there was all this population and cultivation down the river and that it would of course be madness to dam up its mouth'.[62]

As Dobbs wryly commented, Buchanan would have known this had he read Dobbs's report on the area or Dobbs's comments on his scheme.

Dobbs was well aware of the heavy toll that poor logistical support and the lack of medical facilities took on the troops. He saw this first hand at Ctesiphon and many other examples while working with or near the military. There were repeated failures to provide any protection from the searing heat. When one of the officers complained that he had nothing to shelter his troops from the relentless sun, because there were no bamboos or wooden posts to prop up reed mats to provide shade, Dobbs got the swamp tribes to cut stout reeds and had them sent to the soldiers.[63] Dobbs also tried to help make good a shortage of sun helmets for the Cossacks who had arrived in response to the British request to the Russians for help. A steamer, carrying helmets which the British had agreed to provide but which had been consigned 25 miles upriver where the Cossacks had originally been going, docked. The British military rejected Dobbs's suggestion to unload them and sent them upriver with a request that they be sent back. By the time the helmets returned, the Cossacks had left.[64]

This minor episode was typical of the sort of mismanagement that the Mesopotamia Commission later identified on a large scale. British public opinion had been shocked by the defeats in Mesopotamia and the failure to relieve Kut. The government in London responded in July 1916 by setting up a parliamentary enquiry – the Mesopotamia Commission – to look into what had gone wrong. The commission criticized almost every aspect of operations during this period of the campaign from the inadequacy of resources and preparations to the judgement and competence of the military, the reluctance to commit the necessary resources, the confused government oversight, including lack of clarity over the Government of India's precise responsibilities and the absence of agreed objectives.[65] Dobbs, on his brief visit to India, had noticed a general lack of interest in the campaign: the Government of India 'made no particular effort to help'. Dobbs was subsequently told by Sir George Buchanan, who had been working in India, that censorship had been used to prevent difficulties in Mesopotamia being reported to the Indian authorities, and that requests from

Mesopotamia were routinely refused by heads of departments in India and had never reached the commander-in-chief or the viceroy.[66]

On the civil side however, Dobbs was very proud of the fact that he had managed to make a surplus on his revenue and civil administration, 'in time of war and in a new country with trade suffering and everything upside down, and with half the taxes being remitted and not recovered'.[67] The future of the country was uncertain and people were 'apprehensive and doubtful', which made it hard to get anything done. The situation was exacerbated by the military stagnation that followed the Battle of Ctesiphon and the failure to relieve Kut. As Dobbs remarked in January 1916, 'We cannot expect the leaders to settle down and feel comfortable until they see which side is going to win. It is absurd to expect anything else.'[68]

At least as trying for Dobbs as these practical problems were his disagreements with the head of the civil administration, Sir Percy Cox, over what administrative and judicial arrangements should be put in place. Cox strongly held the view that a permanent British-controlled administration with an Anglo-Indian flavour was essential to safeguarding Indian and British commercial interests, an approach that was actively supported by the viceroy.[69] He also thought British control should be free from any 'Turkish taint'. Cox and his private secretary, Arnold – later Sir Arnold – Wilson's aim was to replace the systems operating in the Ottoman Empire with regulations and direct colonial rule on the traditional British Indian model and in a form that took no account of intermittent pressure from London on British India to increase native participation in government. They wanted to employ in Mesopotamia administrators from British India who would be more familiar with practices where they came from, rather than relying on the local population. Furthermore, the viceroy, Lord Hardinge, supported colonizing Mesopotamia with Indians, a proposal which Cox and Wilson were sympathetic to. Dobbs however did not agree that British India's centrally prescribed governing systems and laws were necessarily best or appropriate in the circumstances. For example, he preferred to administer tribal areas through local chiefs on the Sandeman model as he had done in Balochistan. He also expected general pressure for some degree of self-government to increase.[70] Dobbs moreover was operating in war zones, recently seized by advancing troops. For him, it was more practical and politically acceptable to carry on with the surviving Ottoman arrangements and use what was already in place, especially when it was the system that such officials as remained in post were used to.

Dobbs's differences with Cox surfaced a few weeks after his arrival. The Indianization policy[71] which Cox was taking forward was completely at odds with Dobbs's approach and he opposed it vigorously. He wrote:

> If I hadn't intervened, they would have had all the Arab landowners ousted in about 6 months, and a nice problem of infuriated, dispossessed Mohammedans to deal with. I am sorry to say that I was betrayed at a Conference into telling them that they were contemplating government by blind man's buff; which seemed to give some offence. But it really was so. There they sat without having consulted a single person of the country, looking to impose a brand new set of Indian laws on a mixed population of Arabs, Kurds, Turks, Jews, Armenians, Chaldeans, Sabalans, Persians without any idea of their laws of land, or inheritance or marriage or contract. The whole country would have been bouleversé no one knowing who had a right to what, whether they had legally inherited, whether they had to pay their debts or not, and so on. It still makes me very angry to think of it all – sheer stupidity and obstinacy which might easily have lost us the province by creating a mutiny of every inhabitant.[72]

Dobbs was also concerned that Cox's programme conflicted with British legal obligations under the Hague Convention. These required the occupying force to respect existing laws until the occupied territory, in this case Mesopotamia, was formally annexed. Cox had from his arrival assumed that the newly conquered territories would be annexed.[73] Indeed, he had drafted a proclamation for General Sir Arthur Barrett to announce that the British were annexing Basra, in other words, making it part of the British Empire. This was not British government policy and the government had not endorsed this statement. This being the case, Dobbs pointed out that Cox's proposed introduction of Indian regulations would conflict with the British government's obligations under international law.[74]

By the middle of May 1915, Dobbs believed he had 'won the fight on Indian laws' and that what would be in place was Turkish law and Arab custom administered by British officers.[75] Within the British government, there was increasing sympathy and support for Arab aspirations and corresponding unease over applying the Indian colonial model.[76] Ministers in London had decided to transfer the Government of India's responsibility for Mesopotamian operations to the War Office at the beginning of February 1916 and the Arab Bureau was becoming ever more influential, although departmental and ministerial responsibility for Mesopotamia in London still lay with the India office and the secretary of state for India. The senior official heading the Political Department at the India Office, Arthur Hirtzel (later Sir Arthur Hirtzel), had made clear to Cox as soon as he had arrived in Mesopotamia that following the Indian district model was unlikely to be acceptable in the longer term.[77] Thereafter, Hirtzel had frequently reminded Cox and Wilson of the gathering pace of support for self-determination, and the move towards an 'Arab State policy' which the Arab Bureau advocated. He was later to comment to Dobbs on Wilson's 'singular lack of political sense'.[78] However, the various indications that government policy in London was moving in the direction of self-government did not make the slightest difference to Cox, supported by Wilson. Undaunted, they continued to press on with introducing direct rule on the Indian model, including detailed Indian regulations like the Indian Penal Code – the Knox Code. Dobbs believed that with relatively little experience in civil administration – previously Cox had been mainly concerned in negotiating with semi-independent rulers or Persian sub governors – and as a military man with an obsession for controlling the detail,[79] Cox was more at home with following prescribed codes rather than with studying, applying and improving local laws and customs.[80] Dobbs had tended to find Cox more sympathetic without Wilson, and ascribed some of his particular difficulties to the latter, 'a fairly efficient creature'[81] who tightly controlled access to meetings with Cox and decided which papers he saw. His 'gatekeeping' activities also included Gertrude Bell and even Lady Cox.

The continuing policy differences between Cox and Dobbs led to constant disagreements between them, 'I see so much going wrong'[82] wrote Dobbs, but he had two consolations. The landholding system in rural areas which he had done a lot of work to put on an orderly basis with his Tribal Disputes Regulation was firmly in place, and he had a very sympathetic listener in the form of Gertrude Bell. Gertrude had arrived in Mesopotamia in March 1916 from the British government's recently created Arab Bureau based in Cairo. She was joined briefly by her colleague from the bureau, T. E. Lawrence. They and the bureau were moving towards encouraging an Arab revolt against the Ottomans and supporting Arab self-determination – Lawrence was to become actively involved with the Arab revolt. All three were admirers of the Arabs and sympathetic to their aspirations. Lawrence suggested that Cox shared this view,[83] perhaps having in mind Cox's successes in persuading Arab leaders to support the British. However, Gertrude found that in Mesopotamia, the Indian colonial approach pressed by Cox and Wilson was in the ascendancy. She had known Dobbs for some years and was very supportive of his opposing views – she had often met him when in London at his cousin Alfred Lyall's house. 'She absolutely understands and won't be muzzled.'[84] Lawrence, who was generally highly critical of the approach to running Mesopotamia, commented separately on Dobbs's achievements, also that Dobbs had strong views and was one of the most interesting people he had met in Mesopotamia.[85] Indeed, Dobbs had thought early on that 'It would be much better for the Arabs here to be under officers who knew Arabic and Arab traditions', and that was 'the only way to save it permanently from cramped and wrong-headed Indian officers determined to administer on fixed Indian lines'.[86]

The Indian colonial approach which Dobbs so strongly opposed was to be overtaken as the momentum behind self-determination gathered pace. It was to become Allied policy at the Versailles peace negotiations in 1919 to be put into effect through the mandate system under their newly created League of Nations. These developments and the lack of tangible progress fuelled Arab nationalist opposition to the British regime in Mesopotamia and were a factor in the serious disturbances in 1920, which realized one of Dobbs's fears. In 1916, he had voiced concerns about the dangers of causing 'needless offence to influential persons ... Perhaps it doesn't matter a hang what the Arabs feel; but general discontent and a tendency to join against us must surely be a military danger.'[87] The rebellion was suppressed with some difficulty and at considerable cost.

Dobbs however was now beginning to plan for his departure from Mesopotamia at the end of July 1916 to take long overdue leave in Ireland. As in his previous posts, he worried about how best to ensure that what he saw as worthwhile advances were built on and not put at risk after he left. Accordingly, he was anxious to see someone of similar seniority to himself, who might stand up to Cox, appointed as his successor. This led to a furious row with Cox. Although Dobbs persuaded the military commander to support him, his intervention made no difference. Wilson told Dobbs he had been too independent and Cox appointed H. St J. Philby. Dobbs described Philby as 'a young bounderish civilian of 8 years' service not very experienced, working in PZ [Cox]'s office and licking his hand'.[88]

Back in Ireland, Dobbs had to spend much of his time recovering from the malaria and jaundice from which he had frequently suffered in Mesopotamia. Perhaps surprisingly, Cox urged him to return to Mesopotamia and Gertrude Bell pressed him to join them. He was advised against going for health reasons. He was also clear that he was not willing to go back until he would be in a position to do things his way. He got his chance in 1922 when he returned to what was then Iraq. He succeeded Cox and presided over its development for six years as its second and longest-serving high commissioner.

However, Dobbs's next move in the spring of 1917 took him back to India. There he was to draw on his experience of tribes and frontiers first in charge in Balochistan where he became chief commissioner and agent to the governor-general and then, as foreign secretary to the Government of India, when he negotiated a lasting peace with Afghanistan.

5

On the edge of India and in Afghanistan
1917 to 1921: From governing Balochistan to concluding the 1921 Anglo-Afghan Treaty

Dobbs left for India at the end of March 1917. He had spent seven months, much of the time in Ireland, trying to recover from the various illnesses he had contracted in Mesopotamia. The doctors advised that he was not strong enough to return there and instead he had gone back to Balochistan and to a post he had held earlier as revenue and judicial commissioner. He was though still much preoccupied with the situation in Mesopotamia.

Hardly had Dobbs arrived in India and set off for Balochistan (Quetta) via Simla, when he heard that Cox had 'wired urgently that he must be sent to Mesopotamia and Gertrude Bell was hysterical with joy'.[1] He refused to go, partly because of his health but also because of his fundamental disagreements with Cox and his deputy Arnold Wilson over policy. Dobbs had strenuously but ultimately unsuccessfully objected to their 'Indianization' policy (see Chapter 4). Dobbs was also strongly opposed to Cox's approach to controlling one of the fiercest tribes, the Muntefiqs. Cox had wanted General Maude to take 10,000 troops and 'smash them'.[2] When in Mesopotamia, Dobbs had visited that tribe accompanied only by a friendly sheikh. He believed that they could have been won over by peaceful means and saw the later problems with them as an example of matters being mishandled. It was another reason why Dobbs did not wish to return to work for Cox. In the event, nothing was done about the Muntefiqs because Maude refused to spare the troops. Cox had seriously fallen out with the general over the division of responsibilities between them to the extent that Cox considered resigning.[3] He was furious with Maude over the Muntefiqs and the foreign secretary to the Government of India, Sir Hamilton (Tony) Grant made him angrier still by suggesting he needed a rest.[4] On his possible Mesopotamia posting, Dobbs commented, 'in vain is the net spread in sight of the bird. I would not for anything put my head into the noose again'.[5]

Previously in Balochistan, Dobbs had devoted a lot of energy to promoting projects which he hoped would bring economic benefits to the area (see Chapter 3). After his return, the reverberations of the Great War dictated his first economic initiative even in this remote area. British munitions manufacturers were desperate for chromite ore because they needed chromium to temper the steel used in producing the big guns to fight at the front. Quetta had become the only available source of supply for this essential war product. However, when Dobbs visited in June, all mining had stopped. Dobbs found himself 'coping with ignorant European mine managers, cunning council contractors and rebellious workmen' and drafted in one of his own staff to take charge.[6] Chromite ore began to 'pour steadily down to Karachi'[7] and by September, there were 7,000 tonnes of ore awaiting shipment. Another Dobbs project was to improve the quality of the local wool and so increase its export value (wool made up over half the value of Balochistan's exports). Earlier, he had introduced merino sheep from Australia and he now developed a complex scheme to improve quality at the various stages of wool production. It included establishing a cooperative for processing the wool at Harnai powered by coal from the local mines.[8] A woollen mill operated there until 2004.

In September 1917, Dobbs heard that he was to take over in Balochistan and would succeed the present agent to the governor-general (AGG) and chief commissioner, Sir John Ramsay, in December. Dobbs's appointment prompted him to reflect on vice-regal performance and on what was needed to make a success of being in charge in Balochistan:

> What a number of viceroys I have now seen pass like shadows – Elgin, Curzon, Minto, Hardinge, and now Chelmsford. I liked Curzon best. Although frightening, he worked very hard himself, understood everything and knew what other people's work was worth, and exactly what he wanted. I am coming more and more to the conclusion that nothing much matters, so long as one gives perfectly clear orders and sticks to them. Uncertainty is the bugbear of most people; and they don't mind what you tell them to do so long as everything is clear and settled. So I don't think that even when you have made a mistake, unless it is immensely important you should ever alter. I shall try to follow this plan in governing Baluchistan. I wonder what sort of job I shall make of it.[9]

Dobbs's new responsibilities would now also include political oversight of eastern Persia (now eastern Iran) which the Government of India had transferred to the AGG in Balochistan from the resident in Bushire. The British government's focus on Persia was being driven primarily by concerns about how Turks and even more so Germans might use Persia as a springboard for undermining the British position in both India and Afghanistan during the war.[10] Persia had also long been seen as an important area for British India's frontier security because it could open the way to an attack on India by Russia. This had been a cause of concern throughout what was later described as the 'Great Game'[11] and remained so for Lord Curzon, then acting foreign secretary and a die-hard Russophobe who continued to see Russia as a serious and additional threat. These concerns had led the Government of India to authorize the extension of the Quetta to Nushki[12] railway into Persia itself.

Dobbs had taken an interest in Persia since his travels there in 1903 and believed its rich civilization would only benefit India. He saw Balochistan as a doorway to Persia and was keen to encourage contacts in every way. He wanted to revive Persian education in Balochistan and, thinking of fourteenth-century caravanserais, his vision was of an eventual new railway system replacing caravans and camels. He envisaged that it would take traffic from Balochistan across Persia and Mesopotamia to the shores of the Mediterranean so that the new rail transport system would be 'enriching and reviving' the countries it passed through. 'Quite a revival of Eastern civilisation' he hoped.[13]

Dobbs's interest extended to Persian politics, which he had enjoyed discussing with the locals in Tehran on his private visit in 1908. On that occasion, shortly after his departure, the majlis (Parliament) was bombarded by Russian troops with the encouragement of the shah. Detentions and two executions of the more revolutionary elements followed. Although constitutionalist forces secured the reinstatement of the majlis, it was shut down again in 1912 in response to Russian pressure to dismiss its American financial adviser Morgan Shuster and his team. Before 1908, the British government had supported the majlis and Persian democrats against the shah. However, after Britain had agreed that northern Persia would be a Russian sphere of influence under the 1907 Anglo-Russian Convention, the British government had acquiesced in the Russian suppression of Persian democrats and of the majlis for fear of antagonizing their Tsarist ally.[14] Dobbs believed that the democrats felt betrayed by Britain. Consequently, the British had lost support and had become much disliked with the result that the Persians were very ready to intrigue with Turkish and German agents.[15] In November 1917, Dobbs had written both to Curzon, the acting British foreign secretary, and to the viceroy about what he regarded as Britain's misguided Persian policy. The Bolsheviks were repudiating international agreements made by their Tsarist predecessor and in Persia they called for self-determination, favouring the establishing of a republic. Dobbs wanted the British government now also to take the side of the Persian democrats against the shah. He believed that had the British government thus changed its policy, the resulting Persian goodwill towards Britain would have made it unnecessary for British troops to continue occupying southern Persia. Dobbs was in fact uncomfortable with the uninvited British military presence there. It cast Britain in the role of a foreign occupying power in Persia when in 1914 Britain itself had regarded the occupation of Belgium by foreign troops as so unacceptable as to prompt its declaration of war on Germany.[16] A month later, in December 1917, Dobbs had a discussion in Delhi with the visiting secretary of state for India, Edwin Montagu, who told Dobbs he had sent his note to Curzon but said 'we seemed to have no policy in Persia and he didn't know what Curzon would make of it'.[17] Dobbs however knew that his views would be dismissed because of Curzon's Russian phobia and the great fear and general horror of Bolshevism which had replaced concerns about Tsarist Russian aggression. He was undaunted:

> I expect I shall get a furious snub from Curzon as his policy consists in keeping a few corrupt ministers in by bribery and downing the democrats. However I don't care if he does snub me. I have written what I thought right and necessary, both from the point of view of justice towards Persia and the safeguarding of India from attacks through Persia. 'Ruat coelum'.[18]

Dobbs went on tour to see for himself what the situation was among the Persian tribes. He describes what he found on his visit in May 1918:

> I went out to Eastern Persia about 110 miles beyond our extreme Eastern [surely Western?] frontier to a place due South of Sistan last week and held a durbar of wild Persian tribesmen who have broken loose from Persia and are at present under me! They are much afraid of being put back again under their Persian Governors and I had to talk very warily. We had to take them over as German agents had got among them and raised them against us and also our own tribes next door. One of my tasks was to liberate a number of Persian slaves – women and children – whom these horrible Balochi tribes have recently taken in raiding forays towards Kerman. They tied children together in each camel saddle bag, made marches of 60 miles a day back to their homes and turned out one or two dead each day and reached home with only about 10% of the women and children whom they had seized. I was met outside the place I was going to by about 600 robber chiefs of sorts mounted on their camels – a curious sight and

I pranced in with all these behind me across the lower slopes of a huge smoking volcano, the Kuh-i-Taftan [Taftan] with snow on its crest.[19]

There were also concerns about hostile activities in the other country bordering Balochistan, Afghanistan, where Germans and Turks were similarly active. There, Dobbs had increased the numbers of agents reporting to India on the situation[20] although Amir Habibullah had in fact kept Afghanistan neutral. As to Russia, Dobbs believed that at that stage, it was too preoccupied with internal fighting following the 1917 revolution to be able effectively to threaten India through either Afghanistan or Persia. In general Dobbs regarded the Government of India and indeed the military as prone to exaggerate the dangers on India's northwest and western frontiers.[21] Even if there was a war with Afghanistan on that frontier, Dobbs was confident that India had the capacity to deal effectively with it, as was indeed demonstrated when the next amir launched the Third Afghan War.

Two months after taking up his appointment as AGG Balochistan, Dobbs was faced with a serious tribal uprising. The Marri tribe was particularly hostile to the British and was being encouraged against them by German agents.[22] Discontent was also being increased by serious shortages of basic necessities such as flour, cloth and firewood. The shortages were caused by the lack of railway transport which had been diverted to build the extension of the Nushki railway towards Persia.[23] At the same time, under pressure from the Government of India to raise more troops for the Great War, Dobbs had encouraged efforts to recruit from the tribes. He commented that these efforts 'provoked much feeling against us. They don't feel it is their war and are terrified of accounts of gas, bombs and aeroplanes'.[24] In February 1918, Dobbs received reports that a large Marri force was about to attack. He was sceptical and asked for more information. In the meantime, the local military had become very nervous, the political agent moved into Fort Gumbaz and the Marris mounted a savage attack. Dobbs described what happened from the eyewitness account Colonel Gaussen gave him:

> The howling was horrible like thousands of mad jackals. The Marris were so mad with fanaticism that ever so many bullets couldn't stop them. One had 8 in him and still came on. Gaussen and McConaghey fought with shot guns which they found most effective at such short range. There was a faint moon, constantly behind clouds; and through the dim light came howling the mad Marris with their scaling ladders and swords and rifles – one attack after another through the night – Marris inside the fort, Marris outside the fort and now and again some managed to get on the roofs and parapets and run from one side to another

at the defenders. The worst time was when the ammunition ran out and the sowar[25] sent to open the spare box down below in the centre of the fort had his throat cut by a Marri sword. The key of the box was in his hand and was lost and Gaussen had to get down among the swarming Marris and keep them off and break open the ammunition box with a hatchet. The 75 sowars fired 60,000 rounds that night. Of course it was all in the dark or one would wonder at such a large expenditure of ammunition.[26]

Matters were made worse when the Marris were joined by another tribe, the Khetrans and the combination created a particularly dangerous situation. It was sufficiently serious for women and children to be evacuated from two centres at risk, Fort Sandeman and Loralai, and Dobbs was planning the evacuation of Quetta.[27] He was by now anxious to have reinforcements but was having difficulties with Delhi. Because of the large number of foreign agents who were active on the Indian frontier, Dobbs commented that the Foreign Department of the Government of India 'had taken fright and wired that no military intervention was to take place in the present delicate juncture'.[28] Dobbs then allowed the Marri to attack the Quetta railway because he knew that this would induce Delhi to send troops.[29] These were much needed. There were a series of engagements throughout March and the Marri were frequently bombed. Their main force was defeated on 4 April. Dobbs had kept in touch with the Marri Nawab but he could not control his tribe. They surrendered on 2 May. Dobbs considered that Balochistan had been very effectively pacified and consequently it posed little risk when the Third Afghan War broke out a year later in May 1919. Although glad that the Marri revolt was over, he regretted having seen no action and that he had been required to remain at the centre: 'I hate not being on the spot and being reduced to sending telegrams and receiving them and issuing orders.'[30]

Dobbs had little opportunity to advance his plans for Balochistan. First, much of his time had been taken up with the Marri and Khetran troubles. Although these were over at the beginning of May 1918, he was still extremely busy in August 'mopping up all the debris of the rebellions of my tribes and writing reports upon the operations'.[31] His wife had joined him in January 1919 – her arrival had been much delayed by the difficulties of securing a sea passage and concerns over the risks of travelling during the war. Hardly had she reached Quetta than the viceroy, Lord Chelmsford, asked Dobbs to take the post of foreign secretary to the Government of India. Although he was 'ready to go where public interest required',[32] he did not look forward to life in Simla and Delhi. He saw the influence of the Indian Foreign Department as somewhat reduced – exemplified by their loss of responsibility for Mesopotamia to London.[33] He also much wanted to settle down and not to keep changing positions. However, he recognized that it was 'an interesting period to be foreign secretary with the future of Persia and Central Asia unsettled and various urgent Afghan questions' and liked the fact that the decision had effectively been taken out of his hands so 'I shall only have Providence to reproach and not myself if things go wrong.'[34]

Henry Dobbs arrived in Simla in June 1919, soon after the amir of Afghanistan had sued for peace in the Third Afghan War, and took over his responsibilities in September. Some ten months later in April 1920, he wrote to his mother that he had been 'heavily overworked in rearranging the whole of our frontier policy'.[35] Dobbs was trying to get acceptance for changes to India's long-established policy towards Afghanistan. In the agreement that ended the Third Afghan war and was signed at Rawalpindi in August 1919, Dobbs's predecessor as foreign secretary, Tony Grant, had formally ceded British India's control of Afghan foreign relations. Grant took this major decision entirely on his own authority to meet Amir Amanullah's demands and ensure an end to the hostilities.[36] Grant claimed that the military had insisted that there must be no risk that fighting would restart because the army was too weak to continue, a claim the military later denied.[37] A key objective of Amir Amanullah's had been to free Afghanistan from any British oversight and secure the complete independence he had promised to Afghan nationalists.[38] In order to achieve this, he had to obtain its release from British India's prohibition on contacts with other states, originally imposed at Gandamak in 1879. This had been a cornerstone of British policy for the last forty years.[39] The government in London was furious at not being consulted in advance on such a fundamental policy shift and the establishment in British India was unwilling to admit any necessity for this change.[40]

Dobbs thought the Government of India should accept that after Grant's settlement there was absolutely no realistic prospect of reclaiming the control of Afghan foreign relations, which it had previously enjoyed. Dobbs recognized that, in the volatile post-war international situation, Britain appeared significantly weaker in light of its increasing difficulties in Mesopotamia, the Turkish successes under Mustapha Kemal (known as Atatürk) as well as the unrest in Ireland at the heart of its empire. Amanullah saw further signs of weakness in the British eagerness to settle with the Afghans at Rawalpindi and their apparent readiness to give up control over Afghan foreign relations – on which hitherto they had always insisted – without even trying to obtain anything in return. The permanent secretary at the India Office, Sir Arthur Hirtzel, commented privately to Dobbs, 'It looks to me as though your predecessor has got us into an almost insoluble difficulty'.[41] In all these circumstances, it was practically inconceivable that Afghanistan would willingly return to its previous subservient relationship with British India in return for financial support and protection from Russian aggression.

Indeed, Dobbs expected growing international support for self-determination led by the United States and reflected in the Allies' decisions at the end of the Great War to become irresistible. It reinforced Amanullah's resolve – he had even suggested he should be invited to the Allies' continuing discussions. Dobbs was also sympathetic to Afghanistan's aspirations, just as earlier he had been to those of the Arabs when he was in Mesopotamia. Furthermore, Dobbs was sensitive to the fragility of Amanullah's position within Afghanistan. Following his father Habibullah's assassination, Amanullah had succeeded as amir in dubious and precarious circumstances. He had stirred up nationalist sentiment, and advancing Afghan independence would much increase his standing with his people.[42]

Far from the earlier Afghan fear of Russia, Amanullah was looking for a possible alliance with the government that was assuming power there. He was in touch with Bolshevik representatives and had felt able to ask for Russian support during the Third Afghan War.[43] According to a Foreign Department note, policy should no longer be based on 'what was practical politics in the mid-Victorian era'. Afghanistan had become 'a petty state sensitive of its independence on the borders of a powerful neighbour'.[44] It was actively taking many diplomatic initiatives and seeking new alliances. In Dobbs's view any future arrangements would need to take account of these realities.

In contrast with the situation for much of the previous century, Dobbs did not at this juncture see Russia as posing any serious threat to British India. The Bolshevik regime was still comparatively weak and had many other preoccupations and problems. Dobbs was also relaxed about Afghanistan's international ambitions. He was somewhat sceptical about how well the Afghans would succeed in managing their diplomatic relations:

> They have a passion for posing as a civilised nation. Let them pose; and let them assemble as many ambassadors as they can at Kabul – French, Russian, Persian, Chinese, Turkish, Siamese, Japanese, German and British. Their intrigues ought to neutralise one another and put the Afghans in a fix; and they will all hate the Afghans after a short experience of them.[45]

The tactic would be simply to give the Afghans 'rope' in order for them and their various allies to fall out. More important was Dobbs's assessment that British

India would still be able to dominate because of its proximity and significant strengths relative to other countries, even if these strengths were not as great as they had once been.

Dobbs saw the tribal situation on the Indo-Afghan border as a much greater risk to the security of British India than any Afghan international entanglements. He believed that the amir's ability to incite the border tribes against India was, 'our heel of Achilles'.[46] Amanullah, in his role as the head of the first independent Muslim nation state, was also raising his profile with the tribes by his public support of the rights of Muslims everywhere. As a Muslim champion, he encouraged Indian followers of the Khilafat (Caliphate) Movement in the United Provinces to migrate to Muslim-controlled Afghanistan.[47] His aspirations played to fears long held in British India that jihad might unite against it all the tribes on its borders. For Dobbs, bringing the border tribes under control would make it possible to look on India's difficult neighbour with comparative indifference.[48]

In October 1919, a month after Dobbs had taken over formally as foreign secretary, the amir approached the authorities in London and Delhi about opening talks. The Rawalpindi Agreement signed on 8 August 1919 had provided for negotiations in six months' time about a possible friendship treaty to settle the many issues outstanding between India and Afghanistan. Now that Afghanistan was an independent state, an agreement could be in the form of a treaty between two states. Previously, agreements had been made personally with the amir. A precondition for opening the talks had been for Afghanistan to demonstrate their wish for British friendship. However, the Afghans were busily expanding their contacts with those known to be hostile to British India, notably the Bolsheviks. Amanullah was also welcoming in Afghanistan many leading opponents of British rule in India where opposition to British control was increasing. Nevertheless, internationally, Britain was facing a deteriorating situation – most notably the unrest in Mesopotamia – and Dobbs saw significant advantages in trying to establish closer relations with India's difficult neighbour, Afghanistan. The British government was then persuaded that discussions should be held to 'clear away misunderstandings'.[49] A conference between the British and Afghan delegates was convened and opened at Mussoorie on 15 April 1920. This was the start of negotiations that concluded with the Anglo-Afghan Treaty, eventually signed in November 1921. Henry Dobbs was the chief British negotiator and led the discussions first at Mussoorie and then in Kabul. Apart from the last six months of 1920, he was entirely occupied with these difficult and sensitive negotiations.

Figure 5.1 Delegates to the British-Afghan Conference at Mussoorie, 1920. The chief British representative was Dobbs and the chief Afghan representative (on his right) was Tarzi (both front row centre). They later went on to negotiate in Kabul. Courtesy of Henry Wilks.

The Government of India's objectives for Mussoorie were very limited. They were essentially to get a better understanding of Afghan demands and priorities and to make clear to the Afghans the limits of any possible British concessions – India's 'red lines'. The talks would also 'tide over the critical period of the next hot weather' when the army was most vulnerable.[50] Dobbs told his mother that the conference was 'only to make time and he had no great hopes of it'.[51] The signs were not encouraging. For months beforehand, the Afghans had been negotiating with the Russians to conclude an offensive alliance against the British. Only when the Russians had refused did the Afghans confirm their delegation. Dobbs commented that 'this characteristic exhibition of Afghan duplicity formed an ill prelude to our discussions'.[52]

The Afghans interpreted their new freedom on the international scene as allowing them to double-deal as much as they liked in what Dobbs described as a 'spirit of treacherous opportunism'.[53] They did not have sufficient resources to pay their troops fully and the loss of the British subsidy, a key issue to be renegotiated after Rawalpindi, exacerbated the situation. Their 'money hunger' made them 'anxious to sell [their] friendship in the dearest market and at the moment when it is most valuable'.[54] They also very much wanted to be seen as playing a significant role in support of Muslims internationally and therefore wished to show they were influencing British and Allied negotiations involving the Turks. Dobbs describes various elements in the Afghan position on international issues:

> They are very difficult to deal with. They came down with all sorts of extravagant ideas and demands and tried to bluff me into yielding territory and every kind of thing by making out that the Bolsheviks were begging them to conclude an alliance with them and invade India. As we have managed to get every detail of their negotiations with the Bolsheviks, and know quite well that the Bolsheviks are most anxious to avoid an entangling alliance with Afghanistan and to come to an understanding with us, I was able to receive their threats with smiling calm and to let drop a few words that showed them we knew everything. Then after sulking for some days, they turned round and asked me to make an offensive alliance with them against the Bolshevists and pay them a large subsidy for the purpose. Of course we don't have to be letting ourselves in for a new central Asian adventure; so this too I turned down …
>
> We really are on a volcano and shall be, until the Turkish peace is signed and the Mohammedans settle down if they ever do. I have the greatest difficulty in preventing the Afghan delegates from intriguing with the Indian Mohammedans. The Afghans pretend to be deeply interested in the Turkish question and I have hitherto successfully managed to prevent their formulating demands about it, in the hope that the Turkish peace terms would be published.[55]

Dobbs touches here on an important factor in the negotiations: the often critical information British intelligence sources provided. The British had the cipher code for the Russian communications, so were well aware of Afghan double-dealing. The Afghans were also busy spying. Later, Dobbs recounted his own efforts to use Afghan undercover activities to his advantage. When he was in Kabul, he suspected the doorkeeper of spying because he noticed him taking an unusual interest in the contents of Dobbs's wastepaper basket. Dobbs was finding the Russian military attaché particularly tiresome, so scribbled and threw away a faked draft despatch to his government warning that the attaché was planning a coup. Within a week, the attaché was on his way back to Moscow as unacceptable to the Afghan government.[56]

In the talks at the Mussoorie conference, Dobbs took a firm line on control of the border tribes from the start. While discussions were beginning, incidents were taking place on the frontier which Dobbs saw as Afghan attempts 'to intimidate us'. Dobbs immediately suspended the conference without consulting the viceroy and it did not resume for seven weeks. In the subsequent discussions, he made it absolutely clear that 'we would not tolerate the intrigues of the past' to which the Afghans admitted and the British would not cede any territory. 'I insisted on the impossibility of our ever yielding up to a nation of whose permanent friendship we had no assurance the keys of our frontier gates'.[57]

When the conference broke up at the end of July 1920, Dobbs thought it had achieved its limited aims. He commented that the Afghans had moderated their more extreme demands and 'learnt the limits up to which they can go; the differences between the two governments have been discussed in the frankest possible manner'.[58] The talks had also helped to maintain the peace at a difficult time of year for the army. The Afghan delegation left with a rough draft of a possible treaty. Dobbs indeed was persuaded by Tarzi, the leader of the Afghan delegation and the amir's foreign minister, that they would be interested in signing a treaty at that point. Dobbs recommended this to the viceroy, Lord Chelmsford, partly because he saw hostile influences gaining ground in Kabul as Russian representation increased, and the arrival of the Turkish general, Jemal Pasha, as an adviser was imminent.[59] The viceroy however did not accept Dobbs's recommendation, and it was the Russians in Kabul who offered the Afghans a treaty promising them a generous supply of money and arms. However, the Afghans were beginning to have doubts about the Bolsheviks' reliability and their commitment to support Muslim rulers following their expulsion of the amir of Bokhara. The Russian treaty with Afghanistan still had to be ratified by Moscow and the amir began to worry that he might not get a treaty with either Russia or the British. By now he was unable to raise enough cash to pay his troops, and on 6 October 1920, he asked for a British mission to be sent to Kabul to conclude a treaty of friendship which he expected to include a subsidy.[60] This time the viceroy, Lord Chelmsford, agreed. He thought the time was right and shared Dobbs's view that India would be more secure if its relations with Afghanistan could be put on a positive and formal basis.

However, the Government of India faced strong opposition from the British government to sending a mission. The government in London remained reluctant to acknowledge that Afghanistan had become a free agent in foreign affairs and that this implied it had every right to negotiate a treaty without either telling the British government its terms or seeking its approval. They now refused to allow a mission to go to Kabul unless the Afghans were first prepared to disclose the terms of their draft treaty with Russia, most of which were in any event known to the British from their intelligence sources.[61] Dobbs and Chelmsford did not regard non-disclosure as any barrier to opening negotiations and, despite the opposition of the Cabinet, eventually won a 'snarling and grudging' acquiescence from the secretary of state for India, Edwin Montagu.[62]

It had taken until December – some three months – for the governments in London and Delhi to reach agreement. Despite his fears that leaving in December would risk their motors getting stuck in the snow, Dobbs, now Sir Henry, and the members of his mission successfully reached Kabul on 7 January 1921. Dobbs's instructions were to negotiate a treaty on the lines of the draft provisions in the aide-memoire drawn up after the Mussoorie Conference. These were believed to have been generally acceptable to the amir. The draft gave effect in broad terms to the agreements that the Indian government had negotiated with Amanullah's predecessors apart from the critical difference that it did not provide for the Government of India to have control of Afghanistan's foreign relations. The main subjects for negotiation were a subsidy from the Indian government, understandings that Afghanistan would not incite tribesmen within British boundaries against India, and would observe the requirements of 'neighbourliness' which included restraining those within Afghanistan from mounting hostile action against British interests.[63] The treaty would recognize Afghanistan's independence, and provisions were therefore needed to define this newly sovereign state's future relationship with British India on a range of matters, from the exchange of ministers to customs regulations.

Before Sir Henry opened the formal discussions in Kabul on 13 January, he had a private meeting with the amir and his foreign minister, Tarzi. At this meeting, he revealed that Britain knew all about their exchanges with the Russians and others, thus undermining the Afghan negotiating position and leaving the Afghans in no doubt that their double-dealing was unlikely to go undiscovered.[64] When Dobbs arrived, he had found 'Kabul simply swarming with Bolsheviks, Turks, Germans and Austrians'[65] and believed that the Turkish general Jemal Pasha was encouraging trouble on the Indo-Afghan frontier. However, the treaty the Afghans had negotiated with the Russians in Kabul a few weeks after the conference at Mussoorie meant that they now felt free constantly to push the British for better terms. Discussions nearly broke down over Dobbs's refusal to make any concessions to the Afghans' 'extravagant demands' on territory and control of the tribes.[66] The importance of controlling them was underlined by Amanullah's later admission that the tribes on the Indian side of the border had been his best troops in the Third Afghan War.[67] After a month, Dobbs outlined the limits of his position, threatened to leave if the Afghans did not give way on the tribes and summoned motor cars from Delhi – a tactic he was to use on three further occasions – and they arrived on 15 February. 'I shall then be ready to shake Afghan dust off our feet at any moment ... I hardly expect them to budge; but the procession of motors may frighten them.'[68] He rightly suspected that the Afghans, 'however much they may wish to play us off against the Bolshevists, can hardly relish the idea of our cutting off all relations with them, as they will then have no bogey of English friendship to frighten the Bolshevists with.'[69] The mission did not leave and both sides agreed to continue discussions.

The Afghans constantly changed their demands depending on how much pressure they believed the British government was under, how well their own negotiations with others were going and how strongly placed they judged their potential allies to be against the background of ever-changing international developments. Dobbs commented, 'It is difficult to exaggerate the effect of such events on the changeable and hesitating views of the politicians of Kabul.'[70] At this point, the Afghans were getting increasingly nervous about Bolshevik setbacks and delays in Moscow, and became ever more afraid that they would end up with no treaty at all. Delays in Dobbs's receiving his instructions meant he was frequently unable to take advantage of changes like this in the strength of his negotiating position. Dobbs commented, 'really this diplomacy by spasms and waiting for weeks every time one gives a knock out blow is impossible.'[71]

These delays were in part due to the slowness of the communications systems at Kabul, 'our wireless collapses almost every day and the most vital telegrams are delayed for 24 hours.'[72] Many more serious and lengthy delays arose from fundamental differences of opinion between Dobbs, Edwin Montagu, the secretary of state for India in London and the viceroy, now Lord Reading, advised by his acting foreign secretary, Denys Bray. The differences between Delhi and London had to be resolved in order to settle the negotiating strategy and instruct Dobbs.

Dobbs's negotiating position in the continuing discussions after the February stand-off was being made increasingly difficult by the demands and actions of the British government in London. First, Dobbs was instructed that no treaty could be considered if the Afghans accepted anything from the Russians – a complete change in the British position.[73] Secondly, Curzon had made public the British requirement that the Afghans must provide the British mission with the full text of their treaty with the Russians before the mission could discuss any friendship treaty.[74] Curzon's long-standing Russophobia was now reinforced by general British establishment horror at Bolshevik schemes. Dobbs however did not regard Bolshevik revolutionary ideas as a reason to rule out making agreements with them. He commented in the context of Persia, 'We are not keeping out Bolshevist ideas by refusing to clasp the Bolshevists' hands.' He did not consider Afghan contacts with Bolshevik Russia as a great cause for concern provided that the Afghans did not agree to let the Russians base hostile activities near India[75] – the Russians were proposing to open consulates close to the Indo-Afghan border.

After Dobbs's threat to leave Kabul in February, there had been almost no progress. The Afghans were 'avoiding conversations' because of their uncertainties over the Russian position and Dobbs was awaiting instructions. At the beginning of April, the Afghans made 'impossible demands' which they said were their 'last word' and Dobbs again prepared to leave. He expected a day of 'storm and stress'. The amir responded by saying he would receive a 'visit of condolence' from Dobbs following his favourite uncle's death. Dobbs described the meeting:

> The interview lasted nearly five hours. The Amir and Tarzi sat there in complete collapse out of fright at my threatened departure. The Amir talked and talked about the virtues of the deceased and about everything under the sun and could not bring himself to the point. Tarzi simply babbled. I refused to help them out. At last the fountains of talk ran dry and we sat in absolute silence. I looked at Tarzi and Tarzi at me with glazed and reproachful eye. Then he took the plunge and said to the Amir that His Majesty had perhaps heard that there were some small differences of opinion between us and that I was, he could not think why, thinking of going away. Then the Amir said he could not understand why, if both governments wished to be friends there should be all this difficulty. I said Tarzi had sent me officially an impossible draft and said it was the last word. So there was nothing for me to do but to go. The Amir said it was all a mistake and was not the last word. Amendments were possible.[76]

After Tarzi had admitted that the Russians wanted the consulates so that they could stir up the tribes and opposition in India to British rule, the amir went out to pray. Debate then resumed. They finished by agreeing that detailed discussions on the clauses of the draft treaty would continue and Dobbs would ask whether the British government would commit to helping Afghanistan if attacked.

The April talks that followed these discussions soon reached another impasse on tribal matters. Progress was yet again being much held up by the length of time it took to issue Dobbs with the formal instructions he frequently needed to authorize his stance. The British government in London was ultimately responsible for India, but it preferred not to overrule the viceroy on matters regarded as primarily for British India of which frontier questions were one. Nonetheless, the Government of India had to agree Dobbs's instructions with

Figure 5.2 Amir Amanullah of Afghanistan. Courtesy of Henry Wilks.

the secretary of state for India in London, Edwin Montagu, and then Simla had to issue them. The delays in this tortuous process had been compounded by the appointment of the new viceroy. Lord Reading had taken over from Lord Chelmsford, whom Dobbs had worked well with despite occasional and sometimes significant differences of view. Reading was a distinguished lawyer, a former attorney general and lord chief justice. He had been influential with Prime Minister Lloyd George, who had sent him to Washington with the delicate task of increasing US support for Britain in the Great War, but he had virtually no experience or knowledge of India. He appeared indecisive to Dobbs and he generally took the advice of his acting foreign secretary, Denys Bray. Dobbs soon found that Reading preferred to settle matters orally in the style of a cross-examining barrister rather than by considering written briefing. Dobbs however did not hesitate to send him a note setting out 'some simple and fundamental truths about the Afghans which a baby should have known'.[77] He pointed out that the questions about the amir's legitimacy left him in a vulnerable position, that the country itself was weak and 'short of money and arms' and that a treaty might steady Afghanistan provided it did not, as had happened at Rawalpindi, 'lower our reputation for nothing'.[78] Reading's working preferences made him particularly dependent on Bray. Bray's views were generally in conflict not only with those of Dobbs but also with those of Edwin Montagu, the secretary of state for India. Bray was convinced that a 'friendship' treaty must be concluded on any terms and must include a subsidy so that the threat of its withdrawal could be used to enforce its provisions. Dobbs would have welcomed a treaty with these provisions but not if weak concessions were the price for concluding it because he was convinced that weak concessions would encourage Afghan aggression.[79] Montagu was generally sceptical about the claimed damaging consequences of failure to sign a 'friendship' treaty and about the effectiveness of a subsidy in securing compliance with its provisions. Dobbs wrote, 'I now have three parties to contend with, the Afghans, Lord Reading and Edwin Montagu.'[80]

Between April and September, the negotiations on the 'friendship' treaty made very little progress. Made bolder by their draft agreement with Russia, the Afghans continued to press for ever more advantageous terms. While Moscow was still deciding whether to ratify their treaty with Afghanistan, Dobbs proposed a most generous offer, provided the Afghans cut their links to Russia. However, this was not passed on promptly and by the time authorization arrived from the secretary of state for India to take this line, the Russians had ratified their treaty, the Afghans had signed and it was too late. At the end of May:

> Arrived a copy of an angry telegram from Edwin [Montagu] asking what on earth they [the Government of India] meant by not telegraphing on to him some of my telegrams which had now reached him with printed papers by post! If they had reached him earlier, he says he would have given much earlier and more emphatic orders in the sense which I had suggested; and he ends up by saying 'HM Govt has the fullest confidence in Dobbs'. ... It is rather unusual for the Secretary of State to support publicly an officer against the Govt of India and to censure them in this open way. These quarrels in high places make it rather difficult for me; and the dreadful delays still worse ... It is bad enough to have all our natural opponents at Kabul and to deal with them; but when you have your own people at loggerheads, it is much worse.[81]

By sending papers by post, the viceroy's office had delayed their receipt by about six weeks. Indeed, the permanent secretary at the India Office subsequently told Dobbs that the government in London had pointed out to Reading that the Government of India's actions had led to an important lost opportunity and that Montagu had privately warned him about Bray's interference.[82]

Dobbs's relations with the Afghans were again being made more difficult by actions in London. Afghan suspicions that the British government was not prepared to deal with them as an independent state were fuelled by the behaviour of the Foreign Office under Curzon. As well as continuing to insist that Afghanistan was handled by the India Office which dealt with dependencies, an objection was made to Italy signing a commercial treaty with Afghanistan because it was part of Britain's 'sphere of influence'. The Foreign Office then added to these insults by continuing its refusal to allow the title 'majesty' to be used when British officials were addressing the Amir.[83]

Throughout the long weeks of negotiation and stalemate, Dobbs and his party took every opportunity to develop friendly relations with the Afghans outside the formal negotiations and add to their understanding of the country. They had done this from the moment they crossed the border. After the mission had been formally received by the amir's representatives led by General Sami, one of the amir's closest advisers, they joined the British in their cars and drove together to Kabul, General Sami travelling with Sir Henry. The Afghans were courteous and communicative and talked about the areas they were passing through.[84] Two months after the mission arrived, when Dobbs had already made one of numerous threats to break off and leave, the mission was invited to the amir's accession durbar. During a lengthy reception, members of the mission talked to the Afghans, some joined the Afghans at bridge tables and others at chess games – Dobbs had help with his chess game from Tarzi, the foreign minister.

In contrast, the Russians who were unable to converse with their hosts sat by themselves and little attention was paid to them.[85]

Although angry exchanges with weeks and months of little progress frequently characterized the formal proceedings, informal socializing still continued. The mission was asked to shoot with the amir who was 'a fine shot' and drove Dobbs in his Rolls Royce.[86] They were invited to go to the Id festivities,[87] to play tennis[88] and to Afghan Independence Day celebrations where they joined the amir at the races. Dobbs sat in front of the amir, next to his little daughters. The amir liked to bet heavily, leaving others to bet against his choice. He insisted on being paid in gold sovereigns and if these were not immediately paid over, required a pledge, so he retained Dobbs's gold watch and chain until his debt was paid. If the amir lost, he paid in Afghan currency worth half the value.[89] The mission members took every opportunity to improve goodwill – perhaps Dobbs felt they needed to after the amir had candidly told him early in the negotiations that he didn't like the British and he was thinking of a treaty purely out of political necessity.[90]

The negotiations became ever more difficult especially after 19 July when the Afghans celebrated signing their treaty with the Russians. Events led to the British again suspending talks. Their mailbag was stolen on 31 July and discussions were adjourned until it was returned three weeks later. Dobbs was then instructed to leave if the Afghans continued to refuse full disclosure of the terms of the Russian treaty and did not withdraw two insulting letters to which Dobbs had already replied in 'suitably outrageous terms'.[91] Dobbs did not expect the Afghans to comply and wrote 'so we part at last. It is unfortunate; but the Afghans have been so treacherous and so insulting that there's nothing more to be done.'[92] However, the Afghans did withdraw the letters but, as Dobbs knew from intelligence sources, they provided an incomplete version of the treaty. Nonetheless, yet again, talks resumed.

Over the most difficult period from July to September, compromises and such concessions as Montagu was prepared to allow were put forward but these never went far enough to satisfy the Afghans. The Afghans constantly prevaricated and Dobbs decided on his own authority 'or in excess of it' to set a deadline for decision and 'damn the consequences … We can't hang on forever here with the chance of the Afghans playing some trick behind our backs.'[93] A deadline would also reduce the Afghans' scope to 'play the auctioneer' by encouraging a sort of bidding war with other treaty signatories, Russia and Turkey.[94] Although Dobbs hoped that Curzon and Montagu would pull back from the 'rotten weak compromise' now on the table, he assured Bray and Reading that 'I shall continue to press our original policy with the utmost determination to the end; only giving way at the very last moment, when my foot is in my motor-car.'[95]

Dobbs had little sympathy for the Government of India's fears that no treaty would be concluded: 'Bray is in a great state of funk lest I should kick over the traces; and keeps sending frantic telegrams bidding me to remember what a dreadful thing it would be if we came away without a treaty, and that we must have one at any price. Lord R[eading] has also sent me a private telegram.'[96]

The British government in London now began to consider a different approach. The secretary of state for India, Edwin Montagu, like Dobbs, found objectionable the humiliation of continually giving way to Afghan pressure by offering the Government of India's proposed concessions in repeated attempts to agree a 'friendship' treaty. At the beginning of August, the government in London suggested that instead of the 'friendship' treaty with its subsidy, the mission should try for a 'neighbourly' treaty and not offer a subsidy. Moreover, without a subsidy the required disclosure of the Russian treaty terms was not necessary as there would be no risk that British money would be used against them in a joint offensive with a hostile power. The 'neighbourly' treaty would simply reflect India and Afghanistan's mutual respect and define the relationship in terms of two independent nation states with provisions for reciprocal rights, envoys and so forth.[97]

The Government of India however still continued to press their case for the 'friendship' treaty. Dobbs made one last attempt to deliver this. Without making further concessions which Montagu had refused to allow, he got nowhere and it was agreed that Dobbs should leave. On 12 September, as the mission was preparing for its departure, Dobbs requested and got permission to suggest the 'neighbourly' treaty.[98] He instructed his officials to put it forward provided they could do so 'without loss of dignity'.[99] The Afghans were shocked by the absence of a subsidy and the amir himself said he could not consider the 'neighbourly' treaty because it gave no advantages to Afghanistan. His response was a promise to repudiate the Russian treaty for a treaty of friendship with the British. He also decided that he would conduct the negotiations himself without his foreign minister, Tarzi. Dobbs was highly sceptical about Afghan undertakings to break with the Russians and recommended that the British continue their discussions on the 'neighbourly' treaty basis, but the Government of India was extremely reluctant.[100] Dobbs however wanted to avoid 'the ill results of a rupture'. He put another suggestion to the viceroy. This was a simple exchange of ministers, confirming recognition of Afghanistan's new independent status. Dobbs argued that not breaking off talks on numerous earlier occasions had 'made the Amir think we had some friendly feelings'. An exchange of ministers would 'keep the door' open to a settlement, was preferable to 'pressing impossible demands' and we could part friends.[101]

The Government of India was unwilling to move closer to Dobbs's position. Lord Reading wrote privately to Dobbs advocating their line 'as he suspects me of wanting to wreck it'.[102] For the next seven weeks, Dobbs got nowhere with offering an increasingly weak 'friendship' treaty: any agreed concessions were never enough. However, the atmosphere became more friendly after he had arranged to help a party of Afghan students by facilitating the diplomatic permissions they needed to travel and a banquet was held to celebrate their trip.[103] Meanwhile, Dobbs had become extremely frustrated at the long delays in receiving his instructions. He pointed out that:

> negotiations are quite impossible if more than a month is allowed to elapse between a reference for orders and a reply; that the Amir had probably changed round again by now; and that if Lord R[eading] thinks that he can advantageously drag out the conversations through the winter he is mistaken; because that will bring us to the spring again when the frontier is always fullest of unrest and most advantageous for the A's. I expect this will make him very angry; but it is the truth and he may as well realise it. These lawyers and judges seem to think that negotiations are like a suit in chancery which can go on for generations. They don't realise that all the time things are <u>happening.</u> (Dobbs's underlining)[104]

At last on 5 November, the definitive instructions he needed arrived: 'A telegram has just arrived turning down the Govt of India's proposals and bleats finally, and directing me to present the kinglet here with the draft which he has already refused [the "neighbourly" treaty] and to go if he doesn't accept.'[105]

Dobbs then advised the amir that his proposals were not acceptable and was told to leave. Departure preparations were yet again made. A week later, on 12 November, 'I went to say goodbye at 7 pm and was kept till 11 pm by the Amir discussing the [neighbourly] treaty at which he said he would not look.'[106] Dobbs thought there was a 'faint chance' the amir 'might take it'. Dobbs then asked for authority to make amendments on the spot because he thought delays would be fatal.[107] He got the necessary authority and continued the talks. These took place in Persian – Dobbs had been without his key interpreter since May. He negotiated alone with the amir over the next three days:

> Day after day, we have discussed it [the treaty] to exhaustion … On Nov 15th we were at it for 11 hours, from 10 AM to 11 PM with one hour's interval during which I had to draft and translate a number of clauses. He fought hard the whole

time and it was most exhausting. At last at 11 pm he said he would personally
accept the treaty ... Then he started clapping his hands and old General Mahmud
Sami and I imitated him. So we parted. At this moment we presented a strange
spectacle. The Amir with his cap off (he worked the whole time with his head
bare) and his long hair standing straight on end; his face all sunk with fatigue. I
looking no doubt even worse.[108]

The treaty provided for diplomatic representation and effectively excluded
Russian consulates from the border. It covered customs and postal arrangements.
The agreement on tribal questions was set out in a side letter. It contained nothing
to which the British objected and included provisions thought to improve India's
security.[109]

The amir had told Dobbs that he personally would accept the treaty and would
make no amendments if the British did not but that he must get the agreement
of his foreign minister, Tarzi, from whom he said he had so far kept everything
secret. During the four or five days the amir thought he needed, Dobbs got an
unwelcome shock. Concerned over the hostility shown in the Afghan assembly
to his treaty with the British, the amir then announced he would not give back
a border village as he had earlier agreed to do. Luckily for Dobbs, the amir was
sufficiently embarrassed by a particular tribal atrocity that he at once gave up
the village, Arnawai, to Chitral in British India. The treaty was signed on 22
November and British press comment was favourable. In the end, Lord Reading
was complimentary about what Dobbs had achieved. The permanent secretary
at the India Office in London, Arthur Hirtzel, had clearly understood the
difficulties of the situation. The treaty, he wrote:

> is indeed a triumph and a rich reward for the incredible patience and endurance
> which you have shown during the last year, and of your skill in handling these
> contrary ruffians. I can quite appreciate what your feelings must have been as
> H.M.G. and the G.of I. continued to wrangle and events at Kabul took their
> course regardless of the wrangling. You, on the other hand, will, I think, have
> appreciated how difficult it was for HMG flatly to overrule the GoI in a matter
> of such importance and in existing conditions, until the last hope of agreement
> between them had disappeared.[110]

The treaty, Dobbs commented, 'was a treaty of friendship in all but name and
gives us what we had wished for far more cheaply than had been contemplated'.[111]
For Dobbs, it was the tribes and the frontier that mattered. As he said after
Mussoorie, 'for many years we must be ready to show our teeth on the frontier'[112]
and when it came to the amir, 'Strength immediately beneath his eyes in our

dealings with the frontier tribes will make the greatest impression on him'.[113] The treaty achieved more than its immediate objective of securing 'two and a half years of uneasy peace' at a time when India regarded her forces as not well prepared for further fighting. Dobbs's negotiations and the treaty that followed provided the basis of the relationship between India (and subsequently Pakistan) and Afghanistan until the 1970s.

Dobbs returned to Simla where he wrote his report on the negotiations and packed up to leave India because he thought he might not return. This made him very melancholy especially as he was doing it on his own. He thought his wife would be with him when he made his final farewell to India 'and now I have to do it alone. It is horrible ...'.[114] He was right. He did not return to India. He first went to Ireland for long overdue leave with his family. He then moved on to another country, Iraq, that like Afghanistan aspired to fully independent status, and where he was to be its longest-serving high commissioner.

6

Iraq at last 1922 to 1924: Appointment as high commissioner; expelling Turkish elements from northern Iraq; winning Iraqi support for the unpopular 1922 Anglo-Iraq Treaty

In November 1921, Dobbs had finally concluded an enduring treaty with Afghanistan against all expectations. Back in Simla he was eager to complete his report on the negotiations as soon as possible so that he could start for Ireland, see his family and begin enjoying a lengthy period of long overdue leave.

Dobbs was very clear about what he did not want to do next and what he would like best. He had made up his mind he would not return to his post as foreign secretary to the Government of India, which had been kept open for him. One important reason was his strong dislike of the then viceroy Lord Reading's working methods. A lawyer who became lord chief justice, Reading conducted business as if he were still a cross-examining barrister.[1] He refused to read written briefing or notes and expected his officials to come to him 'at all hours to explain things to him verbally'.[2] Indeed, Dobbs had to abandon his Christmas lunch in Simla to go to Delhi for yet further discussions with Reading about the possibility of the Prince of Wales meeting the amir on his visit to India. Dobbs therefore preferred to take his chance on either an appointment in London or what he most wanted, the possibility of returning to Mesopotamia, now Iraq. Ever since he had left in August 1916, Dobbs had remained interested in shaping the future of that country. On the frequent occasions when he was considering his next move, Dobbs many times made it clear to his family that he was 'keener on being Chief Administrator of Mesopotamia than anything else'. There were a number of reasons why it was six years before Dobbs returned. First, he refused to work as a subordinate in an administration whose policies under Sir Percy Cox he strongly disagreed with. Secondly, once the British government had taken over responsibility for Mesopotamian operations from the Government of India early in 1917, they were reluctant to appoint Indian Civil Servants to top posts because of their developing differences with the Government of India over the approach to governing Arab countries despite the fact that Dobbs had for some time made clear his view that the 'Indianizing' policy in Mesopotamia must be reversed.[3] Thirdly, the Government of India had their own ideas for deploying Dobbs: in January 1919 when he accepted appointment as foreign secretary to the Government of India, he wrote that he had 'received a rapid succession of offers. The truth being that I should have been really well-pleased by the opportunity of advising about the administration of Mesopotamia … and that it seemed was not going to be offered to me.'[4]

Dobbs's approach to governing Mesopotamia had been fundamentally at odds with that taken by Sir Percy Cox, the civil commissioner, supported by Arnold Wilson (later Sir Arnold Wilson). Cox had brought in Indian administrators to operate Indian colonial practices and replace indigenous officials applying local laws. In the absence of positive guidance from London, Cox and Wilson also continued their policy of imposing direct control on Indian lines. However, drawing on his experience in Balochistan, Dobbs had pressed for leaving traditional systems in place and making local tribal leaders responsible to the British for law and order. As he pointed out to Gertrude Bell, who was very sympathetic to his approach, one advantage it had was that this worked. In writing to her in January 1918, he also argued that having the 'big men' on their side whom he saw as more powerful and influential than was generally acknowledged 'outside the East' would be a key element in controlling the country and building future friendly relations. In addition, before the First World War's victorious Allies had endorsed the policy at Versailles, Dobbs had been clear – perhaps in part because of his sensitivity to Arab aspirations – that some form of self-determination would have to be introduced. 'You must set up some system of <u>self-government</u> in Iraq; because that is the basis of our whole policy and of our conquest. Whether we like it or not, it is almost certain that at the end of this war we shall have to abide by the decision of the occupied territories as to what Government they wish to remain under' (Dobbs's underlining).[5]

Dobbs's sentiments were in the vanguard of changes in outlook that shaped Allied policies towards former Ottoman territories. Increasing pressure from Arab nationalists, the growing influence of the British pro-Arab faction and Woodrow Wilson's advocacy of self-determination were greatly strengthening support for some form of Arab self-government. The ideas for a new world order agreed at Versailles would advance this through the 'mandate system' under the newly established League of Nations (see Chapter 1). Iraq was to be a Class A mandate. This was defined as 'a community whose independence could be provisionally recognised subject to the supply of advice and assistance by the mandatory power until the community could stand alone'.[6] The British government under League oversight had taken on this responsibility for Iraq as its mandatory power following formal agreement at San Remo in April 1920.[7]

This changing policy climate had made little impact on how Arnold Wilson was running Mesopotamia. In January 1920, the most senior London official then responsible for Mesopotamia, Arthur Hirtzel at the India Office, commented privately to Dobbs that 'Wilson made a great mistake in not running the Arab state policy for all it is worth … It is the only practical policy in existing conditions and moreover we are committed to it head over ears'.[8] Wilson, who had become acting civil commissioner in Cox's absence, was unwilling to make other than nominal concessions to Arab aspirations and this was one of the factors leading to the serious and widespread unrest in Iraq in the summer of 1920. Doubts were increasing in London about Wilson's handling of the situation for which he had been sharply criticized by the foreign secretary, Lord Curzon.[9] The government in London that had sent Cox to Tehran to negotiate a treaty with Persia, therefore decided he should return to Baghdad to restore order and set up a provisional government. They then appointed Sir Percy as high commissioner to start overseeing the process of supporting Iraq to independence under the British mandate. Earlier in Mesopotamia, Cox's authority had been challenged by General Maude, and in accepting the appointment, he stressed that 'military government must end' and he must have direct ministerial access.[10]

The Allies' idea for advancing self-determination and independence through their 'mandates' system was long on principles but short on practical guidance. In January 1921, Winston Churchill, recently moved to the Colonial Office and whose remit now included the mandated territories, immediately set up a new department to take over government responsibilities for the Middle East. He had accepted appointment on condition that he had the widest possible powers to include civil and military matters in this new Middle East Department.[11] He was keen to reduce the scope for others, and particularly the military, to block his schemes.

In February 1921, Churchill convened a conference in Cairo to draw up a plan for the Middle East. He invited the relevant officials, Britain's 'men on the spot' and Middle East experts. Notable participants included Gertrude Bell, T. E. Lawrence and Sir Percy Cox. A top priority for Churchill was cutting expenditure. He wanted immediately to reduce the heavy cost of controlling the area by deploying fewer troops and relying more on the use of air power, and by accelerating the change to Arab-controlled states. These changes would greatly reduce expenditure and he hoped promote good will for Britain.[12] At the same time, Churchill aimed to find arrangements that somehow reconciled the various conflicting commitments the British had made – vague promises of an Arab state in the Hussein–McMahon correspondence, the division into French and British spheres of influence under the Sykes–Picot agreement and the commitment in the Balfour declaration to a Jewish homeland.[13] He was persuaded that the answer was the 'Sharifian solution'.[14] Under this, two sons of King Hussein (the Sharif of Mecca) would be installed as amirs, one in Iraq the other in Transjordan, to be created out of Palestine. The promised Jewish homeland would be in what remained of Palestine.[15] Advocated by Lawrence, Churchill's most trusted adviser, by Cox and Bell, the scheme won the conference's support and with other decisions created a new framework for the Middle East.

For Iraq, Churchill accepted his advisers' recommendation that Faisal, seen as a charismatic Arab leader, should be installed in Iraq as a constitutional monarch. The largest of the prospective states, this was thought might be helpful in persuading the Arabs that the settlement was fair, an important consideration for Churchill.[16] However, Faisal's lack of any associations with Iraq meant he would have a hard job to establish himself. Persuaded by Lawrence, Faisal agreed to take on the kingdom of Iraq but only if it could be shown that the people wanted him. In the summer of 1921, Cox organized a referendum in Iraq: 96 per cent of the views expressed had supported the election of Faisal as king.[17]

Churchill was determined to reduce expenditure there immediately. In February 1920 as secretary of state for war and air, he had estimated the costs of controlling the Middle East at £20 million a year[18] and restoring order in Iraq that summer had been very expensive. It was agreed at the conference that troop numbers should be reduced and greater reliance placed on air power, a change that had been strongly opposed by the commander-in-chief in Iraq, Sir Aylmer Haldane.

Also discussed was the position of the Kurds in northern Iraq, Turkey and Iran and Churchill's support for a Kurdish state. Cox and Bell persuaded conference members that Iraq would not be viable without the northern provinces. Bell argued that the area was Iraq's breadbasket and that the Kurds' views should be sought. Dobbs and the League were to find themselves grappling with both these subjects.

Cox had continued to urge Dobbs to return to Iraq. Although there had been bitter disagreements between them in Mesopotamia, Cox had on several occasions pressed the case for him to be appointed as his successor and had told Dobbs from time to time that he looked forward to his succeeding him.[19] In February 1922, on his way back from India, Dobbs was asked to meet ministers and officials in London who had an interest in British policy in Iraq and the Middle East. He spent a morning giving his views to several members of the government including on this occasion Austen Chamberlain, chancellor of the exchequer, Edwin Montagu, secretary of state for India, and Worthington Evans, secretary of state for war.[20] Until the end of the year, Dobbs, who was living in southern Ireland with his family, was frequently in London in order to meet more government officials and ministers including the then colonial secretary, Winston Churchill. Dobbs also had an audience with the king. This lasted forty-five minutes. The king, wearing a frock coat (by then considered rather old-fashioned) and 'a gorgeous satin tie', sat facing the light so that he could 'search [Dobbs's] countenance' and 'really talked more than he listened'. Dobbs reported that Winston, looking very middle-aged and statesmanlike, hoped the arrangements for him to go to Iraq could be agreed.[21]

Decisions about Iraq were further complicated by disagreements within the then ruling coalition government led by Lloyd George about what Britain's future involvement should be. The Conservatives were moving in favour of reducing Britain's foreign commitments and forced an election in October 1922.[22] This they fought on promises of cost-cutting and non-interference abroad while the popular press waged a campaign in support of quitting Iraq. Dobbs had by then been appointed to succeed Sir Percy Cox as high commissioner of Iraq but his departure was delayed so that he could meet the new secretary of state for the colonies, the Duke of Devonshire.

During his tortuous discussions with government representatives about Iraq and his possible appointment, Dobbs had been living in southern Ireland where the war of independence against the British gave place in June 1922 to the Irish civil war between the 'Free Staters' and the Irish Republican Army (IRA).[23] IRA bands roamed the countryside temporarily billeting themselves on larger local properties. On several occasions, the republicans visited Dobbs's mother's house where she and his sister Mildred lived. On the last of their calls at the end of October 1922, four IRA men appeared and told Mildred that if she had been a man she would have 'got a leaden message' for her less-than-warm welcome. She allegedly retorted that they were only there because they knew they would be facing a woman, gave them the slip and cycled through the rain to Lismore to summon the army, which imprisoned the four IRA men.[24] Dobbs himself seems to have been little troubled by IRA activities beyond having his horse stolen, although communications were difficult. Road and railway bridges were destroyed and there was no postal service and no newspapers. Although maintaining that Mildred exaggerated the dangers, in December 1922 Dobbs was sufficiently alarmed to advise his wife in a letter written in Hindustani as he left Ireland not to allow Mildred to stay at their house.[25] His fear, like Mildred's, was that the IRA would look to take their revenge.

On 9 December 1922, Dobbs arrived in London on his way to Iraq. The new colonial secretary, the Duke of Devonshire, gave him the government's general instruction: 'the basic principle underlying relations between the two governments is co-operation towards a common end, namely the progressive establishment of an independent government of Iraq friendly to and bound by gratitude and obligation to His Britannic Majesty's Government'.[26] Dobbs had also hoped to be told the government's decision on whether Mosul would be included within Iraq but that issue was to remain contentious within the British government and unresolved internationally for some time. Indeed, Dobbs was soon to be directly concerned in influencing the outcome.

Nine days after leaving London, Dobbs reached Iraq. He had travelled uncomfortably for part of the way in an RAF plane with his cases roped beneath its wings. When he arrived in Baghdad he stayed with the outgoing high commissioner, Sir Percy Cox, and his wife in the residency. It was very cold, the downstairs rooms so dark 'as if in a London fog' but it had a nice garden, seven suites of bedrooms, sitting rooms and marvellous baths. He wrote that there is 'a splendid view of the river and the opposite frontage from the great raised esplanade outside the offices; and the whole river is gay with boats. This house stands on the right bank of the River Tigris, half way between two bridges of boats and looks across at the bulk of Baghdad, with ever so many blue tiled domes and minarets fronting it'.[27]

Dobbs had arrived three days before Christmas. His formal appointment was set to begin only in September 1923 with Cox's official retirement but he effectively took over as high commissioner in mid-January, when Cox went to London. Among the high commission staff, its best-known member, Gertrude Bell, the oriental secretary, was eager to renew their acquaintance. She frequently lunched at the Residency in circumstances that were not entirely comfortable for Dobbs. 'We were interrupted in the afternoon by Miss Bell, whom Lady Cox hates. Miss B comes to lunch every day and talks in a loud voice to Sir Percy (when he is here) or to me, quite ignoring Lady C. When I have her alone, I enjoy her company; but with the two of them, it is awkward.'[28]

Figure 6.1 Sir Percy Cox and staff at the Residency Baghdad, taken to mark his departure in May 1923: Cox (centre), Dobbs on his left, Lady Cox on his right and next to her, Gertrude Bell. Courtesy of Henry Wilks.

Dobbs met King Faisal in early January. He found him very pleasant to talk to and preoccupied with the news from Lausanne. The Lausanne Conference had been convened at the end of 1922 between the Allies and Turkish representatives in order to agree the boundaries of the new Republic of Turkey. These had implications for Iraq's northern frontier. They involved Turkey's claims to Mosul and the surrounding predominantly Kurdish areas. Lord Curzon, then Britain's foreign secretary, argued forcefully at Lausanne for the Allies' position and made a strong case for including these territories within Iraq. As Dobbs feared, the talks were not going well notwithstanding Curzon's 'boastful communiqués'.[29] Curzon's negotiating position was difficult because opinion among British ministers was so divided. Not all were committed to remaining in Iraq and although the prime minister and some other British ministers recognized the advantages of retaining Mosul and the adjacent area for both Britain and Iraq, they above all wanted to avoid risking a fight with Turkey. Now, under Mustafa Kemal known as 'Atatürk', the Turks had been aggressively expanding their territory. Faisal was concerned primarily because of the importance of these northern areas to Iraq's future economic viability. As the leader of a Sunni government in a country where they were outnumbered by the Shias, Faisal had another interest: their population was predominantly Sunni.[30]

Dobbs soon faced a potential crisis in this northern area. Cox had left Iraq to advise ministers in London, and Dobbs was effectively in charge. The Turks had been making raids into the Iraqi territory around Mosul and into the predominantly Kurdish area as far as the Iranian border. Dobbs explained to his wife that on 21 January, two days after Cox's departure, Sir John Salmond, who was in charge of all British forces in Iraq, had been told about large numbers of additional Turkish forces on the frontier. Salmond as air officer commanding[31] was responsible to Dobbs who was effectively high commissioner and commander-in-chief. He and Dobbs decided to 'send up to Mosul at once what troops could be scraped together so as to forestall any sudden attack or rising of tribes; and this has now been done amid a good deal of excitement'. Dobbs did not think that the Turks meant to fight but 'only to threaten and give trouble by inducing the Kurds and others to make incursions'.[32] About a month later, he told his wife that regretfully he had had to authorize the bombing of the principal Kurdish town, Sulymaniya (Sulaimaniya), with 14,000 inhabitants. 'It is sickening, but there is no way out of it, as their ruling man [Sheikh Mahmud] is preparing to attack us with Turkish backing and we have to get in first.'[33]

Operations to dislodge the Turks and take over this area of the country continued intermittently until 22 April. Dobbs saw establishing control here as crucial to strengthening the British position in the detailed negotiations on international boundary questions that were about to start at Lausanne. He explained to his wife the importance of taking control of the disputed territory at that precise moment:

> Our troops in Kurdistan are I believe entering Rowanduz [Rawandaz] today and turning the Turkish irregulars out. This is the last day on which they could do so; as the Lausanne negotiations begin tomorrow (April 23) and we shall have to pledge ourselves to maintain the status quo i.e., each side to remain where they are and go no further, when once the negotiations begin. And as these Turks have been sitting about 40 miles within Iraq territory and raising the tribes against us for the last two years, without our venturing to turn them out, we should probably have had to give over all that tract for good, unless we had now turned them out in the nick of time. This would have meant that in the end they would probably have made it impossible for us or the Iraq government to hold Mosul. So I am very glad of the result so far.[34]

Dobbs also told his wife that he and Sir John Salmond had been doing this 'on the quiet with barely the briefest information to the Government at home.' Throughout his career Dobbs had frequently taken the actions he judged necessary to achieve policy aims without seeking authorization and making the most of the freedom distance and difficult communications gave 'the man on the spot'. He was taking a considerable risk on this occasion since the Turks under Mustafa Kemal's leadership had frequently shown they were ready to fight for any territory they decided to claim. Fortunately, as Dobbs had told his wife, about that time they were preoccupied with Syria. Dobbs was also well aware that bombing raids in particular – and these too were not authorized by London – were likely to prompt hostile parliamentary questions. Indeed, the Labour MP George Lansbury, a disarmament supporter had asked one referring to 'this Hunnish and barbarous method of warfare against unarmed people'.[35]

The calculated risk and bold decisions which Dobbs had taken paid off. He commented that now, 'we may be in effective possession of all the territory which we claim before we begin to bargain'[36] at Lausanne. Although broad agreement had been reached in February on the treaty proposals in general, the Turkish delegation had wished further time to consider them.[37] The conference delegates therefore had agreed that discussions would be suspended and the representatives would reconvene on 23 April 1923, making this a critical deadline.[38]

Settling the frontiers of Iraq was one important precondition for the British government making a successful application for Iraq's joining the League of Nations as an independent member state. Another was for Iraq to ratify their treaty with Britain (the 1922 Anglo-Iraq Treaty, 'the treaty') and give effect to its provisions. Cox had told the British government in February 1923 that he had ensured Faisal was in no doubt about the treaty requirement. Having been much preoccupied with the frontier issue, Dobbs next focused on getting this treaty and associated agreements ratified.

At Versailles, the Allies had described in 'mandates' the terms on which they expected the former imperial territories to be administered and supported to independence by the 'mandatory' or supervising power. However, in the case of Iraq, these were set out not in a 'mandate' but in a treaty between Iraq and Britain. This was because the mandate was so unpopular in Iraq that Sir Percy Cox had seen no prospect of securing its acceptance as the League of Nations required. Recent experience of British rule had lent credibility to the belief among Iraqis that whatever was said, the British would be looking to increase and not reduce their powers. In addition, Faisal had stipulated that he would only accept the throne if the unequal status implied by a mandate were to be replaced by a treaty. Sir Percy Cox, enthusiastically encouraged by Gertrude Bell, had decided to press for the mandate to take the legal form of a treaty. The hope was that this form, normally used between sovereign states, would help to lessen Iraqi dislike of the mandate's humiliating requirements.[39] However, the League had been opposed to Britain putting the terms of the mandate into the form of a treaty,[40] fearing it would be resented by other members and suspecting that the British might be trying to gain some advantage. The treaty terms had to mirror the requirements of the mandate. Consequently, the terms in the treaty required by the Colonial Office could not disguise Iraq's essentially subordinate relationship with the mandatory power, Britain.[41] In this situation, Faisal, eager to demonstrate his commitment to independence, was building support with the anti-treaty groups, and was only induced to endorse the Treaty after the assurances Churchill gave that the British government would make every effort to secure Iraq's admission to the League of Nations as an independent state at the earliest possible moment.[42] By October 1922, Faisal's ministers were prepared to support the treaty but insisted, despite Cox's strenuous resistance, on a clause making it subject to ratification by an Iraqi constituent assembly.

The Conservative government that had assumed office in November 1922 took until April 1923 to decide whether or not Britain should remain in Iraq on any terms. Their election promises of non-interference abroad and drastic economies meant the government was sympathetic to the continuing campaign in the popular press by Lords Rothermere and Beaverbrook to give up the British mandate and to 'quit Mesopotamia'. A number of ministers were unwilling to go against the opinion of the press barons and indeed many MPs and some members of the government were supporters of the evacuation of Iraq.

The government set up a cabinet committee to consider the options. Papers from Lord Curzon, then foreign secretary, and from Sir Percy Cox eventually persuaded first the committee and then the Cabinet that Britain should retain the mandate and stay in Iraq. Their arguments included Iraq's strategic importance to the region, British commitments, together with economic and commercial benefits including Mosul's oil. Cox wrote privately to Dobbs that the prime minister 'is out not to flout Rothermere and Beaverbrook', that one cabinet member was 'in Rothermere's pocket' and that the decision could go either way.[43] Important to persuading the Cabinet were undertakings that costs would be cut by running down British forces quickly and by shortening the length of time Britain's commitments to Iraq would last. These were now to end four years after the border with Turkey was settled as compared with the original twenty-year period during which Britain was committed under the mandate to supporting Iraq to independence. In addition, Cox had assured the Cabinet that there would be no problem in securing Iraq's agreement to the terms of the treaty and subsidiary agreements.[44] At the end of April the Cabinet agreed to the proposal that Britain should remain in Iraq with reduced forces and on an accelerated timetable for leaving. A protocol to the treaty was drawn up to reflect the shorter timetable.[45]

Both Cox and Dobbs thought that as long as the policy of remaining in Iraq continued to be unpopular in Britain, there was always a very real possibility of its being reversed, and that any failure to deliver would provide the ideal excuse. Dobbs was sufficiently concerned about which way things would go that he threatened to return to India in September 1923 if the Colonial Office did not agree to his compensation terms in the event of early termination of his Iraq appointment.[46] Cox in London had played down the difficulties of meeting the conditions in the treaty and subsidiary agreements as part of his efforts to secure a British government decision to retain the mandate and remain in Iraq. The promised speedy reduction of British forces was also likely to be problematic. Dobbs wrote unenthusiastically to his wife that Cox 'has got away in the nick of time and in a blaze of glory, leaving all the half difficult work undone ... It is easy enough for him to promise for his successor.'[47] On the agreements Dobbs commented:

> There are a number of agreements subsidiary to the main treaty which carry out the treaty and are the only things that matter. They all have to be negotiated with the Iraq Ministers and King and then to be ratified by the Iraq Assembly; and as the Colonial Office want one thing and the Arabs here something quite different, it will be very hard to reconcile matters.[48]

On the desired troop reductions, he remarked, 'Cox has promised to abolish all British forces in 4 years, a quarter each year, although during his time he was unable to do anything but increase them.'[49] Questions and disagreements over the British forces in Iraq and their role were to recur throughout Dobbs's time in Iraq but the problem of securing the treaty and all the necessary agreements was to dominate the next eighteen months. Differences within the British government over future policy in Iraq and within Iraq itself between the British high commissioner and the recently installed King Faisal made it difficult to make progress on getting the agreement of both countries to the treaty. Its terms defined the relationship between Britain and Iraq and established Iraq's new legal and constitutional framework. Its acceptance was thus crucially important to Iraq's future and to Britain's relationship with that country.

It had been made very clear to Faisal that the British government would only move towards supporting the independent status of Iraq once the assembly had ratified the treaty – an endorsement the League of Nations also required. Within Iraq, King Faisal's situation and sympathies were not helpful to securing this result.[50] Having supported Faisal and his family in the Arab struggle against the Ottomans during the Great War, the British government hoped that he would be friendly towards them and, at the same time, would appeal to the Iraqi people. He had impressive Muslim credentials: through his father, the Sharif of Mecca, guardian of the holy places, he was descended from the Prophet Mohammed. He had headed the Arab revolt against the Ottomans and Faisal himself had led the fighting and championed Arab self-government during his brief reign as king of Syria. In Iraq, where he was not known locally, Faisal was in a very sensitive position. He had no natural constituency and saw his independence credentials as essential to winning over the Iraqis. At the same time, he was entirely dependent on practical support from the British. From the start as part of his efforts to build a stronger position for himself, he appealed to the nationalist, anti-mandate, anti-British groups. Dobbs was in fact sympathetic to the difficulties of his position. He pointed out, 'He has had to guard above all against the allegation that he is a puppet king propped up by our bayonets. He can hope to strike roots in the soil only by an attitude of independence.'[51]

Faisal himself realized that in the current circumstances, he was dependent on British forces. He faced serious threats from the Turks in the north and from tribes on the southern border with Ibn Saud's territories. There was also a degree of unrest in and around Baghdad. For the moment, the king, as Churchill tartly commented, had apparently recognized that he needed the British if he was to retain his throne,[52] so he himself did not oppose the treaty or any of its provisions openly.

Faisal had signed the treaty (which, however, did not include the vital subsidiary agreements) and the protocol which the British government had added in March 1923. He was delighted with the prospect of a shorter timetable of four years instead of twenty for Iraq's acceptance as an independent state. Dobbs's focus was on securing ratification from the constituent assembly of the entire treaty together with its protocol and related agreements. Faisal recognized that this was the next stage in Iraq's advance to full independence. Cox had warned the king and his ministers that 'Iraq must realise that [the treaty's] rejection or any indication that it was not appreciated by the people of Iraq, would be regarded by the British Government of the time as a justification for getting rid of their commitments in Iraq'[53] and furthermore he had told the

Figure 6.2 King Faisal I of Iraq in 1921. Sueddeutsche Zeitung Photo/Mary Evans.

British government that Faisal understood this. Dobbs's oft-repeated view was that it would not take much to make the present British government decide to exit Iraq. Consequently, he saw the assembly's ratification of the treaty as vital to Iraq's continuing relationship with Britain and its advance towards independence. His focus until he set off for leave in Ireland in July 1924 was to secure the necessary ratification.

The constituent assembly did not meet until 27 March 1924 although Faisal had issued the Iradah (decree) needed to hold elections in October 1922. The first obstacle was the opposition of the Persian Shia clerics to the elections. They were guardians of Iraq's most holy shrines, and in November 1922 they had issued a fatwah prohibiting participation. Initially this influenced primarily the tribes in the Euphrates area. However, the Persian clerics in the shrines first at Kadhimain then at Karbala and Najaf actively fomented opposition to the regime. The king and his ministers became increasingly concerned as did the high commissioner. After hostile demonstrations at two of the shrines, Faisal and his government were encouraged by Dobbs to deport the troublemakers who were Persian nationals. Dobbs wrote, 'we are trying to expel the Persian priests who threaten to excommunicate everyone who dares to vote for King Faisal'.[54] Although Dobbs wanted to engineer their departure, he was very keen not to be associated with the decision and to see the action ascribed entirely to Faisal's government, 'although I had been behind the scenes, I didn't want to get openly mixed up in it. I flew off to Mosul and then to Rowanduz [Rawandaz].' Dobbs described what happened: 'all the priests are marching off into Persia as a protest … The indignant and emigrant priests were met by Arab police bundled across the Tigris and into a special train and whisked off into Persia before they were able to make any disturbance.'[55]

This was at the beginning of July 1923. Dobbs was well aware that these developments would adversely affect relations with Persia where the priests made a 'sad fuss'.[56] Sir Percy Loraine, British Minister in Tehran,[57] flew down and spent a week trying to persuade Dobbs to take them back. Loraine seemed to think that Iraq's treatment of the priests would result in a dangerous level of unrest among the faithful, and Dobbs describes taking him to the main shrine:

> To give him an idea of how calm we are here, I took him out driving by motor yesterday to the heart of fanatical Kazimain [Khadamain], whence came the priests whom we have arrested and deported, and stopped our motor by the door of the great mosque where intense religious excitement should according to all the rules of the game have been prevailing. Of course everything was quite

quiet; but my own quiet was much disturbed by the fact that a large stork flying high above dropped something horrid on my nice white trousers; so I couldn't get out and walk about.[58]

Dobbs explained to his mother how he dealt with Sir Percy:

As I knew that no diplomatist could resist an 'aide memoire', I finally presented him with an 'aide memoire' which if necessary I shall follow up by a 'Protocol'; and he flew back to Teheran fairly content, clasping his beloved aide-memoire to his bosom, but without having persuaded me to take back the priests. I am afraid he will have a very cold reception from the Shah.[59]

He then explained succinctly why he had refused: 'I cannot have Mesopotamia thrown into disorder by Persian priests to please Persia. Now perhaps we shall get our elections through quietly and get an assembly elected which will ratify the Treaty with Great Britain and we can then begin the long process of our withdrawal which will occupy the next four years.'[60]

The king's government and the high commissioner agreed that the return of the priests would be reconsidered after the assembly elections had taken place but in fact Faisal, who would have liked to build support with the Shia community, soon began contacting the priests, which Dobbs discouraged at this juncture.[61] For the moment however the way was clear to hold elections to the constituent assembly and seek ratification of the Anglo-Iraq Treaty.

The complex electoral process began at once with the registration of those entitled to vote in the primary elections – basically all male taxpayers over twenty-one. They would then elect a group of secondary voters to select the members of the constituent assembly.[62] The king set out to tour the country to win support for participation in the elections. The high commissioner followed to demonstrate that Iraq and Britain shared a common purpose.[63] He first made a round trip by river from Baghdad going as far south as Basra. He travelled on a small gunboat (a monitor) which got stuck in the mud and where the temperature in the cabins was 150°F (65.5°C): it was so hot that his soap melted.[64] He also flew north to the Mosul area where in addition to elections, he was preoccupied with questions over the future status of the predominantly Kurdish areas. His northerly trip by aeroplane proved more hazardous. On one occasion, his plane crashed into the rocks on landing and fell to pieces around him but he and the pilot emerged unhurt. He commented that there was more concern over the plane's fate than his, but he himself seemed most worried that it might have created a bad impression on the Kurdish chiefs who were waiting to receive him.[65] Returning to Baghdad in another plane,

> I felt the heat become almost unbearable and then I saw the pilot yelling and pointing to the side of the aeroplane. Looking over as we circled round, I saw it had caught fire from a spark in the engine; so poured two water bottles on it and it sizzled until we got down. I was very glad to get out of it.[66]

Back in Baghdad, Dobbs was very busy working with the Iraq government to complete the subsidiary agreements that were part of the treaty and which also needed to be ratified by the constituent assembly.[67] They were highly contentious and covered a number of subjects that were both extremely sensitive and critical to the operations of the British high commission and the Iraq government.[68] Among the most difficult areas were finance, the army and the role of British advisers. Control of defence was to be with the British and advisers placed in each ministry.[69] The British looked to the last two to give them what they regarded as adequate control while the Iraqis sought to enlarge their scope for operating independently. The detail in the provisions particularly about British advisers and the powers of the high commissioner brought home the many different and tiresome ways in which the Iraqis would be constrained while they remained under the mandatory power. The military agreements posed extremely difficult questions of command and control, while both on military costs and financial arrangements more generally Iraq was being asked to take on unaffordable levels of debt. As the complex process for completing the elections to the constituent assembly ground slowly on through the autumn, Dobbs told his mother he was 'lying low and saying nothing' as much as possible and that 'the country was quiet'.[70] He did though have a 'cabinet crisis' to cope with, which was sparked by the resignation of Faisal's prime minister, Abd al-Muhsin al-Sadoun, because of differences with the king. Dobbs was 'rather in a fuss' because he believed Faisal 'wanted to dismiss the whole of his Cabinet which would make a dreadful mess of things and perhaps prevent the Treaty between Great Britain and Iraq from being passed'.[71] Dobbs's concern was that changes would bring in a government that would be more difficult to work with at this critical time than that headed by al-Sadoun. In fact, Faisal and his government recognized that the treaty probably offered the country the fastest route to independence and the difficulties were to come less from the new prime minister, Jafar al-Askari and Faisal's ministers than from the critics of the treaty within the assembly and beyond. During these months, there was also something of a political crisis going on in Britain where a split in the Conservative party over introducing protectionist policies had led to a general election. This had returned a hung Parliament. Labour under Ramsay Macdonald formed a government in January 1924 and Dobbs commented, 'We are all agog to know whether the Labour Government will abandon Mesopotamia or not.'[72] He wrote to Sidney Webb, who had been appointed president of the Board of Trade but was one of the more influential members of the government, 'descanting on the magnificence of Britain's mission here'.[73] In fact, Dobbs soon got a telegram from Jim Thomas, the new colonial secretary, assuring him of his 'sympathy and cooperation'[74] and so assumed correctly that the government's Iraq policy under Labour would remain unchanged. Meanwhile in Iraq, elections to choose the members of the constituent assembly had continued to be held. Registration of primary electors was completed in December, and secondary elections to select the assembly members began in February 1924.[75] Both the king and British administrators had sought to influence electors' choices. As part of his efforts to strengthen the basis of his support and increase his leverage with the British, Faisal had covertly encouraged groups opposed to the Treaty while British administrators had secretly sought opportunities to secure more sympathetic representatives.

By the time the assembly met on 27 March 1924, Faisal's new government had signed the subsidiary agreements which formed part of the treaty, and the whole document was thus ready to be considered. Opening the proceedings, Faisal in his speech from the throne urged members to ratify the treaty, vote for the 'organic law' – or constitution – and pass an electoral law. The reasons he gave for supporting the unloved treaty were that it provided a swift route to independence and that British support was presently needed to help secure Iraq's disputed borders with Turkey to the north and with Ibn Saud to the south.[76] Neither Faisal's exhortations from the throne nor the British government's accelerated timetable for Iraq's independence and its efforts to secure Mosul for the country succeeded in dampening opposition to the treaty. Almost from the moment the assembly convened, the deputies faced nationalist demonstrations outside the chamber. Anti-treaty agitation gathered pace. Three weeks later there was an attempt to assassinate two pro-treaty sheikhs. At the start of May, Dobbs wrote to his mother, 'We have had a prolonged political crisis, the Assembly elected to ratify our Treaty with the Iraq Govt shirking the responsibility of ratification and I don't know at the moment whether it will end in the British Govt deciding to evacuate or not.'[77]

The options open to either the Iraq government or the high commission to bring about the desired result of ratification were extremely limited. It required a majority of assembly members to vote in favour of the treaty and the subsidiary agreements. Among assembly members, the treaty was opposed for a variety of reasons. Its most articulate and influential opponents were the nationalists. They were against the British, the mandate and the treaty. Many of their more specific criticisms – mainly of the subsidiary agreements to the treaty – were reflected in the assembly's report on the treaty. They opposed the powers of the high commissioner, and the extent of British control over the army and the administration. They argued that the military costs and financial obligations placed on Iraq were greater than the country should be asked to bear. In the face of some cogent criticisms and the general nationalist sentiment, Faisal's government under Prime Minister Jafar al-Askari was not sufficiently strong to be able to engineer much support from the deputies.[78]

The ways open to Dobbs to try and influence assembly members were greatly limited by the constraints within which he was required to operate. He had to avoid giving grounds for any suggestion that the high commission had exercised undue influence because the British government needed to be able to demonstrate to the League of Nations that, as the mandatory power, the high commission, its agent, was supporting the democratic process.[79] It was not helpful that the British government had been left by Cox with the clear expectation that the treaty and associated agreements would be ratified without difficulty. Dobbs himself believed that any alterations to the treaty itself would certainly result in delaying Iraq's independence because renegotiation would have had to follow and many sections had been contentious.[80] A more far-reaching consequence in his view was that asking for changes would have risked ending the British government's commitment to Iraq by providing an excuse to evacuate in line with popular opinion at home. The situation meant that Dobbs had in practice no scope for accepting changes which could have helped reduce opposition.

Dobbs told Faisal that no modifications could be made to the treaty in a letter which the king published in the *Baghdad Times*.[81] The assembly committee on the treaty first presented its critical report to Dobbs on 16 May.[82] Notwithstanding the prohibition on making amendments, the committee refused its support unless changes were made to both the treaty and subsidiary agreements. The king asked Dobbs for additional 'explanations and reservations' and repeatedly tried to get alterations made 'in line with the will of the people'. Dobbs responded by saying 'everyone had quite enough of explanations' – and refused all changes.[83] Dobbs was however sympathetic to some of the criticisms particularly on the financial arrangements where he recognized that Britain was asking Iraq to shoulder financial burdens beyond her capacity to do so. He promised to obtain an undertaking from the British government that, after ratification, they would reconsider Iraq's financial obligations.[84]

This concession by Dobbs did little to dampen the anti-treaty agitation and he soon began exchanges with the Colonial Office about possible courses of action if the assembly failed to ratify the treaty. He described these to his wife. He had to oppose the first suggestion from the Colonial Office that he should carry on without the assembly as impractical and outside the powers he had then been given. The Colonial Office then proposed giving the assembly the deadline of 11 June to accept the treaty, when they were due to make a report to the League of Nations.[85] At that point Dobbs believed that the Colonial Office had accepted his earlier suggestion that if the assembly did not ratify the treaty, the British government would 'make other proposals for the disposal of Iraq'. Dobbs thought that the threat that the British might leave Iraq would be more likely than anything else to persuade the assembly to pass the treaty by the deadline, because this would have put early independence for Iraq and even its survival at risk. However, the Colonial Office promptly forbade Dobbs from publicly stating that Britain might evacuate Iraq[86] since the government had not decided on any such policy at that point. They took about ten days to respond to his various proposals. This indecision and delay which added to Dobbs's difficulties may have been due in part to the head of the Colonial Office's Middle East Department, Sir John Shuckburgh. He was appointed by Winston Churchill from the India Office whose senior official, Arthur Hirtzel, had refused the position. He commented to Churchill that Shuckburgh's 'only fault perhaps [is] a tendency to excessive caution'.[87]

While awaiting the Colonial Office decision, Dobbs had told the king that plans for a British evacuation were in place (they had been made while his predecessor, Sir Percy Cox, was high commissioner). He also confessed to his wife that on 16 May, the day the assembly presented to him their criticisms of the treaty:

> I began a series of slashing articles (anonymous of course) in the *Baghdad Times* pointing out how advantageous it would be for the British to evacuate Iraq. These are having a great effect and have produced such excitement that Mr Cameron, the Editor, tells me his circulation has more than doubled already. They are greatly alarming the King. I point out in these articles how much more convenient it would be for us to have our flying centre at Kuwait and to transfer our alliance to Bin Saud, the Sultan of Najd (who is Iraq's greatest enemy).[88]

Dobbs was ignoring the spirit if not the letter of the Colonial Office's opposition to using the threat of evacuation. His hope was that raising this possibility would persuade the assembly that the treaty was a lesser evil and they would accept it.

Some ten days later Dobbs received the Colonial Office's revised instructions on what to do if the treaty was rejected. These required him immediately to make public the measures they would take in the event of rejection. Dobbs told the Colonial Office that would result in the king losing support and having 'to go back to direct rule which would have been very difficult. I said No.' Dobbs's counter-proposal was, 'promulgate the Treaty and constitutional law by order, dismissing the Constituent Assembly; then elect a regular Parliament to carry on the ordinary administration'.[89] In fact Dobbs received no further instructions from the British government. As he had told his mother, 'It is very difficult to get the Cabinet to give any decision, with so many other things for them to attend to.'[90] Dobbs was thus left to manage matters in his own way. He was ready as he had always been in the past to take full advantage of whatever freedom the situation allowed.

In Iraq, opposition to the treaty continued to escalate throughout May. Dobbs had a meeting with leading deputies including Abd al-Muhsin al-Sadoun, previously prime minister and now speaker, and Yasin al-Hashimi, who chaired the committee that had drawn up the critical report on the treaty. They told Dobbs 'in as plain language as they dared that they wished to depose Faisal and have a republic and much else'.[91]

> On the morning of 29 May, there was a demonstration of low persons outside the Assembly and the Deputies were hustled and insulted and ordered to vote against the Treaty. The police were mismanaged; owing to … everyone shouting different orders and finally Nuri Pasha [Minister of Defence] called out his troops and placed a machine gun on the roof of the Assembly and a few shots were fired and one or two homeless pilgrims were killed. Altogether quite a lot of excitement.[92]

Faisal's ministers responded to the unrest by asking Dobbs to sign an order giving them powers to arrest and imprison without trial. He refused on the grounds that this would give the deputies an excuse for breaking up the assembly and claiming they had rejected the treaty because of the high-handed action of the British. Dobbs then arranged for the Baghdad governor (mutassarif), to have sole responsibility for 'issuing orders and keeping the peace in Baghdad'. Since then, Dobbs wrote, 'there has been perfect peace'.

The military commander of the British forces, now Air Vice-Marshal Higgins, was however less confident, and two days later put double guards on the residency. Dobbs, undaunted, went alone to the assembly where he refused to accept amendments to the treaty:

Instead of returning to the Residency from the Palace, I drove slowly through the streets to the Assembly and interviewed the majlis there, as I heard they were just going to pass a resolution which they fondly imagined I should accept. I told them it would constitute rejection; was very well received and left; though my visit caused much excitement in the military mind. They seemed to think I had escaped from my guard like a naughty child. It was rather funny – the Residency bristling with soldiers and I driving slowly into the heart of the supposed danger.[93]

The situation continued to worsen. At his regular meetings with the king, Faisal continued to press modifications to the treaty. Dobbs commented 'so silly and persistent' but he also observed that the king was 'glum' and 'frightened'. He told the Colonial Office that 'there was practically no chance of getting the thing through'.[94] On 5 June, Dobbs received a report that anti-treaty sheikhs and townspeople had got together and decided to proclaim a provisional government, and that large numbers of tribesmen would be brought into the city in order to enforce this. Dobbs wrote, 'We are still in uncertainty, but the Assembly is going to reject the Treaty or do something decisive before the day after tomorrow [7 June] and the Government at home have still not made up their minds. It makes me feverish.'[95]

Dobbs, again admitting authorship only to his wife, then put about a rumour that the British government were now very anxious indeed for the assembly to reject the treaty at once as they would be free from any obligation to defend Mosul against the Turks and could make their own bargain with Turkey. 'At this the whole Assembly behaved like an Irish pig and bolted in the opposite direction.'[96] They voted down the extremists who were pressing for rejection of the treaty, and adjourned until 9 June.

Dobbs gave his wife a detailed account of the tensions and dramas that eventually ended with the assembly ratifying the treaty. First, he and the air vice-marshal discussed 'measures' to maintain order, and Dobbs reluctantly agreed to let him keep double guards on the residency. 'Everyone began buzzing around and devising formulas, none of them proper acceptances of the Treaty, which they wanted to bring me. I followed my usual tactic of hermitically sealing myself in my house and refusing to see anyone and again forbade Gertrude [Bell. Dobbs's Oriental Secretary], to her grief, to see people.'[97]

Dobbs went to see the king. 'He hadn't the heart to try another formula on me. I told him he must keep himself aloof like me and show no more concern in what was going on ... He was very glum.'

Once the assembly had met on 9 June, Dobbs announced to his staff that if the assembly rejected the treaty, the high commission would take over. Faisal

Figure 6.3 Sir Henry Dobbs, who as high commissioner was also commander-in-chief of British forces stationed in Iraq, reviewing the troops. Courtesy of Henry Wilks.

was told that if the assembly did not approve the treaty by the government deadline – effectively midnight on 10 June – Dobbs would ask him to take powers to dissolve the assembly and to do so at once.[98] The following day (10 June), when the assembly met, they had less than twenty-four hours to ratify the treaty and satisfy the British government deadline. Dobbs explained what happened. There was

> great public excitement, all the deputies receiving threatening letters. They began first of all by sitting for two hours in secret session, while the public remained outside in the heat. Then the public session began and the King in the Palace was taken with panic once more, hearing they were going to reject the Treaty, and telephoned down to Jafar [the prime minister] to get the Assembly adjourned again, if he possibly could, until June 11th. Then the king telephoned to me from his palace what he had done and begged me to let them be for another day. I was furious and telephoned back a snappish reply that, unless a decision had been reached by midnight, I should dissolve the Assembly myself. I said the King must get the adjournment of the morning cancelled and call the deputies back for an

evening session. Then there was a frightful fuzz buzz everyone running hither and thither and saying the deputies had all dispersed and it was impossible.[99]

Next, 'Jafar [prime minister] and Yasin [vice-president of the assembly] appeared at the Residency quite green in colour and presented another footling and impossible formula which they begged me to accept. I merely said "What's the use of wriggling" and entered my car to drive to the Palace.'[100] At 4.00 pm Dobbs saw the king and gave him a written ultimatum. British support for him would only continue if, with his council of ministers, he immediately took power to dissolve the assembly, put guards on the assembly building and sent the dissolution order to its speaker, Abd al-Muhsin al-Sadoun, before 7.00 am next day. At 8.00 pm, Dobbs received 'a final pleading telephone appeal from Jafar to say there was no hope of getting any deputies to attend the evening session. They were frightened and the extremists were keeping them away. He begged I would give 24 hours longer. I refused.'[101]

Dobbs returned to the residency. Faisal's chamberlain then rooted out a number of deputies and told them that the assembly would be dissolved if they did not go and vote. Others were collected in taxis organized by the police. Meanwhile, Dobbs

> sat down with little Holt [Vyvyan Holt, his private secretary – in fact a very tall man] in the drawing room. Little H slept and I played Patience. I knew at once that I was going to get the Treaty as all my Patiences came out, one after another and I was left with nothing to do ... I drank till 11.30 pm then the bell rang again and Drower [one of Dobbs's officials] who was sitting alone with the King said the deputies had passed the Treaty by 48 votes to 25. So I said he could leave the Palace and went to bed. Everyone woke up next morning astonished at the news.[102]

As Gertrude Bell colourfully put it, 'We beat Cinderella by half an hour – the Treaty was ratified last night at 11.30.'[103] Dobbs, as he frequently warned, had thought it unlikely the Treaty would be ratified. When it was, he wrote to his wife, 'I have pulled the moon out of the bottom of the sea.'[104] He judged that it had been much more difficult to achieve this result than it had been to conclude a satisfactory treaty with Afghanistan. He was somewhat annoyed that the Colonial Office, unlike the viceroy and the India Office, did not offer congratulations nor did they even comment. He wondered if it was because they disliked him because 'I pay them so little attention and don't tell them much of what I am doing. But why should they want to know?'[105] He added to his office's regular summary of events, 'Some comment has been aroused in Baghdad by the fact that HM's Government were moved neither to satisfaction nor to regret by the news.' Dobbs himself saw the treaty as a significant milestone, 'Considering that of the three Arab countries, Egypt, Palestine and Mespot [Iraq], this is the only one in which an elected assembly has been induced to pass a treaty with the British.'[106]

He also considered that the British government's line had reduced the effectiveness of the tactics he was able to adopt. He had wanted to be able either to suggest that Britain was not particularly interested in remaining in Iraq, or, going rather further effectively to threaten publicly that Britain would leave Iraq if the treaty was not ratified, in the hope that the assembly would see the Treaty as the least worst outcome: 'I have maintained an attitude of complete indifference, as if I showed myself over anxious for its acceptance, they would think that the British Govt was longing to remain here at all costs.'[107] Forbidden by the Colonial Office from making any public statement of this kind, he believed that 'they are lucky to get the Treaty at all, after all that has happened and after refusing to leave Iraq in the event of rejection. For that really deprived me of my weapons.'[108] In the circumstances he thought the Colonial Office could not really complain about the rider that the assembly had inserted. This was to make the treaty conditional on Britain defending Iraq's rights to Mosul 'in their entirety'.[109]

Once the assembly had ratified the treaty, it went on to pass the organic law or Iraqi constitution and the electoral law which provided for elections to Iraq's Parliament. Formally settling her borders was the next set of issues that needed to be resolved before the League of Nations would recognize the country as an independent state. The question of Iraq's northern borders and relationship with its northern neighbour, Turkey, was to become Dobbs's main preoccupation over the next two years.

7

Moving towards independence for Iraq 1924 to 1929: Securing Mosul for Iraq; concerns over minorities; death of Gertrude Bell; Mustafa Kemal (Atatürk) confides in Dobbs; tensions over finance and military questions; progress towards independence

After a couple of months' leave in Ireland, Sir Henry Dobbs returned to Baghdad in September 1924. Elections to the Iraqi Parliament were being held under the recently promulgated constitution and were going ahead smoothly. He commented on the general good feeling.[1] This contrasted with all the difficulties and dramas before he left over the Anglo-Iraq Treaty and associated agreements. These had been hotly disputed until the assembly's grudging acceptance.

The most urgent problem now facing Dobbs was Iraq's northern border with Turkey. The constant unrest in the area – mainly sporadic fighting with Turkish forces which Dobbs described as 'our semi-war with the Turks'[2] – posed a continuing potential threat. As well as wanting to end this, the high commissioner knew that without settled frontiers, Iraq would not be considered for membership of the League as an independent state. Furthermore, international recognition of its northern border drawn to include Mosul within Iraq was also a top priority for King Faisal and his government.

Turkey's borders had been called into question as a result of the Turkish nationalist leader Mustafa Kemal's refusal to accept the humiliating terms the sultan had agreed in August 1920 in the Treaty of Sèvres. Later known as Atatürk, he effectively headed Turkey's government after his various military successes against the European powers, and in November 1922 he abolished the Sultanate. The boundaries of Turkey, including Iraq's northern frontier, then had to be discussed afresh with Mustafa Kemal's representatives at the Lausanne Conference convened by the Allies in December 1922.[3]

Lord Curzon, the British foreign secretary, led the negotiations for the Allies. At that point, the British government was reconsidering its commitment to Iraq and its prime minister, Bonar Law, wanted above all to avoid war against the successful and aggressive Mustafa Kemal. These considerations did not stop Curzon from arguing strongly that Iraq should include Mosul together with the Kurdish territories in the north.[4] Even after an adjournment, the reconvened conference members could not reach agreement.[5] Curzon however persuaded the Turks to accept League of Nations arbitration but only on the understanding that any arbitration decision needed the approval of league members.[6] However, this had to be unanimous and effectively allowed Turkey to veto the arbitration decision if they were not happy with it. Once the dispute had been referred to the League, its guiding principle of self-determination meant that its conclusions had to take account of how the local population wished to be governed.[7] At the end of September 1924, the League appointed the Mosul commission of enquiry to investigate the views of those living in the area of the boundary between Iraq and Turkey and to make recommendations.[8] Both countries said they would accept its decisions.

The British government was divided on how far they should push to secure Mosul for Iraq, but Dobbs was in no doubt that it was essential to the country's future viability on both strategic and economic grounds. He believed that the country's security was enhanced if it was delineated by a physical barrier, the mountains on this frontier and that Baghdad would be vulnerable if Iraq did not control these northern areas. He also suggested that Iraq could not pay its way without the wheatlands of Mosul and Arbil.[9] Although oil is often seen as central to the argument in favour of including Mosul, at this stage Dobbs and others saw the possible oil reserves more as a hoped-for future rather than as a contemporary source of prosperity. In addition, including Mosul was politically important within Iraq. The assembly's agreement to the 1922 treaty had been conditional on Britain defending Iraq's rights to Mosul 'in their entirety'.[10] Later, King Faisal colourfully told the international commission, 'It is impossible for Baghdad to live if Mosul is detached from it.'[11]

The commission's chairman was Carl Einer de Wirsen, a Swedish diplomat. The other commissioners were Count Pal de Teleki, a former Hungarian prime minister and noted geographer, and Colonel Albert Paulis, a retired Belgian officer. They went first to London in November 1924 and arrived in Baghdad in January 1925,[12] where they stayed for ten days with the high commissioner.

The team supporting the commissioners included Belgians, Swiss, Swedish, Hungarians, Italians and Turks. Dobbs thought that, helped by his wife (she was generally with him when the Baghdad weather was cooler) and her command of French, all had gone smoothly.[13]

The commission then set off from Baghdad to visit the disputed frontier area in northern Iraq. Here, as in the country as a whole, there was an extremely diverse population, all of whose views it had to assess. The Turkish request that a plebiscite be held was not supported by the British and judged impractical by de Wirsen.[14] The commission however made strenuous efforts to find out the preferences of all those living in northern Iraq.[15]

The largest of the many different groups whose opinions were sought were the Kurds. They displayed their many divisions and differences to the commission, which led de Wirsen to point out that they were in no way homogeneous, speaking different dialects and barely understanding each other.[16] In addition to the Kurds, there were Arabs, Turks and Assyrians living there, and a variety of religions and sects – Muslim, Jewish, Yazidi and Christian of various sorts.[17] Views expressed by the different groups were fragmented and often contradictory. For example some Turks favoured Iraq, some Arabs favoured Turkey and the Kurds did not want to be governed by either Turks or Arabs. Among the minorities, the commission was particularly concerned about the Christians. Caricaturing their representations and the general European sympathy for them, Dobbs wrote that they had come and howled and sobbed in front of the commission who joined in.[18]

To secure Mosul, the British needed the inhabitants to express a preference to remain within Iraq and the Mosul commission to be satisfied that the position of the many minorities was safeguarded. However, it was vital that the British should avoid appearing to exert any undue influence. The difficulties of being seen to stand aloof were increased by the police presence in the area. Dobbs considered this was 'made necessary by the Turkish brigands whom the Turks had sent here as their 'experts' but really to try to raise a rebellion'[19] and it frequently caused offence to the commission. Dobbs hoped that the authorities would manage to 'bottle things up sufficiently until the reports are written.'[20] However, officials trying to supervise the process sometimes went too far. On one occasion, De Wirsen complained that the commission was being obstructed. Dobbs immediately flew up to Mosul in a snowstorm. This reduced visibility to 20 yards and according to De Wirsen, Dobbs was nearly killed when his plane crashed. De Wirsen reported that 'Dobbs had immediately placed matters on a wholly satisfactory footing whereafter all had gone well.'[21]

Dobbs saw the commission as 'extremely suspicious of us and [they] think, every time that the Arabs make a demonstration in favour of the Iraq government and against the Turks, that it has all been organised by us. Yet, if no demonstration were made, they would say that the people didn't care to what government they belonged.' He also thought 'These small nations belonging to the League of Nations look upon Great Britain as a bully and their instinct is to oppose her. So I expect that the Commission will propose some fantastic frontier which we shall have to oppose before the Council of the League.'[22]

The Mosul commission decided to defer issuing their report from June until September. Dobbs was afraid that this extra delay would mean more trouble on the frontier where the Turks were amassing their troops and intriguing with the Kurds.[23] When the commission's decision was announced, it was not as Dobbs had at one time feared. Mosul was to form part of Iraq, provided Great Britain agreed to stay for twenty-five years or until Iraq was admitted as a full member of the League. There were also to be special administrative arrangements for the Kurds. The Council of the League was to consider the report on 2 September when Britain would be represented by the secretary of state for the colonies, Leo Amery.

Dobbs, however, was very apprehensive that as between the weakness of the London government's commitment to keeping Mosul within Iraq and the uncertain course of any diplomatic discussions at the League, the north of the country might still be lost to Iraq. To help stiffen the British government's resolve, Dobbs pointed out to them that if Mosul became part of Turkey, a large refugee problem would be created for Iraq and that he would require an additional £1 million as well as troops from India to handle it. He also recommended that if Turkey was awarded Mosul, Britain should withdraw from Iraq. Indeed he regarded this as a sufficiently serious possibility to tell his wife that he was 'quite prepared for flight.'[24]

Dobbs expected Turkey to continue to argue that it should be awarded Mosul. He feared that the commission recommendations were 'so very lukewarm' that the Council of the League 'with their craving for compromise' could well propose the alternative of the Lower (Little) Zab frontier.[25] This would place Mosul and the Kurdish areas within Turkey, deprive Iraq of any useful physical barrier as a frontier in the area and leave the border uncomfortably close to Baghdad. Dobbs also worried that in order to veto any decision against them, Turkey would use the proviso Curzon had accepted: a possibility on which the Foreign Office legal adviser had 'poured contempt' when Dobbs raised it. He was furthermore troubled by Amery's very certainty that the Council would find in Iraq's favour: 'So often I have seen British Diplomats enter these conferences with their noses in the air, quite confident that there can be no view other than their own and find to their great surprise that there is great opposition and counter argument, and collapse.'[26]

Dobbs's gloomy prognostications proved all too accurate. First, in response to Turkish objections, the Council immediately proposed the Lower (Little) Zab frontier with all its disadvantages for Iraq. Next, Dobbs writes, 'came another screech from Amery saying the horrid Turks had unearthed Curzon's promise at Lausanne that no decision can be given without Turkey's consent'.[27] The proposal which was then put forward was to refer the matter to arbitration at the International Court at The Hague. Dobbs advised against accepting because there was no reason to expect the Turks to be bound by the court as they had never respected its earlier decisions. Dobbs recommended that since the Turks had repudiated their undertaking to accept the Mosul commission's decision, Amery should do the same. He would thus in effect be refusing to respect their future decisions. To Dobbs's surprise, Amery accepted his rather robust advice.[28] The result was to maintain the status quo until the British and Turkish governments reached a bilateral agreement.

Bilateral negotiations in Ankara between Britain and Turkey's representatives followed. Before they began, Dobbs, on leave in Ireland, went to London to press his views on Britain's ambassador to Turkey, Sir Ronald Lindsay. Lindsay maintained that nothing would be agreed unless half of Mosul province was given up and the Turks compensated with at least £1 million.[29] Dobbs on the other hand 'believed the Turks would give anything to make a treaty with us', that the 'whole thing was bluff'.[30] He argued that no part of the area should be given up and that the cost of frontier operations would justify paying the Turks compensation of £1 million. Dobbs was sufficiently concerned about a land giveaway to Turkey to persuade the Colonial Office that Lindsay should be formally instructed not to offer any territory.[31] In the negotiations, Lindsay indeed gave up no territory and the British agreed to pay the Turks only £500,000. Among the ministerial congratulations Dobbs received for his part in the successful settlement, Sir Samuel Hoare recognized the importance of his 'personal efforts'.[32]

The Ankara Treaty was signed on 5 June 1926, and the frontier between Iraq and Turkey was at last agreed. Six months later, Dobbs met the Turkish leader who had insisted his representatives press Britain hard and was criticized at home for yielding. He wanted to talk to the man who had so successfully opposed his claims. It was only once Dobbs's visit to Turkey had been set up that Mustafa Kemal agreed to receive the British ambassador, Sir George Clerk.

Sir Henry arrived at Ankara with Sir George and 'an Embassy crowd' on 21 November 1926:

> All the party were in the most correct clothes, doe skin gloves, stiff collars, bowler hats and that kind of thing. In fact, I found the diplomatic world very fatiguing in that way. Even in the wilds of Angora, [Ankara] they wore top hats or bowlers and spats and gloves and Claudel canes. Although the party was only going for four days, the train of luggage was so enormous that it took the whole railway station staff about ¾ hour to transfer it to our Pullman.[33]

Mustafa Kemal had declared Ankara the capital only three years before when the new Turkish republic was established. As they drove on 'roads thick with dust' towards a small villa on the brow of a hill where the president lived, Dobbs saw 'an uninteresting city with hills all round it, up which struggled the shoddy little villas of the Turkish officials recently run up in all directions'.[34] Because of the Foreign Office's insistence on their dress code, before his meeting with the president, Dobbs had to exchange his jacket for Sir George Clerk's morning coat as Sir George emerged from another meeting. Mustafa Kemal expounded his views to Dobbs for two hours – believed to be the longest meeting he had yet held with any foreign representative. Speaking in Turkish, which his foreign minister Tewfik Rushdi translated, Mustafa Kemal first explained the reasons for the Ottoman Empire's demise. He ascribed this to 'a fantastic belief that it could rule Asia through the power of the Caliphate and religion' because 'this was pure delusion and had caused the Empire to mix itself in the affairs of distant countries and to make promises to their peoples which it could not fulfil and to be involved in matters which did not really interest it. This policy had brought misfortunes in the Great War.'[35] Atatürk then went on to explain his future policy. He was determined to cut the Turks free from any Arab connection including the Muslim religion and the Caliphate. 'For this reason he was well content that Turkey had lost Iraq' (the territory bordering Iraq that Turkey had been claiming was not predominantly Arab) and he wanted to get rid of all 'unTurkish' races. He also wanted to establish a secular state:

> People had warned him that the Turkish peasants would never stand his tampering with their religion, but when it came to the touch, he found that they had no religion at all and were quite ready to obey a strong government. Now it was a question of changing the whole mentality of the people and this was the object of his decrees against the wearing of turbans and tarbushes and against priests. He was determined to succeed and if the Kurds were unable to assimilate the modern attitudes, they would have to go.[36]

Dobbs 'said very little except encouraging words when the flow seemed inclined to stop. I felt that he wanted to talk, not to hear anything from me.' Mustapha Kemal did however welcome the assurances that Dobbs had given his foreign minister of the Iraq government's friendly attitude to Turkey and the statement that there was no thought of creating Kurdistan in any form or granting Kurdish independence.[37] The Turkish readiness to massacre non-Turks, notably Kurds, which the foreign minister specifically mentioned to Dobbs in his separate discussions, particularly alarmed Dobbs, not least because of the huge refugee problem this would create for Iraq. 'Modern Turkey is founded upon a hecatomb of corpses and there will be many more before she has done. She must be ruthless'[38] said the foreign minister.

Iraq's highly diverse population increased the difficulties of governing effectively. Dobbs described its main components as wandering desert Arabs influenced by Wahabi doctrine, the Shia tribes of the middle Euphrates, the Shia 'divines', Sunni Arab tribes in the northern deserts, Kurds in the north mixed with Christian villages, tribal Kurds in the mountains and the sophisticated town Arabs and Jews of Basra, Baghdad and Mosul. Dobbs commented, 'the perpetual conflict of these jarring elements has kept Iraq disturbed throughout the past two thousand years'.[39] The Mosul commission had given particular consideration to the position of the minorities in northern Iraq. Although the frontier was now settled, the general issue of minorities' rights in Iraq continued to pose very awkward problems for its government and later led to questions within the League about Iraq's readiness for independence.[40]

The minorities were a concern for many European states, now League of Nations members. In Britain, where Gladstone had voiced outrage as far back as 1880, sporadic atrocities against Christians in the Ottoman Empire had been a long-standing issue. Among the worst was the large-scale massacre of Armenians in 1915–17. Assyrians suffered alongside Armenians, many fleeing to northern Iraq. Following the Great War, the Kurds became more rebellious. Their hopes of realizing their dream of independence had been raised when the Allies' self-determination policies led them to consider creating a separate Kurdistan at the Paris Peace Conference in 1919. This proposal was soon abandoned because of insuperable practical obstacles. The Kurds could not agree among themselves on forming a government. Turkey under Atatürk refused to make the gift of Turkish territory to the Kurds envisaged in the conference's follow-up Treaty of Sèvres in 1920. Meanwhile support among the Allies including Lloyd George had leached away.[41] In Iraq, the British tried to establish in May 1921 how the Kurds wished to be governed but failed to find a consensus. They then offered them a degree of autonomy but the Kurds could not agree on what special arrangements they wanted.[42]

In northern Iraq, the Kurds lived side by side with some twenty thousand Assyrian Christians including refugees from the Hakkari Mountains in Turkey.[43] The Assyrians were campaigning for their own 'homeland', a fragmentation of Iraq unattractive to its government. Historically at enmity with the Kurds, the Assyrians were distrusted by Sunni Arabs as too close to the British and liable to work against Arab interests. Many had served in the levies, the first indigenous military force established in British-controlled Iraq and commanded by British officers. They were therefore always identified with the British and mistrusted.[44] Furthermore, the Assyrians did not hide their disdain for the Arabs in which they were encouraged by their British officers. Dobbs tried through the air officer commanding to correct this behaviour but to little avail.[45]

In an incident that the British government succeeded in keeping out of the British newspapers, Assyrians made an unprovoked attack on Muslims in Kirkuk during the Eid festival in 1926 massacring about 120. Dobbs somehow managed to effect a reconciliation. He saw resettlement of the refugees back in Hakkari, their preference, as the best solution, but he could not persuade the Turks to accept them. Repeated efforts to find a homeland for them in the British Dominions or in Syria came to nothing.[46]

In November 1926 the Permanent Mandates Commission (PMC) which was responsible for monitoring the progress in mandated territories on behalf of the League had before it the Mosul commission's recommendations on frontiers and the minorities as well as progress reports on Iraq. The British government was represented by Sir Henry. He was able to maintain to the PMC's satisfaction that the Kurdish community's position was being safeguarded as recommended by the Mosul commission. He cited provisions in the Organic Law (Iraqi constitution) on freedom of religion and on the right to maintain their own schools. He added that Kurdish privileges were 'respected and assured' by the appointment of Kurdish officials.[47]

The PMC then asked about the Assyrians. Dobbs replied that the Assyrians' demand for a separate homeland and the general ill feeling between them and the Arabs posed an insoluble dilemma. Nonetheless, the commission members were generally sufficiently reassured not to press a recommendation that a League of Nations delegate should be based in Iraq to hear complaints from any who thought they had a grievance or were being persecuted.[48]

The PMC was taking an increasing interest in the rights of minorities. In January 1930, a year after Dobbs had left Iraq, their growing anxieties led them to make

Iraq's proposed independence and membership of the League conditional upon adequate safeguards for the rights of minorities. Petitions presented to them on behalf of Kurds, Assyrians and other minorities underlined their concerns. Progress to implement Kurdish rights had been slow. This had been the responsibility of the Iraqi not the British government who had chivvied the Iraqis to little effect. The League persisted and eventually the Iraqi government provided a guarantee of minority rights.[49] It took, in addition, a statement from the then high commissioner, Sir Francis Humphrys, that Britain accepted the moral responsibility for the equal treatment of Iraq's minorities to satisfy the League before it would agree to admit Iraq as an independent member state in October 1932.[50]

These doubts and anxieties were all too well founded. The Assyrians, encouraged by their patriarch Mar Shimun, continued to press for a homeland. In July 1933 some of them, refused asylum in Syria, returned and inflicted casualties on the Iraq army during fighting with the locals. Baghdad authorized the Kurdish general Bakr Sidqi to take action on the grounds that they posed a threat to the Iraqi state. Many Assyrians were massacred by the Iraqi Army with local Kurds joining in. Estimates range from 600 to the 3,000 claimed by the Assyrians. The advice and recommendations of Faisal, then seriously ill, had been ignored and he proved powerless to intervene. He died in Switzerland shortly afterwards. European nations expressed outrage. In Iraq, the campaign was hailed as a triumph for its army, its general, Bakr Sidqi and a victory for the Iraqi state.[51]

Part-way through Dobbs's term and soon after the satisfactory conclusion of the treaty with Turkey (see earlier in the text), he was much saddened by the death of Gertrude Bell. On the night of 11 July 1926, she died in her sleep. Dobbs had remarked on her 'deep melancholy'[52] and noted the money concerns she spoke of as her father's fortune eroded in England,[53] then in the throes of the General Strike. Dobbs oversaw her funeral arrangements, selecting a place in the British cemetery at a spot where water flowed so that roses could grow on her grave. Faisal, who was away, ordered a military funeral. Gertrude was buried in the early evening on 12 July and Dobbs wrote: 'It was witheringly hot. There was a great crowd as if a Queen were being buried. Poor Gertrude; how she would have loved to have seen it. The whole of Baghdad streamed there and stood by her grave. It caught at my throat. It was dreadful.'[54] He also wrote to his mother, 'I am feeling dreadfully desolate over the death of Gertrude Bell suddenly in her sleep … She was almost the only person here with whom one could talk as a companion and who belonged to the great world … She used to lunch with me every day so her going leaves a great gap.'[55] According to Gertrude herself, she and Sir Henry would discuss 'the affairs of the day, public and private' over lunch at the Residency.[56]

Many suppose that Miss Bell and Sir Henry did not get on, but it is clear from Dobbs's correspondence that they did. Certainly, she was not an easy person and Dobbs was from time to time embarrassed by her rudeness especially to other women. For example, the colonial secretary's wife, Mrs Amery, commented to the wife of the high commissioner in Palestine, 'Probably all of us <u>prefer</u> to talk to men but none of us are rude enough to show it except for Gertrude Bell'(underlined in original).[57] Dobbs told his wife, 'I was much touched by hearing that Gertrude had written to you so shortly before she died and had said such nice things about me. Darling, I had not written kindly of her to you, had I? That makes me very unhappy.'[58]

Far from dismissing Gertrude as his Oriental Secretary as is sometimes asserted,[59] Dobbs kept her on in this capacity until she died. They were at one in respecting and looking to build on local traditions. She had strongly supported Dobbs in this approach during his earlier dispute with Cox and Wilson. Within the high commission, she was generally impressed by what she saw of Dobbs's work: 'I have a great admiration for Sir Henry. He is extremely good at his job; I admire his despatches home immensely – they are very courageous and very illuminating. He is a considerable administrator.'[60] Gertrude was also impressed by his 'plans for big administrative works. They interest me very much his schemes and I think them on the whole very good.'[61] 'I stand amazed at his general capacity.'[62] The two did however have their differences. In particular, during the frequent cabinet crises, Dobbs's preference was to make clear the consequences of the various options and then to remain aloof whereas Gertrude liked to intrigue to the extent that Dobbs on occasion instructed her to refrain from seeing people. In Britain, such influence as she had once enjoyed waned as the powerful figures within her impressive network of connections moved on. Dobbs commented 'these are other days and Gertrude's star shines not so brightly as it did'.[63] She herself was aware that she was no longer at the centre of affairs and naturally regretted it.[64] However, Dobbs recognized her deep knowledge of the Middle East[65] and always valued her opinions. In May 1926 she was writing, 'Sir Henry rather leans on me, not so much to *do* things as to talk them over.'[66] Shortly after Gertrude's death, Dobbs wrote to his wife, 'She was a companion, dearest. I railed at her, but I do miss her so, I cannot tell you how much.'[67] 'It was pleasant to be able to discuss things with her, even although I so often differed with her. She could always have an interesting opinion.'[68] and 'I do find it very dull not having her to talk to. She understood what things signified.'[69]

Figure 7.1 Gertrude Bell, a portrait taken *c.* 1900. Dobbs first met her in London probably at about this time. Reproduced by kind permission of the principal and fellows of Lady Margaret Hall, Oxford.

Gertrude's interests were not confined to politics. She had always been a great traveller mainly in the Middle East and had a long-standing interest in archaeology. Appointed honorary head of the Department of Antiquities at King Faisal's suggestion, she inaugurated the Iraq Museum in 1923 and with Dobbs's support found a permanent home for it three years later. The formal opening took place shortly before her death and the king insisted that one wing of the museum should be named after her. Dobbs was certainly right when he wrote, 'We shall not see her like again.'[70]

Dobbs now returned to the many issues outstanding between the king and the Iraq government on the one hand and the high commissioner on the other. 'I have always prophesied that our political troubles will begin here as soon as the Arabs are relieved of the fear of the Turks',[71] wrote Dobbs, four days after the agreement with Turkey was concluded, later commenting that it was the same as with the Americans who 'rebelled as soon as we had banged the French in Canada'.[72] It did indeed so turn out. The disagreements between the British and the Iraqis, which there had always been, increased and became more difficult to resolve as King Faisal and his government felt more secure and were ready to push more aggressively for freedom to act more independently.

An important League and mandate requirement was the creation of an 'appropriate' legal and constitutional framework. Faisal in agreeing to take the throne had been ready to accept the condition, also required by the Iraqi cabinet, that his government would be 'constitutional, democratic, representative and limited by law'.[73] On his visit to Baghdad in 1925, the colonial secretary, Leo Amery, had a long conversation with Faisal about the rights of a constitutional monarch in relation to his ministers.[74] He also sought to impress on Faisal's prime minister (at that point Yasin al-Hashimi) what the respective powers and duties of each were in a constitutional monarchy.[75] Trying to ensure that the king and his government acted within these boundaries was seen by the high commissioner as an important part of his responsibilities.

This was not simply because a constitutional monarchy was the British government's preferred form of government. It was also because the mandatory power had to be able to demonstrate to the satisfaction of the League of Nations that the prospective member had a stable and constitutional government. Dobbs's appearance before the PMC in November 1926 clearly illustrates this. As Dobbs anticipated, 'the inquisition of the Mandates Commission is going to be pretty stiff and the questions will take a lot of answering'.[76] Following the Mosul commission's report, which included their concerns and recommendations on protecting the minorities, Dobbs was pressed in detail on the workings of the constitution, including the legal system and on the exercise of the royal prerogative. It was extremely helpful that he could refer to the legal and administrative safeguards put in place for the minorities. In addition, he was also questioned on many aspects of the new state from public health to diplomatic relations, from its economy and finance to tribal areas and railways.[77]

The secretary to the commission told Dobbs he had provided the best report on any mandated territory.[78]

The constitutional and legal requirements and the League's interest in them did not change Faisal's belief that the country could most effectively be governed by a strong autocratic ruler who should not be limited by the law and the constitution or bound by the decisions of what the king saw as often self-serving politicians. He thought that a strong man was needed to bring his country into the modern era. In this context, Faisal's views inevitably brought him into conflict with the high commissioner with his eye to satisfying the League. In May 1926, Dobbs commented:

> I have always had to fight Faisal for wanting to punish and imprison the people whom he doesn't like by executive order and to exercise arbitrary power; and I can't allow the principle that it can be done in any circumstances, for that would remove the lynch-pin of the whole system of civilised government which we have built up and open the door to every kind of excess.[79]

Dobbs had periodic run-ins with Faisal when he tried to act outside the constitutional and legal framework and ignore its limitations on his decisions. In May 1927, the king overruled the expulsion of students who had rioted and assaulted the police. Dobbs commented, this 'will probably prevent his getting into the League of Nations, just after I had drawn so beautiful a picture of his regime'.[80] A month later, to the fury of the high commissioner, Faisal replaced two provincial governors (Mutasarrifs) on somewhat specious grounds with officials who would be more compliant with his wishes. The king also frequently tried to influence his cabinet and Dobbs many times advised him to follow his own example and 'stand aloof'.[81]

Dobbs had long recognized the general predilection in the East for 'strong men' and was well aware of Faisal's autocratic preferences. The king was a great admirer of Mustafa Kemal who later invited him to Turkey.[82] Atatürk's success owed much to his leadership of the armed forces, and his example underlined for Faisal the importance of controlling a strong and effective fighting force. The military agreements with Britain then in place called for Iraq to take full military responsibility by 1928. Faisal and his minister of defence, Nuri al-Said, wanted Iraq to develop a much larger army and its own air force. This was also thought likely to help bring together the disparate elements in the newly created country. In addition, Faisal argued that unless the Iraq government had full responsibility for the armed forces, the country could not be completely independent.

Nuri ignored Dobbs's suggestion that the British were willing to consider extending their military support beyond 1928 and began to advocate conscription. It offered the prospect of a sizeable army at a relatively lower cost. Faisal and Nuri both 'chafed against constitutional restraints', and Dobbs believed that Nuri's military plans were designed 'to enable him to make a coup d'état in favour of Faisal as an absolute monarch'.[83] Dobbs and the government in London both feared a threat to constitutional government, but in Iraq this was to come not from the monarch but from the leaders of those armed forces. They were to stage periodic coups with fatal consequences for Faisal's dynasty and Nuri himself. The first was in 1936 when General Bakr Sidqi (see earlier in the text), replaced the government with his own nominees and murdered the then minister of defence, Jafar al-Askari.

Dobbs did not accept that military arrangements of the kind the king and Nuri wanted were necessary as part of satisfying the League's independence requirements. He knew that for Iraq to take on the costs of defence even on a modest basis would appreciably add to the already considerable financial pressure the country was facing. He thought that 'Iraq must be content with a kind of gendarmerie for interior defence and … there is no real danger for the present of a war with Turkey',[84] as he told his wife and as he had written in his despatches. He also believed that Iraq would need a 'mercenary air force' which it would pay for whether or not the RAF.[85]

The situation was made more difficult for Dobbs because his stance was also opposed by the inspector general of the Iraq Army, Major General Daly, who reported to the high commissioner. He commented that Daly and most British officers 'all clamour for an army on the German model fit to fight a European foe and of course the country can't afford that. They [get] very angry when told that the army is only needed to keep the tribes in order.'[86] Daly brought forward grandiose plans with the German model in view and he included an expensive infrastructure of support staff. Dobbs on the other hand envisaged 'as big a force of actual fighters as possible'[87] with minimum infrastructure. Daly's scheme was to cost more than twice as much as that of Dobbs.

Daly's ambitious plans were welcomed by Faisal and his minister of defence. Daly continued to press them in the face of Dobbs's opposition. In addition, he also backed conscription. This last was opposed by the British government who supported Dobbs's veto of the Iraq government's draft conscription bill. Conscription was an unpopular policy in rural areas potentially posing a threat to public order, and the British government was not prepared to allow it to be imposed by air policing. These questions led to such heated disagreements between Dobbs and Daly that Dobbs decided their differences were irreconcilable and that one of them must go. To the annoyance of Faisal's defence minister, the colonial secretary decided it should be Daly. Dobbs had found the whole episode extremely disagreeable. He commented, 'I don't think I am a really difficult person to get on with', though Dobbs was known for occasional bursts of temper. He went on to comment on the difficulties of the general situation:

> the peculiar circumstances of service here go to the heads of a lot of people when they get out here. They are all 'Advisers' and everything is vague without any procedure or traditions and each person thinks he has a wonderful field of raw material for untrammelled experimenting and trying his own theories. They can't bear to be criticised and checked and they each think they have an unlimited right to my support against the Iraq Government when the Iraqis don't agree with them, but that I have no right to oppose them when I don't agree with them.[88]

Sensitivities about the respective powers of the British and Iraq governments made the negotiations that were periodically taking place over oil concessions more difficult . The Turkish Petroleum Company (renamed the Iraq Petroleum Company (IPC) in 1929) opened negotiations with the Iraq government in 1923, and in 1925, Dobbs wrote to his mother: 'It is all very difficult; because all I have had [is] crisis after crisis with the Arab ministers over the oil concession in Baghdad and Mosul which they don't wish to give on the terms on which the British Govt insist. It is all very complicated and wearisome.'[89] He described the negotiations between the Turkish Petroleum Company (TPC) and the Iraq government and between a rival and the Iraq government as 'positively boiling'.[90] The concession was awarded to the TPC and in April 1927, Faisal inaugurated their oil field near Kirkuk. Dobbs, who had visited it earlier in the year, was much impressed by the extent of the investment in its infrastructure and by the number of jobs that were being created 'so bringing great prosperity to that part of the country'.[91] Already 50 British and 2,500 Iraqis were involved. A huge gusher was struck in October 1927 at Baba Gugur, and Iraq began exporting oil in 1931.

The country was already enjoying royalties and cheap petrol from the immense Anglo-Persian Oil field at Khanaqin near the border with Persia. Dobbs had earlier feared the negotiations had 'gone wrong' and so had brought in the company's chairman-designate, Sir John Cadman. He was particularly experienced in negotiating concessions with governments and, in May 1926 a deal with the Iraq government had been speedily concluded.[92] Dobbs's part in these various proceedings was essentially that of a go-between, although he may also have helped to moderate the more extreme demands of the parties. He did not have the background knowledge or experience to take a very active part in the oil concession negotiations. He was much more interested and concerned about the position of the tribesmen whose land might be needed for oil drilling. 'I have suddenly discovered that the long-nosed Longrigg has been pertinaciously working for years to enslave nearly all the peasants of the country, declare the land which they have held for generations to be government property and give it out to his townee friends to cultivate with oil-pumps. I only just intervened in time.'[93]

Stephen Longrigg, an official who became inspector general of revenue and later an IPC employee, had scope to do this because of a lack of clarity over tribesmen's rights to the land. Dobbs's main concern was to protect the long-established rights of landholders. He was something of an expert on these subjects. He had introduced regulations on them in 1916 when he was revenue commissioner in Mesopotamia. Relieved of Turkish frontier worries, he now felt 'able to look into things like land tenure which really appeal to me more than anything else'.[94] He soon wrote 'gigantic and monumental notes on land tenures and the rights of tribesmen which Longrigg is trying to take away'.[95] It was a very problematic area because in the absence of records, individual landholders were unable to demonstrate what rights they held. There were few records from the Ottoman period when land was largely government owned and the government granted rights to individuals. While Dobbs's approach provided a very practical way through this complex area, it had various drawbacks.[96] Among these was the scope for abuse because much was left to the larger landholders, and this generally reinforced the position of the sheikhs and codified a system of personal rule. With little supervision, this was often at the expense of the smaller landowners. As it had done in India, this approach reinforced the tribal system in preference to the British system of justice and upholding the traditional approach reduced flexibility to adapt to changing economic circumstances.[97]

However, Dobbs soon had to turn to the question of how long the British would remain in Iraq and what respective responsibilities the two governments would have for the armed forces. In March 1927, Dobbs commented: 'The British Government ... have decided to stick here permanently. They want to keep the RAF here and also to have the perpetual right of sending warships up to Basra and I am now to negotiate a new agreement. We never seem to have done, and I am sure I don't know how the Iraqis will take it.'[98]

Both parties did agree that Iraq would not be ready to meet the full costs of its defence by 1928 and that a new military agreement would have to be negotiated.

An opportunity for somewhat more far-reaching change was also offered in the new treaty the Iraq Assembly had endorsed in January 1926, which had been drawn up to give effect to the Mosul commission's recommendations on the future of Iraq. That treaty included a provision which envisaged the need for a continued British presence for twenty-five years but at the same time allowed Iraq to apply for membership of the League every four years starting in 1928. In early March 1927, Dobbs strongly recommended that the British government support Iraq's entry to the League in 1928 although he thought it most unlikely the League would agree. He had told his wife that 'I have always said we shall have to try and get her in, because otherwise she will doubt our good faith … We must try and try honestly, otherwise the Iraqis will think we are playing to stay here and will never trust us again.'[99] Dobbs himself at the PMC the previous October had done his best to portray Iraq as developing so rapidly that it was now close to satisfying the League's requirements for independence.

Initially, the British government itself had been reluctant to take on the responsibilities of the mandate and had hoped to mitigate its unpopularity in Britain by moving Iraq to independence as swiftly as possible, thus freeing the British government from the costs of the mandate commitment but, it was hoped, leaving behind a friendly state well disposed towards Britain. Now however, Britain was beginning to see a need to retain some degree of control and move more gradually towards Iraq's independence. For Britain, the balance sheet had changed. Iraq no longer represented merely a cost but a country where valuable British and international interests needed to be protected – notably burgeoning oil prospects and the possibility of developing air routes to India via Baghdad.

At the same time, King Faisal and his government saw the post-Mosul treaty as clearing the way to independence.[100] Previously both governments had shared the aim of early independence for Iraq and, despite their differences, relations were generally good. Now, significant shifts in the attitudes of both governments were straining many aspects of the relationship. Faisal, increasingly impatient to move to independence, had always been sensitive about control and always wished to escape from it but it was now beginning to appear as if the British government was increasingly unwilling to let go and tensions increased. Furthermore, international recognition of the Iraqi state depended on its admission to the League of Nations and Britain had to ensure Iraq met the requirements of the mandate, albeit in a treaty format, if its application was to succeed. These requirements were unwelcome to Iraq and further strained relationships.

Figure 7.2 Sir Henry Dobbs in the residency garden with Sir Samuel Hoare (secretary of state for air), on a ministerial visit. The pelican was always jealous of rivals for Sir Henry's attention and sometimes attacked them. Courtesy of Henry Wilks.

By the end of May 1927, there had still been no reaction to Dobbs's recommendation three months before that the British government should support Iraq's early entry into the League, in 1928. Over the previous few months Faisal had become increasingly frustrated. He had got nowhere on conscription and changes to the military agreements, had been at odds with Dobbs over a number of issues and could see no perceptible movement towards furthering Iraq's independence on the part of the British government whose 'willingness' to retain a military presence in Iraq fuelled suspicions. Dobbs wrote, Faisal 'fumes' at the delay. The king then 'set his heart'[101] on going to London. The king and his ministers, Dobbs explains, 'have a feeling that if only they could go home and deal with King George and Amery direct, they would get all that they want in the way of recognition of complete independence and all other fallals'.[102]

Dobbs was becoming increasingly concerned over his difficulties with Faisal and his ministers.[103] He initially opposed Faisal's plan to go to London because he thought a personal visit would achieve nothing and merely add to Faisal's frustrations. His biographer, Ali Allawi, portrays the relationship as being at the point where Faisal and Dobbs could not stand the sight of each other. He suggests that the Colonial Office arranged for Dobbs to take a period of extended leave.[104] In fact, as relations in Iraq deteriorated and after months of indecision on Dobbs's recommendation for Iraq's early entry to the League, the colonial secretary, Leo Amery, sent for the high commissioner. He left Baghdad on 7 July for discussions in London. By the time Dobbs arrived, the British Cabinet had at last reached a decision. It was against the government trying for Iraq's entry in 1928. This timing would have run counter to the De Wirsen commission's support for a more lengthy period of British oversight. It also ran counter to the PMC's general view that oversight would be needed for a long time. Amery, himself an imperialist – indeed Dobbs had earlier described him as 'rather more jingoistic than I approve'[105] – argued that advocating early membership of the League would be seen as sharp practice. This gave him a good excuse to say no, while the head of the RAF, Sir Hugh Trenchard,[106] thought Faisal should be told to shut up.[107] As Dobbs had thought likely, ministers preferred to avoid the controversies that support for Iraq's early entry would prompt.[108] However, Dobbs did manage to persuade Amery to support Faisal's alternative of a revision to the current treaty in a form 'more honourable to Iraq'.[109] Amery sent Faisal a very guarded telegram agreeing to consider this but said he would need to consult cabinet colleagues. In London Dobbs argued that every effort must be made 'to meet his [Faisal's] views and send him back happy, while maintaining the essentials of control'[110] in order to avoid the risks either of Faisal abdicating[111] or being 'seriously weakened in prestige'. Dobbs suggested that each of these results would be 'a disaster'.[112] The first would be seen as a failure of British policy in Iraq and the second risked possibly creating dangerous political unrest. Dobbs's position was that 'having chosen King Faisal as our principal instrument in Iraq, we must somehow see to it that he should make good … . We must make the best of the instruments in our hands just as we did in the native states of India and elsewhere.'[113]

It was agreed to open negotiations on a new treaty and Faisal was invited to London at the end of October. After a series of gruelling sessions in November and December, the general terms of a treaty were agreed. The treaty itself made changes which were little more than cosmetic but it did provide for the military and financial agreements to be renegotiated. These as Dobbs had always maintained were what really mattered – the 'flesh and blood' of the treaty. At the same time, the British government promised to support Iraq for admission to the League in 1932 'provided the present rate of progress is maintained and all goes well in the interval'.[114] Dobbs's main concern had been the risk that the difficulties between the Iraqi and British governments and between the Iraqi

Figure 7.3 Leo Amery, secretary of state for the colonies. Amery was the minister to whom Dobbs principally reported for much of his time as high commissioner. ©Illustrated London News Ltd/ Mary Evans.

government and the high commissioner might jeopardize 'the aim of all our endeavours here [which] is to leave Iraq friendly to Great Britain while securing her well-being'.[115]

It had been possible to paper over the differences between Iraq and Britain about the extent and nature of British control when dealing in the vague and legalistic generalities of the treaty, but Dobbs's last year as high commissioner was spent in fruitless wrangles over very material arrangements in the accompanying military and financial agreements. In London, it had been agreed that in place of the earlier treaty's requirement for Iraq to take full responsibility for internal security and defence from 1928, the British government would pledge to provide such support and assistance as was necessary from time to time. The RAF would remain in Iraq indefinitely and the British government would retain the Assyrian levies.[116]

However, the Iraqi government remained insistent on having a degree of formal control over British forces' operations in Iraq. This was vehemently opposed by Trenchard,[117] who thought the Iraqis already had too much control.[118] Dobbs took an entirely contrary position. He believed that the Iraqi government could not survive the withdrawal of British support and that was the real sanction that mattered. Dobbs's view that the practicalities would count rather more than the formalities arrived at by arguing over paper pledges was lent support by an incident that occurred during his last month in Iraq. A potentially serious situation had arisen on Iraq's border with Ibn Saud's kingdom as a result of tribal raids. Dobbs pointed out that:

> The main reason for the breakdown of the negotiations is that Iraq won't consent to her army coming under the control of the AOC [Air Officer Commanding] at the time of joint operations. In the middle of all this came news from Captain Glubb [later Glubb Pasha] that a terrific raid from Najd [Ibn Saud's territory] was being prepared and Glubb rushes in himself by car arriving from the desert with a crimson nose at 2 AM. Then the King fell into a panic and demanded that the control of the whole of the desert and all the tribes should be put under the AOC [The air officer commanding was in charge of all British forces and reported to Dobbs] which was just what they had refused to do.[119]

The British government however continued to insist on tight controls over all the armed forces in Iraq in the case of combined operations. The British were also equally unyielding on the financial agreements. Britain was demanding that Iraq pay a surcharge which represented the additional costs of stationing British armed forces in Iraq and not in Britain. Dobbs, who commented earlier that

Faisal was much disgusted at this,[120] argued strongly that the Iraqis should not be expected to meet any extra costs because the British armed forces were there to protect British imperial and foreign interests. British intransigence together with earlier disagreements, particularly around developing an independent army, fuelled the fears of King Faisal and his government that Britain's policy was to remain and never leave Iraq.[121] These were also lent credence by the obvious importance to British interests of the now developing air routes via Baghdad and the now massive British and foreign investment in what were being confirmed as extensive oil reserves. Dobbs considered that the disagreements in this changing situation were risking the 'final defeat' of government policy on Iraq, namely to establish an 'independent Iraq friendly and bound by ties of obligation to "H. M. Government"'.[122]

During 1928 Dobbs directed a great deal of effort to persuading the British government to take a more accommodating approach on both military 'control' and on the financial arrangements. However, the colonial secretary adamantly refused any relaxation of control over the Iraqi armed forces and insisted on the arrangements Britain had put forward. Despite Dobbs's efforts to manage the situation there had been frequent resignations of Iraqi ministers.[123] When the then prime minister, Abd al-Muhsin al-Sadoun, who was in general sympathetic to the British, together with his government rejected the British terms and the British government was unmoved, Dobbs decided not to reveal the continued British refusal to compromise in any way and so managed to avoid a total breakdown in relations between the two governments.[124] The unyielding attitudes of the British government and the sensitivities of the Iraq government had resulted in a complete stalemate.

Dobbs was now busy packing up ready to leave Iraq as planned on 3 February 1929. Despite the difficulties created by London's intransigence, Dobbs reported: 'The King has been very kind and bestowed on me his highest order and ever so many other Iraqis have shown great affection. I am really touched. Now I am in the rush of departure and serving drinks and farewells etc.'[125] Dobbs was self-deprecating about his achievements but received warm comments on his time in Iraq in the press and within Iraq. The *London Times* wrote that since his arrival, 'neither rebellion nor civil strife has troubled the waters of the Tigris and Euphrates', referred to the increase in Iraq's prosperity, the importance of securing Mosul and the border with Turkey but recognized that internally Iraq was experiencing the 'troubles of political adolescence', which it hoped Dobbs's successor could resolve.[126] In Iraq, at his farewell dinner for the high commissioner, King Faisal described him as 'the sincere friend of the Iraqis the King and the country'.[127] The *Baghdad Times*, widely regarded as the pro-residency paper, reported 'generous tributes in the Arabic press'.[128] Although *Al Iraq* regretted the pressure Dobbs brought to bear on the Constituent Assembly in 1924, it believed that Iraq would 'always remember with gratitude his honourable stand in the Mosul crisis'.[129] *Al Taqaddum* praised him for convincing his government not to evacuate Iraq and to continue its support over Mosul 'even during the most anxious crisis in Anglo-Turkish relations'. It saw Dobbs as having 'a particular affection for the cause of Iraq' and referred to 'the great efforts which he has made to bring the Iraq and British points of view together during the recent negotiations'. Echoing something of *Al Iraq's* sentiments *Al Taqaddum* recognized that:

> in many matters Sir Henry was obliged by orders from his Government sometimes to follow a policy which was not in harmony with Iraq's interests and that circumstances often prevented him from showing a wider sympathy and encouragement to this country, but we are convinced that Sir Henry is now free from these outside constraints and it is now possible for him to help Iraq.[130]

Al Iraq recalled 'with praise his great work in this country'.[131] *Al Taqaddum* identified his many 'high qualities' and commented that 'he has always done his utmost to foster and encourage big schemes of development, and his advice has played a great part in the progress and development which may be seen all around us'.[132]

Dobbs's successor, Sir Gilbert Clayton, had no more success than Dobbs in trying to persuade the British government to compromise until there was a change of government in May 1929. In June, the new Labour government decided it would set up a cabinet committee to review Britain's policy in Iraq. In fact, Dobbs had previously found the earlier Labour administration rather more sympathetic than Conservative governments to Iraq's requests and much more reasonable on the question of the costs to be borne by Iraq.[133] The government's 'new policy' review was being led by Jim Thomas, now Lord Privy Seal.[134] He had been colonial secretary in Ramsay Macdonald's 1924 Labour government when Dobbs had thought well of him.[135] At that time, Dobbs had also been in touch with Sidney Webb, then president of the Board of Trade who, as Lord Passfield, was now colonial secretary. Dobbs was in London in June 1929 when the Labour government was beginning their policy review. He was a keen advocate of early independence for Iraq and what he saw as the best course for that country and for Britain. He had a long private discussion about these questions with the new colonial secretary, Lord Passfield.[136]

At the end of July 1929, Clayton submitted to the government in London his summary of what the two parties wanted in Iraq. Britain wanted security for imperial communications, the continued presence of the RAF and an assurance that all foreign officials should be British. Iraq wanted its payments for the high commission and British forces suspended, the Foreign Office and not the Colonial Office to handle its affairs and an unconditional statement of support for its entry to the League in 1932.[137]

Six weeks later, the government did make a firm commitment to recommend Iraq unconditionally for membership of the League in 1932 and authorized the high commissioner to tell the Iraqi government. The 'new policy' in Iraq was announced in a white paper published in November 1929 by the secretary of state for the colonies.[138] This acknowledged that the conditional nature of the government's earlier undertaking to support Iraq's candidature for membership of the League had fuelled Iraqi suspicions about British motives: '[The conditions] served to keep alive the belief, never wholly absent from Iraqi minds, that HMG had no genuine intention of ever establishing Iraq in full independence and that their real policy was to "colonise" the country'.[139]

The white paper also recognized that the British government's public commitment to Iraq's early independence had transformed the atmosphere in Iraq and led to 'mutual confidence and goodwill'.[140] These developments were entirely consistent with Dobbs's frequently expressed views. Indeed the senior official in the Middle East Department of the Colonial Office wrote to point out to Dobbs that in his white paper, the secretary of state for the colonies 'has publicly acknowledged your share in pressing a more liberal policy upon His Majesty's Government'.[141]

It was not very long before the more liberal government policy resulted in a new Anglo-Iraqi Treaty and paved the way for Iraq's admission to the League of Nations in 1932 as an independent nation state.

Epilogue

Dobbs's official career came to an end after nearly forty years on 2 February 1929, his last day as high commissioner for Iraq. The following morning he left for Ireland. He had always been deeply committed to his work. Two years earlier, he had written to his mother that he believed he had brought Iraq over 'the most difficult part of the way' and felt that 'having brought it to this stage, I must see it to its final settlement, if I can'.[1] Although Dobbs strongly advocated the early independence of Iraq, which he had done everything he possibly could to promote, it had to wait for a change of government in London until it was achieved in 1932.

At the same time, Dobbs had also told his mother, 'I shall be very glad to have done with it all and to be able to settle down at Camphire [his family home in Ireland] and look after my own business and see more of my family without any more responsibility for big things.'[2] Indeed as his letters show, sometimes rather poignantly, he greatly missed his wife and family. Concerned about his wife's health, and looking ahead to impending retirement, he wrote, 'What a tragedy it would be if after our long separation we were to follow one another into early graves and have no time to enjoy reunion.'[3] Sadly however, he died in May 1934. He had been ill for many months and back at home for only five years.

After leaving Iraq, Dobbs spent most of his time in Ireland. He worked on changes to his gardens (he was a keen botanist and plantsman), wrote newspaper articles and gave occasional lectures on Iraq. In February 1933, at a meeting in London of the Royal Empire Society, Sir Henry gave his retrospective on what the British had achieved in Iraq and its future prospects. He described how from the outset, the British found themselves 'in the thick of political conflict'[4] facing determined nationalist opposition. The pressures for independence and the 'determination of British democracy to spend no more money in Iraq' had made it 'plain' that there would be no possibility of Britain progressively building up the state 'on a well secured foundation'. The only practical alternative had been to 'set the country on its legs as quickly as possible and get out, leaving behind if it might be such kindly memories of our intervention as would secure a generous treatment of our special interests'.[5]

This, Dobbs said, might appear to its critics as 'a policy of jerry building and scuttle'.[6] However, the country's performance had, he argued, transcended these limitations and 'few would deny the success that has hitherto attended this romantic and hazardous adventure'.[7] He ascribed success to the political dexterity of King Faisal, strongly supported in his early years by Gertrude Bell, the qualities of the British officials and the provision of capital for the new state from its oil. Dobbs cited much that had been achieved during the British mandate in the relatively short period of thirteen years: a functioning administration, parliament and army were in place; the police force and judicial service regenerated; roads, bridges, hospitals and schools built; railways extended and water, electricity, telephone and postal services provided in the principal towns.

Dobbs then came to the 'dark spots'.[8] He feared vested interests would make an equitable land settlement unlikely and he was particularly unhappy about the position of minorities – notably the Assyrians and the Kurds:

> So now to raise up this Iraq, we have squandered blood, treasure and high ability. We have bound debts and taxes on the necks of generations of our descendants. We have seemed by the abandonment of the Assyrians and Kurds to sacrifice our very honour. We have suffered the imputation that on the scene of their agony, we living have betrayed the hopes of our dead. You ask, for all this, shall we have our reward? I answer that I cannot say.[9]

Dobbs's gloomy comments[10] contrasted with the rosy picture painted by several of those present, notably Dobbs's predecessor, Sir Percy Cox and the prominent Iraqi politician and former prime minister, Jafar al-Askari. Askari claimed that the minorities lived as peacefully in Iraq as the Scots did in Britain.[11] Sadly however a terrible massacre of the Assyrians took place in Iraq six months after Dobbs's comments at the hands of the Iraqi army abetted by the Kurds.

Presiding over the meeting was Leo Amery, the former colonial secretary to whom Dobbs reported for most of his time as high commissioner. Amery emphasized the 'extraordinary difficulties in creating Iraq' made up of 'desert, swamp and wild mountain ranges', whose inhabitants were conscious of their many differences but not of belonging to a single unit. The creation of this new state had taken place over the relatively short period of thirteen years. Dobbs had been in charge for over six of these. Generally very self-deprecating about his work, he made almost no reference in his lecture to what part in events he played. However, in February 1927, he had told his mother that

> There was nothing but chaos when I arrived at the end of 1922 – all the frontiers out of control, the priests in savage opposition and forbidding elections and the ratification of a treaty with Great Britain; Turkish and Bolshevist intrigue rampant; the country full of British and Indian regiments which were not sufficient to secure peace. Now we have only two regiments in the country and they will go next year together with a great part of the air force.[12]

Leo Amery observed both at the lecture and later that the success of Dobbs's 'great work' in Iraq 'lay in the personal understanding and cooperation between Sir Henry and His Majesty King Faisal'.[13] As Dobbs left Iraq, comments in the Arab press had recognized that it had been British government policy that had at times prevented him from taking a more sympathetic line. Indeed, al-Askari expressed appreciation for Dobbs's efforts to 'ensure a policy which he regarded as the best for the mutual interests of Iraq and Britain'.[14] Faisal himself had described Dobbs as a sincere friend of Iraq and awarded him the country's highest honour – the Blazing Star of the Two Rivers. Amery later wrote that 'to have carried out without impairment of friendship the transition from direct British administration to … Iraq independence was a remarkable triumph of statecraft'.[15]

Amery ascribed success in Iraq to Faisal's and Dobbs's 'peculiar personal qualities'.[16] After Dobbs's death, tributes were paid to his 'brilliant and useful life',[17] his 'great gifts and the charm of his personality',[18] his even making those opposed to him feel 'stronger from contact with strength and happier from contact with so much humanity'[19] – this last, surprisingly, from Sir Arnold Wilson with whom Dobbs had so vehemently disagreed. Dobbs was also described as sympathetic and kind despite his reputation for being irascible.

In addition to these personal qualities, Dobbs had an outlook and set of skills that in combination made him highly effective. Open-minded and never constrained by established views, Dobbs appreciated early on that Britain's traditional approach to its overseas territories was becoming outdated. At home, its international role was being questioned and, abroad, the tacit consent which had enabled Britain to maintain its dominance around much of the world was evaporating as its rule was being increasingly challenged. Leaders of communities overseas now wanted their countries to be treated as independent equals of the European states. Dobbs was quicker than many to realize that this made the colonial-style approach no longer practicable and that Britain would now be better served by supporting self-governing communities in the hope of then enjoying their good will where British interests were concerned.

At the same time, Dobbs also understood that the strength of traditional culture meant that introducing general European practices was full of risk. In late 1928, Amir Amanullah faced an uprising following his reform programme and his insistence on publicly campaigning against the veil[20] and in December Dobbs reminded his wife that in 1922 he had feared the amir 'would get into trouble by going ahead too fast'.[21] In 1929 Amanullah abdicated and fled Afghanistan.

An enquiring mind and natural empathy opened the way to Dobbs's shrewd judgements of context, local sentiments and leading personalities. His astute assessment lay behind his deft handling of the political cross-currents swirling around Iraqi unwillingness to ratify the unloved but key 1922 treaty with Britain. Dobbs devised approaches of his own to break the stalemate and bring about the necessary majority for ratification against apparently overwhelming local opposition. Critical to winning support had been the fear he had created that without ratification, Britain would not continue to support the inclusion of Mosul in Iraq.

Although he often had disagreements with Faisal and key Iraqi politicians, Dobbs won their respect and trust. An element in this was their appreciation that while he was there to protect British interests, he genuinely wished to foster the interests of Iraq as he had done earlier for the communities he was responsible for in India. This empathy with those whom he encountered helped him in his relationships with important regional figures, sheikhs, amirs and leading politicians throughout his career: the head of the Bugti tribe in Balochistan after Dobbs's death described him as 'my greatest friend'.[22]

Dobbs's skills were complemented by his patience and persistence, his charm and firmness. At the same time, not afraid of incurring the displeasure of his superiors, he was confident in his own judgements and dogged in his pursuit of what he thought would deliver the best results. Thus in his negotiations on the 1921 Anglo-Afghan Treaty, he manoeuvred between the different views in London and Delhi with great dexterity to allow himself in the end to negotiate alone with the amir and to arrive at what he considered an acceptable agreement. In the crisis over the 1922 Treaty between Britain and Iraq, Dobbs not only disregarded the unhelpful approach recommended by London but risked using his own wholly unauthorized tactics to achieve a breakthrough.

Ever his own man, Dobbs proved to be a highly effective operator who was able to navigate his way through in the period of turbulent change that followed the Great War. Imaginative and dedicated individuals with the range of personal qualities and skills Dobbs demonstrated are as much needed today as they were then.

Notes

Introduction

1 Secretary of state for the colonies, 1924 to 1929, and later known for his strong opposition to appeasement.

2 Amery is referring to the memorial window now destroyed, which Dobbs's friends and colleagues subscribed to have put in the Mesopotamia Memorial Church, later St George's Memorial Church, Baghdad.

3 Letter, Leo Amery to Lady Dobbs, 29 May 1937, unpublished papers of Sir Henry Dobbs (hereafter unpublished papers).

4 David Gilmour, *The Ruling Caste. Imperial Lives in the Victorian Raj* (London: John Murray, 2005), 1, 10–11.

5 Letter, Dobbs to his mother, 12 April 1913, unpublished papers.

6 Letter, headmaster Winchester College (Dr Fearon) to Dobbs's father, 9 August 1890, unpublished papers.

7 Letter, Dobbs to his wife, 28 June 1916, unpublished papers.

8 Letter, Dobbs to Gertrude Bell, 6 January 1918, unpublished papers.

1 Henry Dobbs in the run of his times: The changing international scene and British policies; the context for Henry Dobbs's achievements

1 Peter Burroughs, 'Imperial Institutions and the Government of Empire' in *The Oxford History of the British Empire, Volume III, The Nineteenth Century*, ed. Andrew Porter (Oxford: Oxford University Press 1999; paperback 2001), 171. Citations are to the paperback edition.

2 Quoted by Wm Roger Louis, 'Introduction' in *The Oxford History of the British Empire, Volume IV, The Twentieth Century*, ed. Judith M. Brown and Wm Roger Louis (Oxford: Oxford University Press 1999; paperback 2001), 5. Citations are to the paperback edition.

3 Robin J. Moore, 'Imperial India, 1858–1914' in *The Oxford History of the British Empire, Volume III*, 427.

4 Ibid., 424–5.

5 Ibid., 435.

6 Judith M. Brown, 'India' in *The Oxford History of the British Empire, Volume IV, The Twentieth Century*, ed. Judith M. Brown and Wm Roger Louis (Oxford: Oxford University Press 1999; paperback 2001), 430.

7 Ludwig W. Adamec, *Afghanistan 1900–1923. A Diplomatic History* (Berkeley: University of California Press, 1967), 15–17.

8 Warren Dockter, *Churchill and the Islamic World. Orientalism, Empire and Diplomacy in the Middle East* (London: I. B. Tauris, 2019), 55.

9 John Darwin, *The Empire Project. The Rise and Fall of the British World-System 1830–1970* (Cambridge: Cambridge University Press, 2009; paperback 2011), 80. Citations are to the paperback edition.

10 Louis, 'Introduction' in *The Oxford History of the British Empire, Volume IV*, 2.

11 Darwin, *The Empire Project*, 260–1.

12 For a detailed account of the foreign secretary's efforts in the summer of 1914, see T. G. Otte, *Statesman of Europe. A Life of Sir Edward Grey* (London: Allen Lane, 2020), chapter 17.

13 Charles Townshend, *When God Made Hell. The British Invasion of Mesopotamia and the Creation of Iraq 1914–1921* (London: Faber and Faber, 2010; paperback, 2011), 264. Citations are to the paperback edition.

14 James Barr, *A Line in the Sand. Britain, France and the Struggle that Shaped the Middle East* (London: Simon & Schuster, 2011; paperback, 2012), 23. Citations are to the paperback edition.

15 Ibid., 25–7.

16 Darwin, *The Empire Project*, 315.

17 Although he had travelled extensively in the Middle East, Mark Sykes spoke no local languages and had little detailed knowledge. Barr, *A Line in the Sand*, 8.

18 Ibid., 7–9, 37–9, 30 and 72.

19 Townshend, *When God Made Hell*, 373–4.

20 Ibid.

21 Susan Pedersen, *The Guardians. The League of Nations and the Crisis of Empire* (Oxford: Oxford University Press, 2015; paperback 2017), 26–7. Citations are to the paperback edition.

22 Barr, *A Line in the Sand*, 70.

23 Margaret MacMillan, *Peacemakers. The Paris Conference of 1919 and Its Attempt to End War* (London: John Murray 2001; paperback 2002), 12–19. Citations are to the paperback edition.

24 Pedersen, *The Guardians*, 28–9.

25 MacMillan, *Peacemakers*, 452–3.

26 Ibid., 463–4.

27 Pedersen, *The Guardians*, 35.

28 Ibid., 408.

2 **Home and away 1871 to 1900:** Family connections; education; early experiences in British India

1 David Wainwright, *Broadwood by Appointment. A History* (London: Quiller Press, 1982).

2 Letter, Sir Alfred Lyall to Dobbs's mother (Edith Juliana Dobbs) 9 November 1892, unpublished papers of Sir Henry Dobbs (hereafter unpublished papers).

3 Henry Dobbs: notes from his housemaster's record book, Winchester College archives.

4 Letters, Dr Fearon (headmaster Winchester College) to Dobbs's father (Robert Dobbs) 18 December 1889 and 9 August 1890, unpublished papers.

5 Letter, Dobbs to John Wainewright (Winchester College friend and contemporary) 23 January 1895, unpublished papers.

6 F. R. H. Du Boulay, *Servants of Empire. An Imperial Memoir of a British Family* (London: I. B. Tauris, 2011), xiv.

7 Letters, Dr Fearon to Dobbs's father, 13 August 1887 and 18 December 1889, unpublished papers.

8 Henry Dobbs: notes from his housemaster's record book, Winchester College archives.

9 David Gilmour, *The Ruling Caste. Imperial Lives in the Victorian Raj* (London: John Murray, 2005), 43–6.

10 Letter, Dobbs to his mother, 21 November 1892, unpublished papers.

11 Ibid.

12 Ibid.

13 Letter, Dobbs to his mother, 1 December 1892, unpublished papers.

14 This province was renamed the United Provinces of Agra and Oudh in 1901 when Curzon created the North-West Frontier Province.

15 Now Udhagamandalam known as Ooty, West of Mysore (now Mysuru) and Southwest of Bangalore (now Bengaluru), itself West of Madras.

16 Now Kodagu district.

17 Letter, Dobbs to his father, 29 January 1901, unpublished papers.

18 Gilmour, *The Ruling Caste*, 76.

19 Letter, Dobbs to his father, 13 December 1892, unpublished papers.

20 Anthony Kirk-Greene, *Britain's Imperial Administrators 1858–1966* (Basingstoke: Macmillan, 2000), 110–24.

21 Gilmour, *The Ruling Caste*, 105.

22 Letter, Dobbs to his father, 13 December 1892, unpublished papers.

23 Ibid.

24 Letter, Dobbs to his mother, 9 January 1893, unpublished papers.

25 Kirk-Greene, *Britain's Imperial Administrators,* 103

26 Letter, Dobbs to his mother, 22 January 1893, unpublished papers.

27 Letter, Dobbs to his mother, 23 March 1893, unpublished papers.

28 Ibid.

29 Letter, Dobbs to his father, 13 December 1892, unpublished papers.

30 Ibid.

31 Letter, Dobbs to his mother, 9 January 1893, unpublished papers.

32 Letter, Dobbs to his mother, 11 August 1898, unpublished papers.

33 Letter sent to his mother.

34 Letter, Dobbs to his mother, 16 June 1898, unpublished papers.

35 Letter, Dobbs to his mother, 8 October 1898, unpublished papers.

36 Letter, Dobbs to his mother, 30 July 1895, unpublished papers.

37 Letter incomplete, Dobbs to unnamed family member, undated, probably December 1892/January 1893.

38 Letter, Dobbs to Wainewright (Dobbs's school friend, see note 5), 13 August 1893, unpublished papers.

39 Letter, Dobbs to Wainewright, 25 July 1893, unpublished papers.

40 Letter, Dobbs to Wainewright, 26 September 1893, unpublished papers.

41 Now Bengaluru, West of Madras.

42 Mildred Dobbs (Henry Dobbs's sister), *Autobiography,* 52–3, unpublished papers of Sir Henry Dobbs. Mildred was in Mysore visiting her brother when the incident took place. Mildred started to write her autobiography probably in 1934 as a record for the benefit of Dobbs's youngest child. A typescript of the unpublished autobiography was found among the Dobbs papers.

43 Letter, Dobbs to his mother, 28 July 1898, unpublished papers.

44 Letter incomplete, Dobbs to unnamed family member, probably mother undated, probably December 1892/January 1893 unpublished papers.

45 Letter, Dobbs to his father, 13 December 1892, unpublished papers.

46 Letter, Dobbs to his mother, 9 January 1893, unpublished papers.

47 Letter, Dobbs to Wainewright, 15 October 1893, unpublished papers.

48 Letter, Dobbs to his mother, 3 January 1894, unpublished papers.

49 Letter, Dobbs to his mother, 30 March 1898, unpublished papers.

50 Letter, Dobbs to his mother, 31 May 1896, unpublished papers. Dobbs had been due to take up the secretariat appointment in May 1894 when the incident occurred and his move was delayed until February 1896. Attitudes towards members of the ICS losing their temper with Indian subordinates is discussed in Gilmour, *The Ruling Caste,* 145–8.

51 Kirk-Greene, *Britain's Imperial Administrators,* 71–3.

52 Letter, Sir Alfred Lyall to Dobbs, 9 November 1894, unpublished papers.

53 Letter, Dobbs to his mother, 29 March 1893, unpublished papers.

54 Letter, Dobbs to his mother, 13 August 1895, unpublished papers.

55 Letter, Dobbs to Wainewright, 3 January 1894, unpublished papers.

56 Letter, Dobbs to Wainewright, 14 June 1893, unpublished papers.

57 Letter incomplete, Dobbs to unnamed family member, probably mother undated, probably August 1896, unpublished papers.

58 Letter, Dobbs to his mother, 2 October 1894, unpublished papers.

59 Letter, Dobbs to Wainewright, 1 June 1896, unpublished papers.

60 Letter, Dobbs to his mother, 19 May 1896, unpublished papers.

61 Kirk-Greene, *Britain's Imperial Administrators*, 114.

62 Letter, Dobbs to his mother, 19 July 1896, unpublished papers.

63 Letter, Dobbs to his mother, 27 September 1896, unpublished papers.

64 Letter, Dobbs to his mother, 19 July 1896, unpublished papers.

65 Letter, Dobbs to his mother, 16 May 1894, unpublished papers.

66 Ibid.

67 Letter, Dobbs to his mother, 30 December 1896, unpublished papers.

68 Letter, Dobbs to his mother, 20 January 1897, unpublished papers.

69 Letter, Dobbs to his mother, 2 March 1898, unpublished papers.

70 Ibid.

71 Letter, Dobbs to his mother, 18 January 1898, unpublished papers.

72 Letter, Dobbs to his mother, 23 February 1899, unpublished papers.

73 Letter, Dobbs to his mother, 4 February 1896, unpublished papers.

74 Letter, Dobbs to his mother, 19 July 1896, unpublished papers.

75 Letter, Dobbs to his mother, 1 February 1898, unpublished papers.

76 Letter, Dobbs to his mother, 23 February 1899, unpublished papers.

77 Ibid.

78 In Persia, now Iran.

79 Sir Antony was appointed permanent under-secretary of Ireland in 1901, where his devolution proposals sparked a major controversy.

80 Letter, Dobbs to his mother, 11 August 1898, unpublished papers.

81 Letter, Dobbs to his mother, 26 May 1898, unpublished papers.

82 Letter, Dobbs to Wainewright, 4 February 1894, unpublished papers.

83 Letter, Dobbs to his mother, 25 December 1892, unpublished papers.

84 Letter, Dobbs to his mother, 31 March 1898, unpublished papers.

85 Letter, Dobbs to his mother, 24 August 1899, unpublished papers.

86 Letter, Dobbs to his father, 29 January 1901, unpublished papers.

3 **Neighbours, frontiers and tribes 1901 to 1914:** Exploring Arabia and Persia; the Russian threat and Afghanistan; working with tribal leaders in British India's northwest frontier provinces

1 Letter, Dobbs to his father, 29 January 1901, unpublished papers.
2 The expression began to be used in this sense in the mid-nineteenth century, was more commonly used after it appeared in Rudyard Kipling's novel, *Kim*, and became more popular in the mid-twentieth century.
3 Letter, Dobbs to his mother, 29 September 1901, unpublished papers.
4 Letter, Dobbs to his mother, 24 August 1899, unpublished papers.
5 Letter, Dobbs to his mother, 7 January 1903, unpublished papers.
6 Francis Rawdon Chesney, *Narrative of the Euphrates Expedition. Carried on by Order of the British Government during the Years 1835, 1836, and 1837* (London: Longmans, Green & Co., 1868).
7 Letter, Dobbs to his mother, 29 December 1902, unpublished papers.
8 Letter, Dobbs to his mother, 18 January 1903, unpublished papers.
9 Letter, Dobbs to his mother, dated 26 January 1903 (covers the period to 5 March 1903), unpublished papers.
10 Ibid.
11 Ibid.
12 Letter, Dobbs to his mother, 3 April 1903, unpublished papers.
13 Ibid.
14 Letter, Dobbs to his mother, 23 April 1903, unpublished papers.
15 Probably Percy Molesworth Sykes' Royal Geographical Society publications and Hon. George N. Curzon MP, *Persia and the Persian Question* in two volumes (London: Longmans Green & Co., 1892).
16 Letter, Dobbs to his mother, 23 April 1903, unpublished papers.
17 Letter, Dobbs to his mother, 26 April 1903, unpublished papers.
18 Ibid.
19 Punishment by caning the soles of the feet.
20 Letter, Dobbs to his mother, 10 July 1903, unpublished papers.
21 Ibid.
22 Letter, Dobbs to his mother, 22 August 1903, unpublished papers.
23 Letter, Dobbs to his mother, 18 January 1903, unpublished papers.
24 Letter, Dobbs to his mother, 16 November 1903, unpublished papers.
25 Ludwig W. Adamec, *Afghanistan 1900–1923. A Diplomatic History* (Berkeley: University of California Press, 1967), 34–7.
26 Dobbs's political journal, entry on 24 October 1903, unpublished papers.
27 Letter, Dobbs to his mother, 16 November 1903, unpublished papers.

28 Letter, Dobbs to his mother, 29 November 1903, unpublished papers.

29 Letters, Dobbs to his mother, 8 and 29 December 1903, unpublished papers.

30 Dobbs's political journal, entry on 20 June 1904, unpublished papers.

31 Letter, Dobbs to his mother, 21 June 1904, unpublished papers.

32 Dobbs's political journal, entry on 12 July 1904, unpublished papers.

33 Letter, Dobbs to his mother, 15 July 1904, unpublished papers.

34 Letter, Louis Dane (later Sir Louis Dane), foreign secretary to the Government of India, to Henry Dobbs, 12 September 1904. The letter records not only Dane's commendation but also that of the governor-general in council (the viceroy). Unpublished papers.

35 Translation of a letter from His Highness the Amir (Amir Habibullah Khan), GCMG, to the address of the foreign secretary, 11 November 1904. IOR/Mss Eur F111/293 (Curzon Papers), British Library (hereafter BL).

36 Adamec, *Afghanistan 1900–1923*, chapter 3.

37 Letter, Dobbs to his mother, 24 March 1905, unpublished papers.

38 David Gilmour, *Curzon. Imperial Statesman 1859–1925* (London: John Murray 1994, paperback 2003), 321–2. Citations are to the paperback edition.

39 Letter, Dobbs to his mother, 22 April 1905, unpublished papers.

40 Ibid.

41 Letter, Dobbs to his mother, 9 December 1904, unpublished papers.

42 Agent to the governor-general and chief commissioner in Balochistan (1905 to 1911) where Dobbs joined his staff. He was high commissioner for Egypt (1914 to 1916). His responsibilities included the Arab Bureau, and he initiated correspondence with the Shariff of Mecca, which led to serious misunderstandings with the Arabs.

43 *Report of Col. Sir Henry McMahon K.C.I.E., C.S.I. Chief Officer on Special Duty with the Amir of Afghanistan* (Simla: Government Press, 1907).

44 *McMahon Report*, 10.

45 Letter, Dobbs to his mother, undated, incomplete, probably February 1907, unpublished papers.

46 Letter, Dobbs to his mother, 7 March 1907, unpublished papers.

47 Ibid.

48 George Rivaz served in India from 1870 to 1897. His last appointment in 1891 was as a divisional judge.

49 Letter, Dobbs to his mother, 7 March 1907, unpublished papers.

50 Letter, Dobbs to his mother, 4 March 1908, unpublished papers.

51 Ibid.

52 Ibid.

53 Ibid.

54 Letter, Dobbs to his mother, 26 January 1903, unpublished papers.

55 H. R. C. Dobbs, *Diary 1908*: Entries for 18 and 25 April, 11 and 12 May, unpublished papers.

56 Letter, Dobbs to his mother, 3 June 1908, unpublished papers.

57 Abbas Amanat, *Iran. A Modern History* (New Haven, CT: Yale University Press, 2017), 349–50.

58 Letter, Dobbs to his mother, 24 May 1909, unpublished papers.

59 Letter, Dobbs to his wife, 21 November 1917, unpublished papers.

60 Letter, Dobbs to his mother, 24 May 1909, unpublished papers.

61 Letter, Dobbs to his father, 19 December 1910, unpublished papers.

62 Letter, Dobbs to his mother, 27 June 1909, unpublished papers.

63 Letter, Dobbs to his mother, 17 October 1910, unpublished papers.

64 Ibid.

65 Letter, Dobbs to his mother, 12 April 1913, unpublished papers.

66 Letter, Dobbs to his mother, 30 June 1913, unpublished papers.

67 Letter, Dobbs to his mother, probably January 1914, unpublished papers.

68 Letter, Dobbs to his mother, 30 June 1913, unpublished papers.

69 Letter, Dobbs to his mother, 10 May 1910, unpublished papers.

70 A reference to the constitutional crisis of 1909–11. This resulted from the House of Lords' refusal to pass the 'people's budget' and concluded with the 1911 Parliament Act which, among other important constitutional changes, removed the House of Lords' power to reject money bills.

71 Letter, Dobbs to his mother, 24 December 1911, and some loose pages probably written a little earlier, unpublished papers.

72 Letter, Dobbs to his mother, 12 April 1913, unpublished papers.

73 Letter, Dobbs to his mother, 21 May 1913, unpublished papers.

74 For a discussion of the 'Sandeman system', see for example Christian Tripodi, *Edge of Empire. The British Political Officer and Tribal Administration on the North West Frontier 1877–1947* (Farnham: Ashgate 2011), 49–69.

75 Letter, Dobbs to his mother, 5 November 1909, unpublished papers.

76 Letter, Dobbs to his father, 19 December 1910, unpublished papers.

77 Letter, Dobbs to his mother, probably January 1914, unpublished papers.

78 Ibid.

79 Letter, Dobbs to his mother, 12 June 1910, unpublished papers.

80 Letter, Dobbs to his mother, 6 February 1914, unpublished papers.

81 Letter, Dobbs to his mother, 5 July 1914, unpublished papers.

82 See, for example, Benjamin D. Hopkins, *Ruling the Savage Periphery: Frontier Governance and the Making of the Modern State* (Cambridge, MA: Harvard University Press, 2020), 28–52.

83 Letter, Dobbs to his mother, 18 January 1914, unpublished papers.

84 Letter, Dobbs to his wife, 13 April 1915, unpublished papers.

4 **Mesopotamia 1915 to 1916:** Administration in a newly occupied territory; Battle of Ctesiphon; working unescorted among the marsh Arabs; opposing the imposition of the Indian model

1 Letter, Dobbs to his mother, 22 July 1914, unpublished papers.

2 Charles Townshend, *When God Made Hell: The British Invasion of Mesopotamia and the Creation of Iraq 1914–1921* (London: Faber and Faber 2010; paperback 2011), 63. Citations are to the paperback edition.

3 Peter Sluglett, *Britain in Iraq. Contriving King and Country* (London: I. B. Tauris, 2007), 9.

4 Letter, Dobbs to his mother, 23 December 1914, unpublished papers.

5 Letters, Dobbs to his wife, unpublished papers.

6 Letter, Dobbs to his mother, 19 August 1914, unpublished papers.

7 Letter, Dobbs to his mother, 14 February 1915, unpublished papers.

8 Ibid.

9 Sluglett, *Britain in Iraq*, 10.

10 *Review of the Civil Administration of Mesopotamia. A Report from the Acting Civil Commissioner Prepared by Miss Gertrude Bell.* Presented to both Houses of Parliament on 3rd December 1920. Command Paper 1061. Great Britain India Office (London: HMSO), 5. (Hereafter Bell Report 1920).

11 Letter, Dobbs to his wife, 14 June 1915, unpublished papers.

12 Letter, Dobbs to his wife, undated, probably 6 May 1915, unpublished papers.

13 Ibid.

14 Bell Report 1920, 7.

15 Letter, Dobbs to his wife, undated, probably 6 May 1915, unpublished papers.

16 Letter, Dobbs to his wife, 25 August 1915, unpublished papers.

17 Letter, Dobbs to his wife, undated, probably 6 May 1915, unpublished papers.

18 Letter, Dobbs to his wife, 26 May 1915, unpublished papers.

19 Letter, Dobbs to his wife, 11 March 1915, unpublished papers.

20 Letter, Dobbs to his wife, 28 April 1915, unpublished papers.

21 Letter, Dobbs to his wife, 25 September 1915, unpublished papers.

22 Letter, Dobbs to his wife, 19 June 1915, unpublished papers.

23 Letter, Dobbs to his wife, 27 June 1915, unpublished papers.

24 Letter, Dobbs to his wife, 6 August 1915, unpublished papers.

25 An Indian measurement of weight.

26 Letter, Dobbs to his wife, 25 August 1915, unpublished papers.

27 Letters, Dobbs to his wife, 8 and 18 September 1915, unpublished papers.

28 Letter, Dobbs to his wife, 5 October 1915, unpublished papers.

29 Letter, Dobbs to his mother, 2 November 1915, unpublished papers.

30 Sluglett, *Britain in Iraq*, 10–11.

31 Townshend, *When God Made Hell*, 142.

32 The ancient Parthian capital, today's Salman Pak named after a companion of the prophet whose tomb was there.

33 Townshend, *When God Made Hell*, 155–7.

34 Groom.

35 Mounted soldiers.

36 Letter, Dobbs to his wife, 24 November 1915, unpublished papers.

37 Ibid.

38 Townshend, *When God Made Hell*, 157–79.

39 For an account of these developments see Townshend *When God Made Hell*, 180–396.

40 Letter, Dobbs to his wife, 9 December 1915, unpublished papers.

41 Letter, Dobbs to his mother, 26 December 1915, unpublished papers.

42 Letter, Dobbs to his wife, 2 January 1916, unpublished papers.

43 Letter, Dobbs to his mother, 26 December 1915, unpublished papers.

44 Ibid.

45 Letter, Dobbs to his wife, 6 February 1916, unpublished papers.

46 Ibid.

47 Letter, Dobbs to his wife, 20 February 1916, unpublished papers.

48 A reed hall where the local Sheikh held meetings and entertained guests.

49 Letter, Dobbs to his wife, 20 February 1916, unpublished papers.

50 Ibid.

51 Letter, Dobbs to his mother, 23 March 1916, unpublished papers.

52 Benjamin D. Hopkins, *Ruling the Savage Periphery: Frontier Governance and the Making of the Modern State* (Cambridge, MA: Harvard University Press, 2020), 67.

53 Letter, Dobbs to his mother, 23 January 1916, unpublished papers.

54 Sluglett, *Britain in Iraq*, 169–71.

55 Letter, Dobbs to his wife 18 September 1915, unpublished papers.

56 Discussed in Chapter 3, 15 to 17.

57 For the wider implications of Dobbs's approach see Chapter 7, p. 142.

58 Letter, Dobbs to his mother, 28 April 1916, unpublished papers.

59 Letter, Dobbs to his wife, 31 January 1916, unpublished papers.

60 Letter, Dobbs to his wife, 18 June 1916, unpublished papers.

61 Letter, Dobbs to his wife, 23 January 1916, unpublished papers.

62 Letter, Dobbs to his wife, 12 June 1916, unpublished papers.

63 Letter, Dobbs to his wife, 28 May 1916, unpublished papers.

64 Letter, Dobbs to his wife, 23 May 1916, unpublished papers.

65 Townshend, *When God Made Hell*, 328–36.

66 Letter, Dobbs to his wife, 12 June 1916, unpublished papers.

67 Letter, Dobbs to his mother, 23 January 1916, unpublished papers.

68 Ibid.

69 John Townsend, *Proconsul to the Middle East: Sir Percy Cox and the End of Empire* (London: I. B. Tauris, 2010), 40, 58, 62.

70 Dobbs's approach is discussed in more detail in Chapter 6, p. 104.

71 Sluglett, *Britain in Iraq*, 9–11.

72 Letter, Dobbs to his wife, undated, probably 6 May 1915, unpublished papers.

73 Townsend, *Proconsul to the Middle East*, 43.

74 Letter, Dobbs to his wife, undated, probably 6 May 1915, unpublished papers.

75 Ibid.

76 Townshend, *When God Made Hell*, 260–82.

77 Sluglett, *Britain in Iraq*, 10.

78 Letter, Hirtzel to Dobbs, 27 January 1920, unpublished papers.

79 Letter, Dobbs to his wife, 6 July 1916, unpublished papers.

80 Letter, Dobbs to his wife, 15 March 1916, unpublished papers.

81 Letter, Dobbs to his wife, 19 October 1915, unpublished papers.

82 Letter, Dobbs to his wife, 15 May 1916, unpublished papers.

83 Townsend, *Proconsul to the Middle East*, 85.

84 Letter, Dobbs to his wife, 28 June 1916, unpublished papers.

85 Townsend, *Proconsul to the Middle East*, 104.

86 Letter, Dobbs to his wife, 14 May 1915, unpublished papers.

87 Letter, Dobbs to his wife, 15 May 1916, unpublished papers.

88 Letter, Dobbs to his wife, 28 June 1916, unpublished papers.

5 On the edge of India and in Afghanistan 1917 to 1921: From governing Balochistan to concluding the 1921 Anglo-Afghan Treaty

1 Letter, Dobbs to his wife, 15 April 1917, unpublished papers.

2 Letter, Dobbs to his wife, 28 October 1917, unpublished papers.

3 John Townsend, *Proconsul to the Middle East. Sir Percy Cox and the End of Empire* (London: I. B. Tauris, 2010), 92.

4 Letter, Dobbs to his wife, 28 October 1917, unpublished papers.

5 Letter, Dobbs to his wife, 25 April 1917, unpublished papers.

6 Letter, Dobbs to his mother, 18 September 1917, unpublished papers.

7 Letter, Dobbs to his wife, 17 October 1917, unpublished papers.

8 Letter, Dobbs to his wife, 11 July 1917, unpublished papers.

9 Letter, Dobbs to his mother, 10 October 1917, unpublished papers.

10 See for example, T. G. Otte, *Statesman of Europe: A Life of Sir Edward Grey* (London: Allen Lane, 2020), 555.

11 The nineteenth century struggle between Russia and Britain for influence in central and south Asia generally in which the British focus was on protecting British India.

12 Nearly 400 miles of track were added, taking it as far as Zahedan in Persia.

13 Letter, Dobbs to his wife, 17 October 1917, unpublished papers.

14 See for example, Abbas Amanat, *Iran. A Modern History* (New Haven, CT: Yale University Press, 2017), 348–52; 367–76.

15 Letter, Dobbs to his wife, 15 November 1917, unpublished papers.

16 Letter, Dobbs to his wife, 5 May 1918, unpublished papers.

17 Letter, Dobbs to his wife, 6 December 1917, unpublished papers.

18 Ibid. (Ruat Coelum: full Latin tag is *fiat iustitia, ruat coelum* – let justice be done though the heavens fall).

19 Letter, Dobbs to his mother, 6 June 1918, unpublished papers.

20 Letter, Dobbs to his wife, 5 May 1918, unpublished papers.

21 Letter, Dobbs to his wife, 15 November 1917, unpublished papers.

22 Letter, Dobbs to his wife, 10 April 1918, unpublished papers.

23 Letter, Dobbs to his wife, 6 December 1917, unpublished papers.

24 Letter, Dobbs to his wife, 5 May 1918, unpublished papers.

25 Horseman, private Indian Army equivalent of British Army trooper.

26 Letter, Dobbs to his wife, 10 April 1918, unpublished papers.

27 Ibid.

28 Letter, Dobbs to his wife, 17 February 1918, unpublished papers.

29 Letter, Dobbs to his mother 6 June 1918, unpublished papers.

30 Letter, Dobbs to his wife, 10 April 1918, unpublished papers.

31 Letter, Dobbs to his mother, 29 August 1918, unpublished papers.

32 Letter, Dobbs to his mother, 21 January 1919, unpublished papers.

33 Letter, Dobbs to his wife, 15 April 1917, unpublished papers.

34 Letter, Dobbs to his mother, 21 January 1919, unpublished papers.

35 Letter, Dobbs to his mother, 5 April 1920, unpublished papers.

36 Letter, viceroy (Lord Chelmsford) to Sir A. H. (Tony) Grant, 28 October 1919, IOR/MSS/EUR/D660/25, British Library.

37 Letter, Dobbs to Sir Arthur Hirtzel, 6 April 1920, unpublished papers.

38 Faiz Ahmed, *Afghanistan Rising. Islamic Law and Statecraft between the Ottoman and British Empires* (Cambridge, MA: Harvard University Press, 2017), 202–3.

39 *Foreign Department Note: Afghan Policy*, March 1921, unpublished papers.

40 Ludwig W. Adamec, *Afghanistan 1900–1923: A Diplomatic History* (Berkeley: University of California Press, 1967), 119, 131.

41 Letter, Hirtzel to Dobbs, 27 January 1920, unpublished papers.

42 Dobbs's views on the situation and the background to it are discussed in Ann Wilks, 'The 1921 Anglo-Afghan Treaty: How Britain's "Man on the Spot" Shaped This Agreement', *Journal of the Royal Asiatic Society* Series 3, 29, 1 (2019): 80–3.

43 Adamec, *Afghanistan*, 116.

44 *Foreign Department Note: Afghan Policy*, March 1921, unpublished papers, 15, 11.

45 Letter, Dobbs to Hirtzel, 6 April 1920, unpublished papers.

46 Ibid.

47 Ahmed, *Afghanistan Rising*, 203.

48 Letter, Dobbs to Hirtzel, 6 April 1920, unpublished papers.

49 *Report on the British-Afghan Conference Held at Mussoorie between the Middle of April and End of July 1920 from the Chief British Representative (H. R. C. Dobbs) to the Foreign Secretary to the Government of India, Simla 6 August 1920, 2–4, IOR/L/ PS/10/811.BL* (hereafter *Mussoorie Conference Report*).

50 *Mussoorie Conference Report 4–5.*

51 Letter, Dobbs to his mother, 5 April 1920, unpublished papers.

52 *Mussoorie Conference Report*, 5.

53 Ibid., 12.

54 Ibid.

55 Letter, Dobbs to his mother, 12 May 1920, unpublished papers.

56 Wallace Lyon, *Kurds, Arabs and Britons. The Memoir of Wallace Lyon in Iraq 1918–44.* Edited and with an Introduction by D. K. Fieldhouse (London: I. B. Tauris, 2002), 136.

57 *Mussoorie Conference Report*, 9.

58 Ibid., 11.

59 Ibid.

60 *Report on the Negotiations Conducted by the British Mission to Kabul during the Year 1921 from Sir Henry Dobbs Chief British Representative to Mr Denys Bray Foreign Secretary to the Government of India.* Secret. Simla. 9 January 1922, 2 (hereafter *Kabul Report*) IOR/L/PS/18/A194 BL.

61 Adamec, *Afghanistan*, 159.

62 Letter, Dobbs to his wife, 14 December 1920, unpublished papers.

63 *Kabul Report*, 10.

64 Ann Wilks, 'The 1921 Anglo-Afghan Treaty', *JRAS* Series 3, 29, 1 (2019): 86.

65 Letter, Dobbs to his mother, 29 January 1921, unpublished papers.

66 Ann Wilks, 'The 1921 Anglo-Afghan Treaty' *JRAS* Series 3, 29, 1 (2019): 87.

67 *Kabul Report*, 8.

68 Letter, Dobbs to his wife, 12 February 1921, unpublished papers.

69 Ibid.

70 *Kabul Report*, 3.

71 Letter, Dobbs to his wife, 11 June 1921, unpublished papers.

72 Ibid.

73 Letter, Dobbs to his wife, 9 March 1921, unpublished papers.

74 Letter, Dobbs to his wife, 1 April 1921, unpublished papers.

75 Letter, Dobbs to Hirtzel, 6 April 1920, unpublished papers.

76 Letter, Dobbs to his wife, 15 April 1921, unpublished papers.

77 Ibid.

78 Telegram, Dobbs to Reading, 19 April 1921, unpublished papers.

79 See for example, *Kabul Report*, 18.

80 Letter, Dobbs to his wife, 15 April 1921, unpublished papers.

81 Letter, Dobbs to his wife, 28 May 1921, unpublished papers.

82 Letter, Hirtzel to Dobbs, 1 June 1921, unpublished papers.

83 *Kabul Report*, 13–14.

84 *Diary of the Kabul Mission 1921*, 5 January, unpublished papers.

85 *Diary of the Kabul Mission 1921*, 3 March, unpublished papers.

86 *Diary of the Kabul Mission 1921*, 17 March, unpublished papers.

87 *Diary of the Kabul Mission 1921*, 8 June, unpublished papers.

88 *Diary of the Kabul Mission 1921*, 12 September, unpublished papers.

89 *Diary of the Kabul Mission 1921*, 8 November, IOR/L/PS/10/957/1, BL and unpublished papers.

90 *Kabul Report*, 8.

91 *Kabul Report*, 13–14.

92 Letter, Dobbs to his wife, 31 August 1921, unpublished papers.

93 Letter, Dobbs to his wife, 8 July 1921, unpublished papers.

94 Letter, Dobbs to his wife, 6 July 1921, unpublished papers.

95 Letter, Dobbs to his wife, 3 August 1921, unpublished papers.

96 Ibid.

97 Secretary of state for India to viceroy. Telegram 3961, 5 August 1921.IOR/L/PS10/955/1. BL.

98 Ann Wilks, 'The 1921 Anglo-Afghan Treaty' *JRAS* Series 3, 29, 1 (2019): 90.

99 *Kabul Report*, 15.

100 Ann Wilks, 'The 1921 Anglo-Afghan Treaty' *JRAS* Series 3, 29, 1 (2019): 91.

101 Dobbs to PS/Viceroy, Telegram 319, 5 October 1921, unpublished papers.

102 Letter, Dobbs to his wife, 5 October 1921, unpublished papers.

103 Letter, Dobbs to his wife, 12 October 1921, unpublished papers.

104 Letter, Dobbs to his wife, 26 October 1921, unpublished papers.

105 Letter, Dobbs to his wife, 5 November 1921, unpublished papers.

106 Letter, Dobbs to his wife, 19 November 1921, unpublished papers.

107 Dobbs to foreign secretary to the Government of India, Telegram 366, 12 November 1921, unpublished papers.

108 Letter, Dobbs to his wife, 19 November 1921, unpublished papers.

109 *Kabul Report*, 17.

110 Letter, Hirtzel to Dobbs, 30 November 1921, unpublished papers.

111 *Kabul Report*, 17.

112 *Mussoorie Conference Report*, 12.

113 *Kabul Report*, 18.

114 Letter, Dobbs to his wife, 21 December 1921, unpublished papers.

6 **Iraq at last 1922 to 1924:** Appointment as high commissioner; expelling Turkish elements from northern Iraq; winning Iraqi support for the unpopular 1922 Anglo-Iraq Treaty

1 Letter, Dobbs to his wife, 15 April 1921, unpublished papers of Sir Henry Dobbs (hereafter unpublished papers).

2 Letter, Dobbs to his wife, 21 December 1921, unpublished papers.

3 See for example his letter to Hubert Young in October 1919 referred to in C. Brad Faught, *Cairo 1921. Ten Days That Made the Middle East* (New Haven, CT: Yale University Press, 2022).

4 Letter, Dobbs to his mother, 21 January 1919, unpublished papers.

5 Letter, Dobbs to Gertrude Bell, 6 January 1918, unpublished papers.

6 Susan Pedersen, *The Guardians. The League of Nations and the Crisis of Empire* (Oxford: Oxford University Press, 2015, paperback 2017), Appendix 1, 408. *The Covenant of the League of Nations, Article 22*. Citations are to the paperback edition.

7 Pedersen, *The Guardians*, 35.

8 Letter, Hirtzel to Dobbs, 27 January 1920, unpublished papers.

9 Peter Sluglett, *Britain in Iraq. Contriving King and Country* (London: I. B. Tauris, 2007), 34.

10 John Townsend, *Proconsul to the Middle East. Sir Percy Cox and the End of Empire* (London: I. B. Tauris, 2010), 140.

11 Warren Dockter, *Churchill and the Islamic World. Orientalism Empire and Diplomacy in the Middle East* (London: I. B. Tauris, Bloomsbury Publishing, 2019), 124.

12 Ibid., 132–3.

13 Outlined in Chapter 1, this volume.

14 Faught, *Cairo 1921*, 84–5.

15 Ibid., 157.

16 Ibid., 104–5.

17 *Report of the High Commissioner on the Development of Iraq 1920–1925. Colonial Office Confidential Print, 6 August 1925*, 10 (hereafter *Iraq Report*) *CO 935/1/11*, National Archives, Kew (hereafter, NA).

18 Dockter, *Churchill and the Islamic World*, 96.

19 In particular, Letter Dobbs to his wife, 10 April 1918, unpublished papers

20 These ministers were members of the liberal/conservative government led by Lloyd George. It lasted until October 1922 when the conservatives withdrew their support and forced a general election which they won in November 1922, then forming a new government.

21 Dobbs to Mary Rivaz (mother-in-law) 22 February and 22 May 1922, unpublished papers.

22 A. J. P. Taylor, *English History 1914–1945* ((Oxford: Oxford University Press, 1965) Paperback, Harmondsworth: Penguin Books, 1970), 254. Citations are to the paperback edition.

23 Their disagreement was over the relationship with Britain.

24 Mildred Dobbs, *Autobiography,* unpublished papers, 122.

25 Letter, Dobbs to his wife, 9 December 1922, unpublished papers.

26 Quoted in Toby Dodge, *Inventing Iraq. The Failure of Nation Building and a History Denied* (London: Hurst & Company, 2003), 26.

27 Letter, Dobbs to his wife, 31 December 1922, unpublished papers.

28 Ibid.

29 Letter, Dobbs to his wife, 23 December 1922, unpublished papers.

30 David Gilmour, *Curzon. Imperial Statesman 1859–1925* (London: John Murray, 1994, paperback edition 2003). Citations are to the paperback edition, chapter 35; also Sluglett, *Britain in Iraq*, chapter 3.

31 Churchill had decided that in the Middle East and similar areas, the RAF should provide the commanding officer; Dockter, *Churchill and the Islamic World*, 105.

32 Dobbs to his wife, 31 January 1923, unpublished papers.

33 Letter, Dobbs to his wife, 1 March 1923, unpublished papers.

34 Letter, Dobbs to his wife, 22 April 1923, unpublished papers.

35 George Lansbury, 12 April 1923, Hansard, *House of Commons Sittings, Series 5 vol. 162 cols 1300–1301.*

36 Letter, Dobbs to his wife, 8 April 1923, unpublished papers

37 Margaret MacMillan, *Peacemakers. The Paris Conference of 1919 and Its Attempt to End War* (London: John Murray, 2001, paperback 2002), 464–5. Citations are to the paperback edition.

38 Letter, Dobbs to his wife, 22 April 1923, unpublished papers.

39 Sluglett, *Britain in Iraq*, 46.

40 Pedersen, *The Guardians*, 263.

41 Charles Tripp, *A History of Iraq* (Cambridge: Cambridge University Press (2000) 3rd edition, 2007), 51.

42 *Iraq Report 1920–1925*, 16.

43 Letter, Cox to Dobbs, 22 February 1923.
44 *Reply by Sir Percy Cox to the Cabinet Committee on Iraq's Questionnaire* (CAB 27/206) IRQ 40 Revised 5 February 1923, NA (Hereafter Cox's response to the committee, 5 February 1923).
45 *Cabinet Memorandum, Committee on Iraq*, CAB 23/45/22, 26 April 1923, NA.
46 Letter, Dobbs to his wife, 8 April 1923, unpublished papers.
47 Letter, Dobbs to his wife, 9 May 1923, unpublished papers.
48 Ibid.
49 Ibid.
50 Ali Allawi, *Faisal I of Iraq* (New Haven, CT: Yale University Press, 2014), chapter 18.
51 High commissioner Baghdad to secretary of state for the colonies, letter, 10 January 1924, CO 730/57/3271 NA.
52 Sluglett, *Britain in Iraq*, 51.
53 Cox's response to the committee, 5 February 1923.
54 Letter, Dobbs to his wife, 1 July 1923, unpublished papers.
55 Ibid.
56 Letter, Dobbs to his mother, 30 July 1923, unpublished papers.
57 Sir Percy later served as high commissioner for Egypt and ambassador to Turkey where he developed a very close relationship with Mustafa Kemal (Atatürk), ending his diplomatic career as ambassador to Italy in 1939.
58 Letter, Dobbs to his wife, 20 July 1923, unpublished papers.
59 Letter, Dobbs to his mother, 30 July 1923, unpublished papers.
60 Ibid.
61 Allawi, *Faisal*, 426.
62 Sluglett, *Britain in Iraq*, 58.
63 Letter, Dobbs to his wife, 5 August 1923, unpublished papers.
64 Letter, Dobbs to his wife, 22 August 1923, unpublished papers.
65 Letter, Dobbs to his wife, 1 July 1923, unpublished papers.
66 Ibid.
67 Letter, Dobbs to his mother, 1 October 1923, unpublished papers.
68 Letter, Dobbs to his wife, 9 May 1923, unpublished papers.
69 Pedersen, *The Guardians*, 263.
70 Letter, Dobbs to his mother, 1 October 1923, unpublished papers.
71 Letter, Dobbs to his mother, 13 November 1923, unpublished papers.
72 Letter, Dobbs to his mother, 17 January 1924, unpublished papers.
73 Ibid.
74 Letter, Dobbs to his mother, 30 January 1924, unpublished papers.
75 Allawi, *Faisal*, 435.
76 Ibid., 436.

77 Letter, Dobbs to his mother, 1 May 1924, unpublished papers.

78 Allawi, *Faisal*, 441.

79 Pedersen, *The Guardians*, Appendix 1, 409. *The Covenant of the League of Nations*, Article 22.

80 *Iraq Report 1920–1925*, 22.

81 Philip Ireland, *Iraq: A Study in Political Development* (London: Kegan Paul, [1937] 2004), 396.

82 Letter, Dobbs to his wife, 21 May 1924, unpublished papers.

83 Letter, Dobbs to his wife, 29 May 1924, unpublished papers.

84 *Iraq Report 1920–1925*, 21–2.

85 Letter, Dobbs to his wife, 21 May 1924, unpublished papers; also high commissioner Baghdad to secretary of state for the colonies, telegram CO/730/59/23489, 15 May 1924, NA.

86 Secretary of state for the colonies to high commissioner Baghdad, telegram CO730/59/22744, 14 May 1924, NA.

87 Martin Gilbert, *Winston S. Churchill Volume IV 1916–1922* (London: Heineman 1975), 524.

88 Letter, Dobbs to his wife, 21 May 1924, unpublished papers.

89 Letter, Dobbs to his wife, 29 May 1924, unpublished papers.

90 Letter, Dobbs to his mother, 1 May 1924, unpublished papers.

91 Letter, Dobbs to his wife, 29 May 1924, unpublished papers.

92 Letter, Dobbs to his wife, 5 June 1924, unpublished papers.

93 Ibid.

94 Ibid.

95 Ibid.

96 Letter, Dobbs to his wife, 12 June 1924, unpublished papers.

97 Ibid.

98 Ibid.

99 Ibid.

100 Ibid.

101 Ibid.

102 Ibid.

103 *The Letters of Gertrude Bell*, selected and edited by Lady Bell, Volume II (London: Ernest Benn, 1927), 698.

104 Letter, Dobbs to his wife, 19 June 1924, unpublished papers.

105 Letter, Dobbs to his wife, 25 June 1924, unpublished papers.

106 Letter, Dobbs to his wife, 19 June 1924, unpublished papers.

107 Letter, Dobbs to his mother, 1 May 1924, unpublished papers.

108 Letter, Dobbs to his wife, 12 June 1924, unpublished papers.

109 Ibid.

7 Moving towards independence for Iraq 1924 to 1929: Securing Mosul for Iraq; concerns over minorities; death of Gertrude Bell; Mustafa Kemal (Atatürk) confides in Dobbs; tensions over finance and military questions; progress towards independence

1 Letter, Dobbs to his wife, 23 March 1925, unpublished papers.

2 Letter, Dobbs to his mother, 16 December 1924, unpublished papers.

3 Margaret MacMillan, *Peacemakers. The Paris Conference of 1919 and Its Attempt to End War* (London: John Murray, 2001, paperback 2002), 463. Citations are to the paperback edition.

4 David Gilmour, *Curzon. Imperial Statesman 1859–1925* (London: John Murray, 1994, paperback edition 2003), 563. Citations are to the paperback edition.

5 Peter Sluglett, *Britain in Iraq. Contriving King and Country* (London: I. B. Tauris, 2007), 73.

6 Gilmour, *Curzon*, 565.

7 Susan Pedersen, *The Guardians. The League of Nations and the Crisis of Empire* (Oxford: Oxford University Press, 2015, paperback 2017), 264. Citations are to the paperback edition.

8 Sluglett, *Britain in Iraq*, 84.

9 Letter, Dobbs to his wife, 11 August 1925, unpublished papers.

10 Letter, Dobbs to his wife, 12 June 1924, unpublished papers.

11 Ali Allawi, *Faisal I of Iraq* (New Haven, CT: Yale University Press, 2014), 453.

12 Ibid., 452.

13 Letter, Dobbs to his mother, 16 February 1925, unpublished papers.

14 Ibid.

15 Allawi, *Faisal*, 453.

16 Despatch (private and confidential), Sir Herbert Dering, 15 April 1925, unpublished papers (hereafter Dering despatch). Sir Herbert was British minister to Romania.

17 *League of Nations Permanent Mandates Commission, Minutes of the Tenth Session from November 4th to 19th 1926: Examination of the Annual Reports for 1923–24 and 1925: General Statement by the Accredited Representative (Sir Henry Dobbs), at meetings seven to ten on November 8th and 9th, Geneva 1926* (hereafter *Mandates Commission*, 1926), 50.

18 Letter, Dobbs to his wife, 26 March 1925, unpublished papers.

19 Letter, Dobbs to his mother, 16 February 1925, unpublished papers.

20 Letter, Dobbs to his wife, 24 April 1925, unpublished papers.

21 Dering despatch, unpublished papers.

22 Letter, Dobbs to his mother, 16 February 1925, unpublished papers.

23 Letter, Dobbs to his wife, 18 May 1925, unpublished papers.
24 Letter, Dobbs to his wife, 23 August 1925, unpublished papers.
25 Ibid.
26 Ibid.
27 Letter, Dobbs to his wife, 17 September 1925, unpublished papers.
28 Letter, Dobbs to his wife, 23 September 1925, unpublished papers.
29 Letter, Dobbs to his wife, 24 May 1926, unpublished papers.
30 According to Ataturk's biographer, Lord Kinross, Mustafa Kemal had no intention of fighting with the British over Mosul. Lord Kinross, *Atatürk. The Rebirth of a Nation* (London: Wiedenfeld and Nicolson, 1964), 409–10.
31 Letter, Dobbs to his wife, 16 June 1926, unpublished papers.
32 Telegram No C. 1547, from Sir Samuel Hoare (secretary of state for air) to Dobbs, 9 June 1926, unpublished papers.
33 Letter, Dobbs to his wife, 23 February 1927, unpublished papers. Dobbs had returned to Iraq via Beirut and his original account had gone astray – he suggested stolen by the French – so he rewrote it.
34 Ibid.
35 Letter, Dobbs to his wife, 2 March 1927, unpublished papers.
36 Ibid.
37 Ibid.
38 Ibid.
39 *Report of the High Commissioner on the Development of Iraq 1920–1925. Colonial Office Confidential Print, 6 August 1925, 31–2* (hereafter *Iraq Report*) CO 935/1/11, National Archives, Kew (hereafter NA).
40 Pedersen, *The Guardians*, 267.
41 MacMillan, *Peacemakers*, 455–9.
42 Sluglett, *Britain in Iraq*, 79–81.
43 *Iraq Report 1920–1925*, 26.
44 Dobbs's statement to Mandates Commission 1926, 60.
45 Letter, Dobbs to George Rivaz (Dobbs's father-in-law), 15 August 1933, unpublished papers.
46 Ibid.
47 *Mandates Commission* 1926, 61–2.
48 *Mandates Commission* 1926, 60.
49 Sluglett, *Britain in Iraq*, 124–35,140–6, 150–1.
50 Pedersen, *The Guardians*, 282.
51 Allawi, *Faisal*, 554–60.
52 Letter, Dobbs to his wife, 17 September 1924, unpublished papers.
53 Letter, Dobbs to his wife, 11 June 1925, unpublished papers.
54 Letter, Dobbs to his wife, 15 July 1926, unpublished papers.

55 Letter, Dobbs to his mother, 14 July 1926, unpublished papers.
56 Gertrude Bell to her father, 18 May 1926, *The Letters of Gertrude Bell*, selected and edited by Lady Bell, Volume II (London: Ernest Benn, 1927), 763.
57 Letter, Dobbs to his wife, 4 May 1926 (comment reported to Dobbs by the wife of Palestine's high commissioner, Lady Plumer), unpublished papers.
58 Letter, Dobbs to his wife, 22 July 1926, unpublished papers.
59 Most recently in Allawi, *Faisal of Iraq*.
60 Gertrude Bell to her father, 9 July 1924, *The Letters of Gertrude Bell*, edited by Lady Bell, Volume II, 703.
61 Gertrude Bell to Lady Bell (her stepmother), 13 May 1926, *The Letters of Gertrude Bell*, edited by Lady Bell, Volume II, 762.
62 Gertrude Bell to her stepmother, 26 May 1926, *Gertrude Bell from Her Personal Papers 1914–1926*, Elizabeth Burgoyne (London: Ernest Benn, 1961), 389.
63 Fragment of letter, Dobbs to his wife, autumn 1925, unpublished papers.
64 Burgoyne, *Gertrude Bell*, 388.
65 Dobbs' Annual Report to the Colonial Office on Gertrude Bell, 1924, quoted in *The Letters of Gertrude Bell*, edited by Lady Bell, Volume II, 686.
66 Gertrude Bell to Lady Bell, 13 May 1926, *The Letters of Gertrude Bell*, edited by Lady Bell, Volume II, 762.
67 Letter, Dobbs to his wife, 15 July 1926, unpublished papers.
68 Letter, Dobbs to his wife, 22 July 1926, unpublished papers.
69 Letter, Dobbs to his wife, 5 August 1926, unpublished papers.
70 Letter, Dobbs to his wife, 15 July 1926, unpublished papers.
71 Letter, Dobbs to his wife, 9 June 1926, unpublished papers.
72 Letter, Dobbs to his wife, 27 May 1927, unpublished papers.
73 *Iraq Report 1920–1925*, 10.
74 *Iraq Report 1920–1925*, 28.
75 Letter, Dobbs to his wife, 21 April 1925, unpublished papers.
76 Letter, Dobbs to his wife, 30 September 1926, unpublished papers.
77 *Mandates Commission*, 44–78.
78 Letter, Dobbs to his wife, 29 March 1927, unpublished papers.
79 Letter, Dobbs to his wife, 12 May 1926, unpublished papers.
80 Letter, Dobbs to his wife, 10 April 1927, unpublished papers.
81 Letter, Dobbs to his wife, 25 June 1925, unpublished papers.
82 Faisal visited Turkey in July 1931. See Allawi, *Faisal*, 529.
83 High Commissioner, *Note on the Internal Situation in Baghdad*, FO 371, B3220/12259, 27 June 1927, unpublished papers.
84 Letter, Dobbs to his wife, 15 September 1926, unpublished papers.
85 Letter, Dobbs to his wife, 26 March 1925, unpublished papers.
86 Letter, Dobbs to his wife, 24 May 1926, unpublished papers.

87 Letter, Dobbs to his wife, 2 June 1926, unpublished papers.

88 Letter, Dobbs to his wife, 20 May 1927, unpublished papers.

89 Letter, Dobbs to his mother, 16 February 1925, unpublished papers.

90 Letter, Dobbs to his wife, 4 August 1926, unpublished papers.

91 Letter, Dobbs to his wife, 20 January 1927, unpublished papers.

92 Letter, Dobbs to his wife, 18 May 1926, unpublished papers.

93 Letter, Dobbs to his wife, 22 July 1926, unpublished papers.

94 Letter, Dobbs to his wife, 28 July 1926, unpublished papers.

95 Ibid.

96 Sluglett, *Britain in Iraq*, 178–81.

97 Benjamin D. Hopkins, *Ruling the Savage Periphery. Frontier Governance and the Making of the Modern State* (Cambridge, MA: Harvard University Press 2020), 65–7.

98 Letter, Dobbs to his wife, 8 March 1927, unpublished papers.

99 Letter, Dobbs to his wife, 18 February 1927, unpublished papers.

100 Pedersen, *The Guardians*, 264.

101 Letter, Dobbs to his wife, 27 May 1927, unpublished papers.

102 Letter, Dobbs to his wife, 20 May 1927, unpublished papers.

103 Letter, Dobbs to his wife, 13 May 1927, unpublished papers.

104 Allawi, *Faisal*, 482–3.

105 Letter, Dobbs to his mother, 10 June 1925, unpublished papers.

106 Air Marshal Sir Hugh, later Lord, Trenchard was the first commander of the newly created Royal Air Force.

107 Pedersen, *The Guardians*, 264–5.

108 Letter, Dobbs to his wife, 18 February 1927, unpublished papers.

109 Statement made by the high commissioner to British officials at Baghdad on 19th December 1927, unpublished papers (hereafter High Commissioner Statement 19th December 1927). Dobbs gave a briefing to his senior staff on a secret and personal basis when he returned from the protracted discussions with Faisal and the British government in London.

110 Ibid.

111 Although Dobbs could envisage circumstances in which Faisal's abdication would have to be accepted, he believed this would be a highly damaging outcome for the British government. He wrote sharply to the Colonial Office when Bernard Bourdillon, acting high commissioner while Dobbs was in London, suggested that the British government should force Faisal to abdicate, 'he knew that this was not my view and I hardly think it wise for a counsellor who is acting for a short time to put forward so sweeping a divergence from his chief's policy', Letter, Dobbs to Sir John Shuckburgh, 31 August 1927, unpublished papers.

112 High Commissioner Statement 19th December 1927.

113 Ibid.
114 Ibid.
115 Ibid.
116 Ibid.
117 Letter, Dobbs to his wife, 19 January 1929, unpublished papers.
118 Sluglett, *Britain in Iraq*, 100.
119 Letter, Dobbs to his wife, 5 January 1929, unpublished papers.
120 Letter, Dobbs to his wife, 16 March 1927, unpublished papers.
121 Sluglett, *Britain in Iraq*, 110–11.
122 Telegram of 31 December 1928, high commissioner Baghdad to secretary of state for the colonies, quoted in Sluglett, *Britain in Iraq*, 113.
123 Sluglett, *Britain in Iraq*, 113.
124 Letter, Dobbs to his wife, 5 January 1929, unpublished papers.
125 Letter, Dobbs to his wife, 2 February 1929, unpublished papers.
126 *The Times*, London, 4 February 1929. Press cutting.
127 Quoted in *The Times*, London, 4 February 1929.
128 *The Baghdad Times*, 5 February 1929.
129 Quoted in *The Baghdad Times*, 5 February 1929.
130 Ibid.
131 Ibid.
132 Ibid.
133 Letter, Dobbs to his mother, 16 December 1924, unpublished papers.
134 Sluglett, *Britain in Iraq*, 118.
135 Letter, Dobbs to his mother, 2 August 1924, unpublished papers.
136 Letter, Dobbs to his wife, 24 June, 1930, unpublished papers.
137 Sluglett, *Britain in Iraq*, 119.
138 *Policy in Iraq: Memorandum by the Secretary of State for the Colonies. Command 3440. November 1929.* HMSO London (hereafter *Command 3440*).
139 *Command 3440*, 2.
140 Ibid., 3.
141 Letter, Sir John Shuckburgh to Dobbs, 21 November 1929, unpublished papers. Dobbs's part in the change of government policy is referred to on page 2 of *Command 3440*.

Epilogue

1 Letter, Dobbs to his mother, 15 February 1927, unpublished papers.
2 Letter, Dobbs to his mother, 12 October 1927, unpublished papers.
3 Letter, Dobbs to his wife, 1 September 1928, unpublished papers.

4 Sir Henry Dobbs, 'Britain's Work in Iraq', *Journal of the Royal Empire Society*, 24, no. 3 (1933): 133.

5 Ibid.

Some argue that commitment of greater resources to Iraq's development over a longer timescale would have created stronger foundations for the new state; for example, Toby Dodge's *Inventing Iraq. The Failure of Nation-Building and a History Denied* (London: Hurst, 2003). Dobbs's comments highlight that this was beyond the bounds of practical politics at the time in London or Baghdad.

6 Dobbs, 'Britain's Work in Iraq': 133.

7 Ibid., 135.

8 Ibid., 139.

9 Ibid., 140.

10 Dobbs, Sir Samuel Hoare (former air minister) Sir Arnold Wilson (former acting high commissioner in Iraq) and a number of MPs had expressed concerns about Iraq's minorities in 1930 and 1931. It took a declaration in June 1931 by the high commissioner for Iraq, Sir Francis Humphrys, that the moral responsibility for minorities must rest with the British government to persuade the League of Nations Mandates Commission that special protection for Iraq's minorities after independence would not be necessary. Susan Pedersen, *The Guardians. The League of Nations and the Crisis of Empire* (Oxford: Oxford University Press, 2015; paperback 2017), 281–2. Citations are to the paperback edition.

11 Ibid., 141.

12 Letter, Dobbs to his mother, 15 February 1927, unpublished papers.

13 *The Times*, London, February 1929. Press cuttings.

14 Dobbs, 'Britain's Work in Iraq': 140.

15 *The Times*, London, February 1929. Press cuttings.

16 Ibid.

17 Letter, Sir Elliot Colvin (Dobbs worked with him in India) to Lady Dobbs, 10 June 1934, unpublished papers.

18 Letter, Sir Arthur Hirtzel, India Office, to Lady Dobbs, 3 June 1934, unpublished papers.

19 Letter, Sir Arnold Wilson to Lady Dobbs, 15 November 1934, unpublished papers.

20 Leon B. Poullada, *Reform and Rebellion in Afghanistan, 1919–1929. King Amanullah's Failure to Modernize a Tribal Society* (London: Cornell University Press, 1973), 82.

21 Letter, Dobbs to his wife, 8 December 1928, unpublished papers.

22 Letter, Sardar Bahadur Nawab Mohd Mehrab Khan, Tumandar Bugti Tribe (Sind) to Lady Dobbs, 27 July 1934, unpublished papers.

Bibliography

Primary sources

1. India office records, British Library

Documents from the series Political and Secret Subject Files 1902–1931 (IOR/L/PS/10).
Private papers of Lord Curzon as Viceroy of India 1904–1905 (IOR/Mss EUR F111).
Private papers of Viscount Chelmsford as Viceroy of India (1916–21) (IOR/Mss EUR D660 and E264).

2. National archives, Kew

Cabinet Minutes CAB 23 (records for 1923).
Cabinet Memoranda CAB 24 (records for 1923).
Cabinet Committees CAB 27 (records for 1923).
Colonial Office correspondence on Iraq 1921–32 CO 730.
Foreign Office correspondence on Iraq 1916–40 FO 371.

3. Winchester college archives, Winchester College

Henry Dobbs: Notes from his housemaster's record book

4. Private papers

Unpublished letters and papers of Sir Henry Dobbs.

5. Published primary sources

League of Nations. *Minutes of the Permanent Mandates Commission 1926 and 1931.* Geneva.
Policy in Iraq: Memorandum by the Secretary of State for the Colonies. Command Paper 3440 (London: HMSO, 1929).
Report of the Commission Appointed to Inquire into the Origin, Inception, and Operation of the War in Mesopotamia. Command Paper 8610 (London: HMSO, 1917).

*Review of the Civil Administration of Mesopotamia. A Report from the Acting
    Civil Commissioner. Prepared by Miss Gertrude Bell.* Command Paper 1061
    (London: HMSO, 1920).
Treaty with H.M. King Faisal, 10 October, 1922. Command Paper 1757
    (London: HMSO, 1922).

Secondary sources

Adamec, Ludwig W., *Afghanistan 1900–1923. A Diplomatic History.*
    Berkeley: University of California Press, 1967.
Ahmed, Faiz, *Afghanistan Rising. Islamic Law and Statecraft between the Ottoman and
    British Empires.* Cambridge, MA: Harvard University Press, 2017.
Allawi, Ali, *Faisal I of Iraq.* New Haven, CT: Yale University Press, 2014.
Amanat, Abbas, *Iran. A Modern History.* New Haven, CT: Yale University Press, 2017.
Barr, James, *A Line in the Sand. Britain, France and the Struggle that Shaped the Middle
    East.* London: Simon & Schuster, 2011. Paperback, 2012.
Bell, Gertrude, *The Letters of Gertrude Bell, Volumes I and II.* Selected and edited by
    Lady Bell. London: Ernest Benn, 1927.
Brown, Judith M., and Louis, Wm. Roger (eds), *The Oxford History of the British
    Empire, Volume IV, The Twentieth Century.* Oxford: Oxford University Press, 1999.
    Paperback 2001.
Burgoyne, Elizabeth, *Gertrude Bell from Her Personal Papers 1914–1926.*
    London: Ernest Benn, 1961.
Chesney, Francis Rawdon, *Narrative of the Euphrates Expedition. Carried On by Order of
    the British Government during the Years 1835, 1836, and 1837.* London: Longmans,
    Green & Co., 1868.
Cowper-Coles, Sherard, *Cables from Kabul.* London: HarperPress, 2012.
Curzon, George N., *Persia and the Persian Question, Volumes I and II.*
    London: Longmans Green & Co., 1892.
Darwin, John, *The Empire Project. The Rise and Fall of the British World-System 1830–
    1970.* Cambridge: Cambridge University Press, 2009. Paperback, 2011.
Dobbs, Sir Henry, 'Britain's Work in Iraq', *Journal of the Royal Empire Society*, 24, no. 3
    (1933): 132–42.
Dockter, Warren, *Churchill and the Islamic World. Orientalism Empire and Diplomacy in
    the Middle East.* London: I. B. Tauris, Bloomsbury Publishing, 2019.
Dodge, Toby, *Inventing Iraq. The Failure of Nation Building and a History Denied.*
    London: Hurst & Company, 2003.
Du Boulay, F. R. H., *Servants of Empire. An Imperial Memoir of a British Family.* London
    and New York: I. B. Tauris, 2011.

Faught, C. Brad, *Cairo 1921. Ten Days that Made the Middle East*. New Haven, CT: Yale University Press, 2022.

Fraser-Tytler, W. K., *Afghanistan. A Study of Political Developments in Central and Southern Asia*. 1950. Revised by M. K. Gillett. London: Oxford University Press, 1967.

Gilbert, Martin, *Winston S. Churchill Volume IV 1916–1922*. London: Heineman, 1975.

Gilmour, David, *Curzon. Imperial Statesman 1859–1925*. London: John Murray, 1994. Paperback, 2003.

Gilmour, David, *The Ruling Caste. Imperial Lives in the Victorian Raj*. London: John Murray, 2005.

Hopkins, Benjamin D., *Ruling the Savage Periphery. Frontier Governance and the Making of the Modern State*. Cambridge, MA: Harvard University Press, 2020.

Hopkirk, Peter, *The Great Game. On Secret Service in High Asia*. Oxford: Oxford University Press, 2001.

Ireland, Philip, *Iraq: A Study in Political Development*. London: Kegan Paul, [1937] 2004.

Kinross, Lord, *Atatürk. The Rebirth of a Nation*. London: Weidenfeld and Nicolson, 1964.

Kirk-Greene, Anthony, *Britain's Imperial Administrators 1858–1966*. Basingstoke: Macmillan, 2000.

Landor, A. H. Savage, *Across Coveted Lands from Flushing, Holland to Calcutta Overland*, Volume II. London: Macmillan, 1902.

Longrigg, Stephen Hemsley, *Iraq 1900 to 1950. A Political, Social, and Economic History*. London: Oxford University Press, 1953.

Loyn, David, *In Afghanistan*. New York: Palgrave Macmillan, 2009.

Lyon, Wallace, *Kurds, Arabs and Britons. The Memoir of Wallace Lyon in Iraq 1918–44*. Edited and with an introduction by D. K. Fieldhouse. London: I. B. Tauris, 2002.

MacMillan, Margaret, *Peacemakers. The Paris Conference of 1919 and Its Attempt to End War*. London: John Murray, 2001. Paperback 2002.

Main, Ernest, *Iraq. From Mandate to Independence*. London: George Allen and Unwin, 1935.

Otte, T. G., *Statesman of Europe. A Life of Sir Edward Grey*. London: Allen Lane, 2020.

Pedersen, Susan, *The Guardians. The League of Nations and the Crisis of Empire*. Oxford: Oxford University Press, 2015. Paperback 2017.

Porter, Andrew (ed.), *The Oxford History of the British Empire, Volume III, The Nineteenth Century*. Oxford: Oxford University Press, 1999. Paperback 2001.

Poullada, Leon B., *Reform and Rebellion in Afghanistan, 1919–1929. King Amanullah's Failure to Modernize a Tribal Society*. London: Cornell University Press, 1973.

Roberts, Lord, *Forty-One Years in India. From Subaltern to Commander in Chief, Field-Marshal Lord Roberts of Kandahar, Volumes I and II*. London: Richard Bentley and Son, 1897.

Sluglett, Peter, *Britain in Iraq. Contriving King and Country*. London: I. B. Tauris, 2007.

Stewart, Rory, *Occupational Hazards. My Time Governing in Iraq*. London: Picador, an imprint of Pan Macmillan, 2006.

Stewart, Rory, *The Places in between*. Revised edition. London: Picador, an imprint of Pan Macmillan, [2005] 2014.

Taylor, A. J. P., *English History 1914–1945*. Oxford: Oxford University Press, 1965. Paperback, Harmondsworth: Penguin Books, 1970.

Thesiger, Wilfred, *The Marsh Arabs*. London: Longmans Green, 1964.

Townsend, John, *Proconsul to the Middle East. Sir Percy Cox and the End of Empire*. London: I. B. Tauris, 2010.

Townshend, Charles, *When God Made Hell. The British Invasion of Mesopotamia and the Creation of Iraq 1914–1921*. London: Faber and Faber, 2010. Paperback 2011.

Tripodi, Christian, *Edge of Empire. The British Political Officer and Tribal Administration on the North West Frontier 1877–1947*. Farnham: Ashgate, 2011.

Tripp, Charles, *A History of Iraq*. Third edition. Cambridge: Cambridge University Press, [2000] 2007.

Wainwright, David, *Broadwood by Appointment. A History*. London: Quiller Press, 1982.

Wilks, Ann, 'The 1921 Anglo-Afghan Treaty: How Britain's "Man on the Spot" Shaped This Agreement', *Journal of the Royal Asiatic Society*, Series 3, 29, no. 1 (2019): 75–94.

Wilks, Ann, 'The 1922 Anglo-Iraq Treaty: A Moment of Crisis and the Role of Britain's Man on the Ground', *British Journal of Middle Eastern Studies*, 43, no. 3 (2016): 342–59.

Wilson, Arnold T., *Loyalties Mesopotamia 1914–1917. A Personal and Historical Record*. London: Oxford University Press, 1930.

Wilson, Arnold T., *Mesopotamia 1917–1920. A Clash of Loyalties. A Personal and Historical Record*. London: Oxford University Press, 1931.

Yapp, M. E., *Strategies of British India: Britain, Iran and Afghanistan 1798–1850*. Oxford: Oxford University Press, 1980.

Index

Milton Keynes UK
Ingram Content Group UK Ltd.
UKHW031007190324
439562UK00004B/80